Your soul
read re
the Holy
God Bless
for you
Sincerely, Sister Mildred Crosby
3/31/18

The above I have not given
Mildred Crosby

VOICES FROM
PRISON WALLS

by
WILLIAM CAWMAN

SCHMUL PUBLISHING COMPANY
NICHOLASVILLE, KENTUCKY

Published by Schmul Publishing Co.
PO Box 776
Nicholasville, KY USA

Printed in the United States of America

ISBN 10: 0-88019-588-6
ISBN 13: 978-0-88019-588-1

Visit us on the Internet at www.wesleyanbooks.com, or order direct from
the publisher by calling 800-772-6657, or by writing to the above address.

Contents

FOREWORD

THE THOUGHT OF BECOMING a state prison chaplain would have been the remotest of ambitions for the first half century of my life. Nonetheless, I look back now at how the great God of Heaven was preparing me in many ways for that which I knew not.

For several years preceding this I had, in the providence of God, been assigned the task of job superintendent of a number of construction projects in which I had to coordinate at times seventy or eighty men, each with his own interest and agenda, and very few caring much about the others. I look back now, and recognize that it was all training for trying to help all types of personalities loaded with every conceivable manner of baggage.

In the year 1994 news came out in the local newspaper that three young boys had committed what the Vineland, New Jersey police department labeled, "the most heinous murder scene they had ever witnessed." Searching for drugs and guns, the boys had broken into the home of an elderly couple and brutally murdered both of them, coming off with thirty-seven dollars for the deed. Although this type of crime was not new, something about the continuing story of the three boys began to haunt my mind and heart. True, there lay two innocent victims of a dastardly deed in death on the floor of their own home, but what about the three victims of our society who had perpetrated it?

This began to trouble me to no small degree. What could be so seriously wrong with our society that three boys, two only sixteen and one seventeen, could be so bankrupt in conscience, morals, and even feelings, to have done such a thing? I had grown up in a small town that did not even need a police department. We seldom locked our doors.

I could get no rest from the boys' situation and so after a few months I did something I had never done before: I called the county court system and asked about the boys. The clerk told me they had been turned over to the state and gave me an inmate locator phone number. I called the number and they gave me the location of two of the boys, but they could not find the third. I wrote a letter to each of the two for whom they had given me addresses.

The first letter returned was from the seventeen-year-old. His opening words were, "First of all, I want to thank you for caring about me." That nearly broke my heart as I began to learn the answer to my nagging question: *What went so wrong.* I pondered how I would feel if no one had ever cared for me. He invited me to visit him and put me on his visitor list. I did so and I believe the Lord really saved him. For as long as I was visiting him he seemed to be finding help from the Lord.

The second boy responded with these words: "If I knew more about you I would tell you more about me." When he found that I was visiting the first boy, he wrote back and said, "If you are visiting him I don't want anything to do with you—ever!" Nine years later I received a letter from him asking me to forgive him and saying he would like to correspond with me.

The first boy told me the location of the one seemingly lost to the state, so I wrote him a letter. I heard nothing back, but continued to write him. One year later he wrote a letter to me and asked me to come and see him. He was imprisoned in a maximum security prison for sixty years without parole.

I entered the visit hall and did not know how I would find this boy, but as the string of inmates began filing into the room, both of us headed for each other; don't ask me how.

We sat down and he said, "I want to ask you a question, but first of all let me tell you something. When you first wrote to me I did not answer you because I said, 'This is too good to be true; no one cares about me.' But when you continued to write to me I said, 'Why don't I give him a try; what do I have to lose?' Why did you write to me?" I told him that when I had read about him, my heart was burdened for him and I cared about him.

The boy then told me that he had been born into a military camp and really did not know his father. He had moved all around and run with the gangs in Miami Beach and Vineland, New Jersey. At the age of sixteen he said to his gang leader, "I'm sick and tired of this." The gang leader said he was, too. One week later they broke into the home and committed the crime.

After this youth was sent to prison, someone told him that God would forgive him if he really asked Him to. That night in a three-man cell and after his cell mates had gone to bed, he got down on the floor and began to ask God if He could forgive him.

Suddenly everything inside of him broke loose. He said that before this time he hadn't cried for years and was so hard that he probably would not have cried, except in anger, if his own mother had died, But that night the fountain of his heart and eyes broke loose and he began to cry and weep and did not care who heard him. He said that night a peace came into his heart that he had never known in all his life. He was now happier in prison with Jesus in his heart than he had ever been out on the street without Him.

As I went again and again over a period of two or three years and visited with these two in the visit hall, I would look around at all the other men, many of them just young men, and my heart began to long to help them.

It may sound strange, but as I would walk up to the red, brick walls of that old prison—at one time a fort—my eyes would almost tear up with a longing, "Oh God, I want in there!" The souls of needy men were in there, men who never had the chance that I had enjoyed, of growing up in the best Christian home in America. I thought continually of what I might have been, had I been raised in their shoes.

For a period of perhaps two years, while I continued to supervise a crew of rough workmen on construction sites, my heart was being drawn to another group of men. I knew down deep inside that God was closing a door and opening another, but I did not know just what and where.

There were times when I would leave the job site and no sooner get in my truck than I would nearly burst into tears, praying, "God, I know that You are bringing a change into my life, but I don't know what it is." I found out when the door finally did open, that the reason it didn't open sooner was, it was not on its hinges yet. I walked into this prison as a volunteer just as the construction crews that built it were pulling away.

But let me go back to the drawings of God. In the early spring of 1998, I was called to hold a ten-day revival in Ohio. The seventeen-million-dollar project I had been working on was nearing completion and a younger superintendent, who had been with me for a month, knew the job well. I knew he could carry it on and I knew God was closing that door for me.

On a Friday morning I went into the office and told the owner of the company that I was leaving for two weeks for a meeting and that when I returned, if I did, I would no longer be serving as a job superintendent. When I walked across the parking lot that Friday afternoon, away from that large high school addition and gigantic auditorium, I saw as distinctly as it had been in the flesh, a huge hand go up against that auditorium wall. I knew I would never return.

The first morning of that revival, after preaching the night before, I went to the basement of the house where we were staying and spilled my heart out to God. I wept; I cried; I laid all my reasons out before God.

"Oh God, You know this is not comfortable to me. I know without a doubt that Your hand went up and that the door behind me is closed. I have walked away from a good salaried job with many benefits and I see no door open before me. I have a family to take care of and I don't know how I am to do that. But God, *I will obey You!*"

With that said, indescribable billows of glory rolled through my soul and I knew I was on the altar completely.

The next morning I went to the same prayer spot and prayed it all over again. Again, the billows of glory rolled and rolled. The next morning I did the same, and the next, and the next— for the whole ten days. At the close of that meeting the same Hand was pointing straight ahead.

I went to the state capital, found the man in charge of all state chaplains, and explained how I was feeling. He looked me over and said, "I'll tell you what to do. Sixteen miles from your house they are building a brand-new prison, the largest one in the state. Go in and volunteer; that's the way in the door."

I did so and was welcomed in, for as yet there was no prot-estant chaplain at all. In the very first service with those men I knew I was gloriously in the center of God's will.

And so, I volunteered and still no door opened for any in-come. A year and a half later we had sold the little farm where we raised our family, and were building a new home a few miles from there.

One day as I was working on the house, an anxiety attack came over me. Our bank account was draining fast and noth-ing was coming into it. You see, a volunteer's paycheck is rather inglorious.

I dropped what I was doing and said to myself, "Somewhere

I have missed God's voice. I know His hand went up. I know He blessed me out of myself when I turned my all over to Him, but somewhere I have missed a turn, for no door is opening. I am going to go upstairs in this unfinished house and pray until I get through to God, for something is wrong."

No stairway was in place yet, but as my foot stepped off the top rung of the ladder onto the upper floor, a huge Hand came down over me.

Son, didn't you turn this over to Me?

"Yes, Lord, I did."

What are you going to do with it now?

"Lord, here! I give it back to You." Immediately those same billows of glory began to roll and roll through my soul. I went back down the ladder and to work again.

A few days later I found in the mailbox a small envelope from someone in another state that I did not know either then or now, and cannot now remember the name. Inside of the envelope was a check made out to my name for five thousand dollars.

I thought, "What is the mistake here?" And here came that big Hand again.

Didn't I tell you I would take care of you?

Just as that was running low, the man I had talked to in the capital a year and half before, stepped into my office in the prison. "Chap, I want to tell you something. When I heard what God is doing with you here in the prison my heart rejoiced. Are you ready? You are going on the payroll today!"

And that is how and why, at the writing of this book, God has led for the past twenty years into what will likely be a "life sentence." The stories recorded in this book are the accumulation of monthly prayer letters that we sent out for the first four years.

Many have been the prayers of God's children around the world in response to those letters, and the stories in this book reveal how effectively God has answered those prayers. To Him be all the glory, and to all who have prayed but have not had the pleasure of reaping and witnessing the answers to those prayers, just wait. There are going to be a number of Blood-washed souls that will greet you in that heavenly land because you prayed and thereby *visited them in prison.*

—WILLIAM CAWMAN

October, 2014

ACKNOWLEDGMENTS

I WANT TO ACKNOWLEDGE with sincere and loving gratitude the precious helpmeet that God gave to me for forty-one years. She stood by me in every sense of the word, and numbers of times accompanied me into the prison services until the men felt she was mother to them all. When God in His infinite wisdom took her home to Him, November 20, 2011, the men in prison were among the most affectionate of my comforters, aside from the precious Holy Spirit, who has never left me for a moment since.

I dedicate this book to her—my precious wife, Peggy Joyce (Carroll) Cawman.

Memory fails me as to who first suggested that I publish a monthly prayer letter as to needs and victories within the prison walls. But after several people had approached me regarding it, I took it to my supervisor and the director of all chaplaincies in the state of New Jersey. Both encouraged me to do so, but to be careful not to give names of inmates or volunteers, nor release information sensitive to the incarceration security. Whoever that was who first suggested or requested the letters, I now give a long overdue thanks, for were I at this point to try to recall all that is here recorded, time and memory would both forbid even a fraction of the content.

We want to thank all of you who have prayed for us and the work in the prison, whether once or every day. God alone has the record of how many of those prayers have been answered. Thank you, every one!

I give thanks from the depths of my heart for the volunteers who have picked up the calling and burden and who have faithfully given their time to fill in for me in the classes and Bible studies and Sunday services when I have been absent in meetings abroad. Their labor has been invaluable and perhaps no one has been more conscious of the fruit of their loving work than the man who follows them up and witnesses it.

We thank Sister Roberta Sarver for her editing and arranging the work that she so graciously offered to do. Numbers of people had asked if we would someday put together these monthly letters into a book, but we confess the requests rather went in one ear and out the other until the Sarvers offered on their own to undertake the task. Thank you, Brother and Sister Sarver.

We thank God, most of all, for so loving fallen, sinful men that He sent His Son to die for them to save and sanctify. Often as we have grown to love and respect these men as dearly as any men on earth, we have been reminded of the Scripture: "And such were some of you: but ye are washed, but ye are sanctified, but ye are justified in the name of the Lord Jesus, and by the Spirit of our God."

Be it clearly understood that human help, human programs and human reform measures all fail dreadfully and pathetically short of lifting fallen, sinful man, but Jesus can! There is not a soul that's fallen so far that Jesus' Blood cannot go farther. There is not a scar so vivid that Jesus cannot heal it. There is not a human vessel so wrecked by Satan that Jesus cannot restore so completely, that not one taint of sin remains. All hail to the Blood of Jesus! And had it not been for that precious

Blood, you would do well to throw this book into the trash unread, for there would have been nothing worth writing about.

Behold the Lamb of God, which taketh away the sin of the world! ...And they sung a new song, saying, Thou art worthy to take the book, and to open the seals thereof: for Thou wast slain, and hast redeemed us to God by thy blood out of every kindred, and tongue, and people, and nation; And hast made us unto our God kings and priests: and we shall reign on the earth.

1
MIRACLES MADE IN A MOMENT

December 4, 1999

I N THE PAST SEVERAL MONTHS we have had several requests asking us to send out a monthly newsletter telling of the workings of God in the prison system. After reflecting upon this and consulting with those over me in the chaplaincy department, I felt it would be a good thing to comply with the requests. We feel in a way, we cannot express a deep gratitude for the support of praying friends, and it would be only fair to share with you the many answers to prayer as well as the requests. So continuing to trust in God for His grace to be outpoured in even greater measures, we will endeavor to give you as often as we can, a report from behind the wall. May the answers to prayer be only to the glory of God, and may the requests kindle in many hearts a passion to answer the great commandment of Jesus, "Thou shalt love thy neighbor as thyself."

From time to time we will endeavor to give you accounts of the struggles and victories of inmates within the prison system who could have been you and me, had we been raised as they were. In doing so, we will, for obvious reasons, conceal their names and any information which could be vital to their identity or security. *These letters will be for one purpose only—to incite to prayer, and to praise God for His answers.*

Let us begin with an account some of you may have heard us tell, but which continues to move my heart as I remember it.

For several weeks I had been busy with inmate requests and had not had time to visit the inmate hospital, located within the prison compound. I began to sense a burden and an urgency to visit there. So, I went into the prison one Sunday afternoon before time for the evening services and went over to the hospital. I went to the second floor and asked the officer if I could visit the inmates who were unable to get out to the religious services. He took me in, and began unlocking the cell doors. I would go in and speak a few words and have prayer, then move to the next one.

As we came to one cell, the officer said, "Do you want to go in here? This one is in bad shape." I said I did. He told me not to make any physical contact as the man was dying of AIDS.

As I entered the cell I realized why the officer had asked. I was totally unprepared for what I saw. Grady's pictures of dead soldiers on the Civil War battlefields could not have looked any worse. He was a man only in his thirties perhaps, and yet was wasted away to a mere skeleton. He left eye was hemorrhaging blood as were his lips. His mouth was open and looked like a dead fish inside. His glassy stare spoke of fear of what lay beyond.

I tried to pray with him, and as I did, noticed he tried to reach for my hand, but then his hand fell back on the pillow. I left him, but the burden did not lift. I confessed to God at having been unnerved to the point that I felt I had not done my best for him.

The next Tuesday afternoon after I was finished with the other inmates, I went back over to the hospital. The nurse asked if I wanted to see D—— again, and I said I did. Entering his cell again, I tried to talk to him, telling him that

Jesus could forgive any sin that he would bring to Him. I told him to bring all the sins of his life to Jesus and ask Him to forgive them, and to take him to heaven. I prayed again with him and then left.

A few days later the nurse saw me and told us that D—— had died only forty minutes after I had left him. Then she looked straight at me and said, "I really think he was waiting for that." I went away feeling overwhelmed at the mercy of our God.

The next morning when my dear father went to the place of prayer, he said he could not pray. He felt the clear witness from God that D—— was in heaven. A few days later as we were telling someone about this, I started to say, "…*if* D—— is in heaven…" and God rebuked me. He impressed me with, *I already witnessed to that.*

How can one fathom the depths of the mercy of our God? Here is a God Who can reach down into the jaws of death and grasp the finished product of sin, only forty minutes from hell, and send him the next moment into the joys of heaven! And I believe that for him too, no doubt, the Father brought out the fatted calf and all the welcoming committee of heaven.

Just who it was that prayed for this man we may never know, nor might the one who prayed; God has the record until the veil is lifted where we shall know even as we are known. Till then, let us rejoice and be glad; another sinner has come home. Next month, it may be your prayer that will be answered.

Recently, a prisoner was brightly saved in the first Christian service he had ever attended in his life. Later, we found that God had whispered his name to a praying man in another state. The praying man told God he knew of no one by that name, but he prayed for him anyway. We do not intend to pass out names for prayer, but if God whispers a name to you, that is His business: pray!

Next month I would like to tell you of the continuing miracle of C—— . If he keeps on going, there will be more to tell by next month, too.

Let me give you a few specific requests for prayer:

1. Please pray for the upcoming Christmas concerts. A good-sized group of young people will be ministering in song and we desire that it speak only of Jesus. We invite a real outpouring of God's drawing power during this time until some can open their hearts to Jesus and have a brand-new life for Christmas. Please pray especially for this.

2. Please pray not only for the inmates but for the staff and the officers.

3. Pray for the many "visions" of the chaplaincy department for the upcoming year. Pray that right will be more aggressive than wrong. And that's a big prayer!

4. Pray for the covering of the Blood of Jesus. We live in a hyper-sensitized society to ever-so-many seen and unseen issues. Pray that we can "walk circumspectly toward them that are without."

Again, I thank each of you from my heart.

Laborers together with God,
William Cawman

January 5, 2000

ONCE AGAIN WE COME to you on behalf of the needs and victories within the prison. First of all I want to relay the many expressions of gratitude I have received for those who came and held the two Christmas concerts on the night of December 23rd. Many of the prisoners have begged me to thank each one who came. It truly was a blessed time as the young people sang and testified to the men, the message of Christmas and salvation.

We held two services back to back so that we would not have more attend than could be seated in the visiting hall. There were over 350 who attended.

During the second service we asked how many could understand Spanish. A number of hands went up, so we told them we had a special treat for them. Then three of the young people sang "Noche de Paz." God's presence really attended as they sang. One very small young man on the front row of seats was so moved that he put his head on his lap, outstretched his arms and just wept. Some said it was all they could do to refrain from going over and putting their arms around him.

As a group of young women sang "At the name of Jesus, the name of Jesus, sin's chains are broken, the captive set free; at the name of Jesus, the name of Jesus, hell trembles and Satan must flee," the entire group of men came to their feet with their hands raised and sang with them. Truly it is the name of Jesus!

We also want to thank everyone who helped us pray for these special services. God honored your prayers and really made Himself known to all who were reaching for Him. One prisoner told me afterward, "Oh I see so much of God in those young people; I want it, I want it!"

Another told me, "Even better than the music was the God I saw in their faces."

Another said, "I am so thankful for real Christians to come and minister to us."

I told you in last month's letter than I would tell you of the miracle of C———. I also told you that if he kept on going there would be more to tell. All glory to the miracle of God's redeeming grace; he has kept right on going. I cannot tell it all in this letter, but here is some of it.

C——— was born in Newark, New Jersey in a drug alley, to a drug addict. He never knew a father and he never knew the love of a mother. His mother seldom lived with him except to come get him to run drug deals with her and steal for her. She left him to be raised by a group of homosexuals who did not care enough about him to hide their lifestyle from him.

C——— was taught very early in life that the only way to satisfy the gnawing hunger in his stomach was to sell himself as a prostitute or to steal. He remembers seeing his mother at one time lying on the floor with her teeth knocked out, her eye socket knocked out, and a huge man standing over her.

C——'s mother slapped him and beat him and shot a bullet through him, but never expressed any love for him. The first time he was caught and went to prison was along with his mother for stealing a car to take her to a drug deal. Four days after they got out of prison, he brought her home the money that she used to overdose on heroin, and she died.

From that time on, C—— was never out of prison for long at a time. That was twenty years ago. As a white man in a black drug alley, he escaped death by only a hair's breadth many a time. At one time a pistol was repeatedly fired right at him and it never went off. *God was not finished with him yet.* He was in many a fight and had his head broken open, his eye smashed, and cuts and bruises everywhere. Amazingly enough, hardly a trace of it remains visible now.

I had seen C—— here and there in the prison for nearly a year or better. He would always speak, but never for long. Several months ago, he came to me and asked if he could have a visit. We went to the chapel. He looked me in the eye and said, "When I first saw you around I thought, 'Oh, just another reverend,' but as I have looked into your eyes I think you are someone I could tell something very few people know." Then he told me briefly, some of the things we have mentioned, and of how long he had spent in prisons.

C—— said that he had become one of the most trusted prisoners in the state; but, he added that there was something very few people knew about, and that was, for the last two years he had been a steady user of the very drug that killed his mother—heroin.

But then he went on to tell me that two months previous to our visit he had awakened one morning so sick of the way he was and so hateful of his addiction that he went into his cell, locked the door and began to read the Bible. He read and read for seven days, and at the end of the seven days not one desire for heroin was left. He went to the men he had dealt with and told them he would not need the heroin anymore. They asked him why and he said he was going to follow God. He waited for two months, and then came and told me about it.

After C—— had told me what happened, he looked at me and said, "Chaplain, would it be right for me to feel that God did that for me?"

What would you have said? I told him there was not a power on earth that could deliver him in a moment from the king of drugs and leave him with a desire to follow God except God Himself. He said, "I wanted to believe that."

That is the last question I have had to answer for him. Friends, Jesus promised that when the Holy Spirit should come, He would guide us into all truth. I have just sat with him over and over and marveled and tried to hold back the tears as I saw the Holy Spirit faithfully dealing with this man.

C—— told me that as he continues to read God's Word, he finds more things which need to be removed from his life, and said he was throwing them out as fast as he saw them. He had kept a supply of tobacco in his locker for a long time. He did not use it himself, but would give it to other inmates who could not afford it. He said God showed him that it was unclean and he should not have it in his locker. He immediately began trading it for cookies and soap, etc. God showed him that he was making merchandise out of an unclean thing. C—— then took the whole mess to the toilet and flushed it down.

While in prison C—— had studied, and through correspondence had gotten a certificate in law so that the prison was using him as a paralegal to help other inmates work on their cases. God began to lay His finger upon the fact that in order to do his job, C—— was having to lie for others. He immediately quit his job, even though it was bringing him good money by prison standards.

One time as we were leaving from a visit, C—— asked me to talk to him the next visit about divorce and remarriage. He said he was divorced. I never had to. The next time we were together he said, "I see what God says about it, and so I promised God that if He would see fit to bring my wife back into my life, I would welcome her back, but if not, I will never consider another woman." It has been consistently that way.

C—— already has read the Bible through several times in the last few months and told me he wanted to read it through every month this year. But then later he told me he might not make it because God kept him so long in Genesis chapters one and two. Oh, thank God for the life-changing power there is in His Word. Obviously, however, one must read it to find it.

After three months, I asked C—— if, really being honest, he would say there was any temptation along the lines of his addiction. His face broke immediately into a radiant smile.

"I was almost hoping you would ask me that. I tell you honestly, I have not felt one single urge or desire for any of it. You could set a whole bale of it in front of me and I would feel no desire for it."

I believe God in His mercy saw a helpless victim whom He knew was not responsible for his condition and removed it in a stroke. Praise His Name.

Recently C—— has been reading about the Holy Spirit, and prayed that God would give him the Holy Spirit. C—— asked God why he could not have Him right now. God impressed him to just stay right in His Word and when he understood the Lord as He wanted him to, He would give him the Holy Spirit. Oh, what a faithful preacher is the blessed Holy Spirit.

Pray that God will continue to lead C—— right into the fullness of the blessing. Or rather, pray that C—— will continue to follow Him without a hesitation. Oh, what a blessing it is to minister to a heart like this. How must the Holy Spirit feel as He ministers to him!

I want to give you one special prayer request. There is a man whom I have worked with for over a year now. I knew that he was not really getting to the bottom of his need, but in the last few weeks he has reached the end of his self-justification and is facing who he is and what he has done. I believe I can say that he is undergoing a case of old-fashioned conviction for sin such as I have not seen since I was a young man. The last three visits with him I have just wept with him as I saw him passing through the throes of Godly sorrow and repentance. I will try to tell you more later, but please pray that repentance will be such that it need not be repented of. How my heart yearns for him. Oh, that it can soon be said of him, too, that weeping may endure for a night, but joy cometh in the morning.

Thank you for listening and thank you most of all for praying. This is God's work; we are just laborers together with Him.

Yours and theirs in Jesus' Name,
William Cawman

+++

February 3, 2000

FIRST OF ALL, I surely want to thank everyone who has held me up in prayer during this past month. It is impossible to describe the support I feel again and again while working with these dear souls, but it is very real to me. It is therefore in a very real sense your ministry as well as ours. Oh, the value of united prayer! May we pray with the disciples, "Lord, teach us to pray."

We thank God the Holy Spirit, for His continuing faithfulness to C—— whom I told you about in our last letter. He told me yesterday, "Oh, I wish we could sit and talk oftener than once a week." From my side, however, I feel I am ministered to more than I can minister to him.

There are some that I try to see every week on a regular schedule and then many others who request a visit and then wait a while, Not all are by any means as bright or rewarding as others,. Oh, the broken lives, shattered emotions, messed up psychologies, distorted concepts of God and of His grace; and these are just a small part of the wages of sin. Many are still in love with some measure of their sin, but no one loves sin's wages.

The man I requested prayer for last month, who was passing through deep conviction of sin, still needs continued prayer. Pray also for me, that God will give me His wisdom in leading this dear man to a real knowledge of forgiveness. He has experienced too deep a measure of conviction to accept anything short of a living witness to his salvation; but the years of false religious teaching which has damaged the simplicity of faith in God, is a real struggle to him. And, as well, the devil is fighting him hard. As long as a soul is content with an emotional religion, the devil will even help him along, but let a soul set out to really find a God who can make him a new creature in Christ Jesus, and he is face-to-face with every devil out of hell.

I must tell you an amazing story of a man we shall call T——. I asked him to write his testimony out for me and I believe he received a blessing doing it. I shall try to give it to you.

He titled his testimony "Twenty Years of Darkness" and then followed it with, "Giving thanks unto the Father, which hath made us meet to be partakers of the inheritance of the saints in light: Who hath delivered us from the power of darkness, and hath translated us into the kingdom of his dear Son: In whom we have redemption through his blood, even the forgiveness of sins" (Colossians 1:12-14).

T—— says that for twenty years he practiced another faith in several sects, and used "all means necessary" to be all his religion demanded. During those years he had a notorious reputation for being a dangerous man in prison and in society. He preyed on drug dealers, pimps, gun-toting robbers and criminals alike. He stood six feet one with a muscular body weighing 275 pounds. No one trusted nor liked him. It was only fear that kept his enemies at bay. Attempts were made on his life, both within prison and without, but the game went on.

It was a Friday in 1997, the Holy Day for his sect. He entered the place of worship and made his prayers. Upon finishing, he sat on the rug-covered floor and listened to the sermon. Suddenly a question struck his mind: *Why are you sitting here listening to this man? After all these years of darkness, when are you going to see the light?*

The sermon and prayer ended; he walked out feeling something he had never experienced before. A Supernatural Force was working on him internally. It was business as usual on the outside. T——'s mind told him all was under control and he could handle himself, but the faithful Holy Spirit had begun His work.

T—— inserts here that for seven years he had been married to a praying Christian woman. (I will add that, thank God, they are still happily married and she is standing right with him.) He loved his wife because she had taught him to love himself. She knew the man inside and prayed and prayed for him.

Three days passed after T——'s encounter with the Holy Spirit in the place his sect worshipped. He tried to push it out of his mind and forget about it. He was still in control, so he thought.

It was six o'clock. He had threatened a man's life because the man had lied on him. T—— lost control of all mental faculties and went into a violent rage. It resulted in a violation of his probation and a warrant for his arrest. His world began to fall apart again.

T——'s wife refused to give up on him. Even so, he kept telling himself that he was still in control, and kept searching all the wrong places to find a way through his troubles. Nothing worked; he gave up completely. T—— turned again to drugs and robbing just as though he had a death wish. This continued about a week, but God's great grace was on its way.

On Sunday morning, T——'s wife was preparing for church. He looked at her and she said, "Will you come to church with me?"

"No!" he said. Then she demanded that he go. He consented—*no big deal*—so he thought.

They entered the church building during the praise and worship. T—— listened as the preacher spoke. All he wanted was to leave. Suddenly, the Holy Spirit took control of him. Before anyone could expect it, he was crying out to the Lord, the Savior Jesus Christ. T—— asked Him to accept him and forgive him for all his sins. He cried and pled like a little child. But the old devil wasn't finished with him yet. Oh friends, this battle for souls is no picnic nor tea party!

In fear and doubt, T—— again made room for the devil to work havoc in his mind. Before nightfall he was doing Satan's work. But, praise God, the Hound of Heaven was still on his trail too.

T—— could not execute his criminal activities with any confidence or pleasure. He felt bad when he used drugs; neither did he want to rob drug dealers. He was experiencing the conviction of the Holy Spirit but did not know it.

Without any warning, the devil compelled T—— to rob a drug dealer. He set out for his prey with someone else driving the car. T—— believed he was the best criminal you could find in his line of work. He inserts, "The vanity of fools is sinful insanity."

As T——'s partner stopped the car in front of some drug dealers, he jumped out. The dealers ran away and T—— became furious. The men continued driving on in search of the drug dealers. All of a sudden a voice said to T——, *Put the safety on the shot gun.* He had never set the safety on his gun; he wanted to be ready. Three times the voice repeated the command. Finally he set the safety.

Only minutes later, T—— told the driver to stop the car and jumped out right in the face of a drug dealer. He put the shotgun in his face and the man grabbed for the gun. Immediately T—— pulled the trigger, but nothing happened. They both stood there for a moment in a state of shock. As the dealer ran off, T—— told the driver to move over and he took the wheel. He let the driver off and never saw him again.

T—— drove straight home under deep conviction. When

he entered the door, he found his wife and some friends gathered in prayer. His wife said, "What's wrong with you? You look like you have seen a ghost."

T—— yielded for a while, and stayed in the house for two days, reading his Bible and praying. The battleground was to see one more struggle, as the man left his house and ran into one of his criminal associates.

The criminal friend had a large quantity of drugs, and offered T—— some. The devil jumped right into his mind and said, "Go ahead and get high; it won't hurt once more." T—— couldn't refuse the offer, and never thought about God.

Joining the group, T—— started shooting cocaine like the rest. He couldn't get high, however. He shot sixty CCs of cocaine into his arm, and suddenly without notice, the voice of God emerged in his mind. The exact words were, *"Go to church!"*

T—— became completely sober and felt as though he had not used drugs all day. He walked away with the men saying to him, "You're crazy."

Entering the church, he was greeted by some people who knew him, and who said, "We have been waiting for you." That very hour, the strong man yielded completely to the Stronger Man.

T—— says he knew exactly what he was doing when he asked Jesus Christ to forgive him of all his sins. He right there confessed to the church that he was a fugitive from the law and that in order to be right with God, he must do the right thing, even if that meant going back to prison.

The first two days after T——'s conversion, he was challenged by the craving for drugs, almost beyond his ability to resist. He cried to God for help and in an instant, God delivered him without any withdrawal, doubts, confusion or fear.

A few days later, T—— was so absorbed in his Bible that he did not see police approach him; he was surrounded by officers who told him he was coming with them.

"Yes," he said, "I am coming with you; God already showed me that."

This new Christian says, "I owe my life to God and my wife...they both loved me first, which came as the result of the greatest sacrifice. First Jesus Christ died on the cross for me." T—— says the end of his testimony is only the beginning of his diligent efforts to share his love for Jesus Christ, the Lord and Savior. He says, "I choose to serve with my life and death."

In the time I have known T——, I believe him to be as sincere a Christian as he was ever a zealot for the devil. I heard him testify in a service that when he was a member of the false religion, he hated what he was and what he did, but he did not know what to do about it. When he met Jesus Christ, he saw that those things were sin, and when he called them sin he found a Savior.

Once again, we thank you for your interest and prayers. Let us work while the day is.

Laborers together with Him,
William Cawman

March 7, 2000

Of all the things we could write to you, I must follow up an incident in the life of T—— which took place since the account we gave of him last month. How wonderful it is just to see God working in a life without that soul having to be told by someone what he should do.

After the story we told of him, T—— asked to see me one day. We visited and prayed for a few minutes and then he said, "There's something bothering me." I asked him what it was. He told me that for some time he had been working on his legal case to try to get back out of prison on parole. He had been studying in the law library and had a number of pages of material typed up. T—— had contacted doctors and lawyers and had all of their papers in his file.

Then he began to feel very heavy about what he was do-ing. He said the thought came to him, "I put my life in God's hands; what am I doing about it now?" T—— had called his wife that morning and told her; she said she felt the same way. He said he would come and talk to the chap-lain and then decide what to do.

As he was relating this to me, I felt a peculiar sense of God's direction in the whole affair. I began to testify to him how well God had ordered my own life when I really turned it over to Him. I told him of a time when something I had placed on the altar began to come back to me with a sense of anxiety. I had taken it to the secret closet, but no sooner did I get there than God just placed His hand on me and said, *Didn't you turn that over to me?*

I answered, "Yes, Lord."

He said, *What are you going to do about it now?*

As we shared this together, we could both feel God's pres-ence settling down around us. I said to him, "T——, I be-lieve if I were you I would put this back in God's hands. I would go ahead and go before the parole board and tell them that they already know your case; they know what your life has been; but tell them that you are a changed man by the grace of God and that whatever their decision is, you are going to live a new life."

With a black face glowing with God's light, he reached over without a word and picked up the whole file containing hours of work, and tore it to pieces. As he did it, I reached over and shook his hand. We both sensed God's witness to what he had done. His life, his future, his case were back on the altar and God was pleased. "Oh how sweet to trust in Jesus"!

Now I want to tell you of another heart-warming miracle. Let me say that it is a good thing God is the judge of who is ready to receive Him. There are hearts we have been working with, and some of them we have expected to really break through to God at any time, but surely R—— was not one of them. He seemed so heathen, so ignorant of God and His nature, so far from any comprehension of the Christian life. But God sees not as man sees.

R—— has requested to see us numbers of times and has told us repeatedly that he did not want to go on living like he was. One day right after we had had a visit, he received the news that his stepfather had passed away with a sudden heart attack. He wanted to see us again right away and was terribly distraught. The first words out of his mouth were, "Why would God do that to me? I just want Him to give my stepfather back to me." It took quite a while to reason with him and point out that God was not what he was picturing Him to be.

A few days ago, R—— had requested again to see me, and I had placed his name on the appointment sheet for the day. He was late showing up, however, and so I took the one that was to follow after him. He came down and when the officer told him he would have to wait, R—— began to act rude and talk back. Then he said he wasn't going to wait, and left. When the officer told me about it I said, "Well, don't call him back; just let him wait until he wants help a little worse than that."

The following Monday morning I went to R——'s unit to see another inmate and when R—— saw me he came over with a big smile and said, "Can I see you?"

"Yes," I said, "I'll be glad to see you but you will have to wait about half an hour."

"Oh, that's fine," he replied

When his turn came, R—— came in the room, and with a smile and a hug, said, "I'm doing wonderful, just wonderful. I got saved." I began to rejoice with him and asked him to tell me more about it.

The dear soul said he had been begging God to take all the rottenness out of his heart and to make it new. At the close of the service the night before, while others were coming forward to give their hearts to God, suddenly R—— just felt his heart break down and God came in. He had been a very radical racist and hated all black people, but he said that for the first time that night he saw no blacks and no whites; everyone was his brother.

Now I would really ask you to pray for R——. I will meet with him often for a while and try to help him get started in walking with and understanding God. He needs a whole new theology. Oh my, how hateful is the shabby religious teaching that the devil has pawned off on the hearts of men.

R—— was already worried about what he would do when he sinned again. I told him he didn't need to sin again.

"Oh," he said, "I will—the Bible says, 'There is none righteous, no not one.'" After explaining to him what that meant, I told him we would read the third chapter of I John together. He wanted to see it for himself and said, "Oh, I'm going to read that again when I get to my room."

You see, the devil had already given him the Scripture he wanted him to believe in, and I'm afraid the devil has many willing workers out there who have rested in that Scripture themselves to the absolute denial of all the rest of the Word of God.

I then challenged him a bit. I asked if he intended or felt he would sin before he left the room. He said, "Oh no." I then asked if he felt he would need to sin on the way back to his room. He again said, "Oh no." So then I told him that he did not have to live without sin six weeks from then; he just needed to live one moment at a time and keep loving Jesus. I asked R—— if he felt a love in his heart for Jesus. He said, "Oh yes I do; I love Him with all my heart."

Will you pray that he will keep loving Jesus with all his heart?

Now I would like to give you two specific prayer requests:

1. Please pray that God will keep the whole chaplaincy department covered with the Blood. The entire chaplaincy department of this state is under fire from a religion which considers Christians enemies. When you consider that in many other countries this sect outlaws Christians, and is actively killing them, it is no wonder that there is tension felt between them here. I do believe that as long as God has a work for us

to do in saving souls, He will keep the door open for us, but I do not believe we can neglect prayer concerning this. The Scripture does predict a time when the night cometh and no man can work.

2. Please pray that God will direct us trying to meet the growing need for aftercare for the prisoners who are released. It is such a burden to see a soul who is yet tender and needy, released back into the world with the same temptations and allurements that he failed under before. The need is so great for a network of compassionate Christians who can and will show these that there is a better way. It seems what little we have been able to do so far, falls terribly short of the great need. We may bring this subject up at a later date, but please help us pray.

Again, we would not forget to thank each one of you for your interest and prayers. May the Lord keep us in the center of His will, sold out to Him completely, and willing to do or be whatever He desires.

Yours and theirs in Him,
William Cawman

2
Rubber Cells and Redeemed Souls

April 3, 2000

As I LOOK BACK over the events of the past month, I wonder how I can relate everything I would like to in this letter. I do want you to know each one that again and again we feel the definite effects of your prayers and see results to them, too.

We don't want in any way, however, to paint a false picture or an all-positive view of prison ministry. I think of the times during the past month when I have been asked to visit inmates in the rubber cell, whose minds are so tormented by demons that they want to kill themselves or someone else. The officer stands by my side and warns me in the hearing of the prisoner that if his hand comes out of the food port in the door, the visit is over.

The prisoner has been so distraught that he is flinging fecal matter at the passing officers, or reaching out to scratch someone. As I begin to talk to him, I see his face soften and his body relax. He gets down on his knees where he can look at my face through the food port and says softly, "Will you pray for me?"

I wish at times I could just open the door and go in and sit down for a while and try to lead him to Jesus, the Healer of soul, mind, and body; but we have to work under the provisions that are made. This is not an isolated case; we see it more often than we wish.

Then there is the inmate who is being tormented in the night by dreams that Satan is standing right over him saying, "I'll get you!" He can't stand it any longer, so he asks for a night job so that he doesn't have to be left alone in the dark. One gets picture after picture of a little of what hell would be like. Some of these poor men are living in hell before they ever get there.

My co-worker, the supervisory chaplain, went to the hospital last Sunday night and found an inmate alone in a cold, dark room—dying. He was all along with his final battle, and perhaps had never had anyone who cared about his soul. The chaplain spoke to him and prayed with him and a tear fell from the prisoner's eye, but that was the only response he could give. The chaplain told me he left and just walked the compound a while to try to compose himself. And at the same time he was visiting this man, he looked across into the yard and there was a twenty-four-year-old man lying on the ground, dying of a heart attack.

No, it is not all bright scenes by any means. "Sin, when it is finished, bringeth forth death."

But listen; God is working! I went to the hospital recently and met a prisoner who was just turning seventy on St. Patrick's Day. He is a Korean War veteran and, as his task was to load the bombs, he inhaled gases which damaged his lungs. As a result, his lungs are enlarged and he needs surgery on them, but his heart is in no shape for lung surgery.

This prisoner became a truck driver after leaving the Air Force and drove for thirty-three years. Just at retirement age he messed up and landed in prison.

I asked this man if he wouldn't want to pray to Jesus and ask Him to take away his sins, forgive him, and give him a new life. He said he would like to do that. Less than two weeks later I went back to see him and he said, "He did it! I asked Him to forgive all my sins and He did. I feel a peace in my heart." I asked the inmate when it happened and he said, "Last Thursday."

Hallelujah what a Savior! "The vilest offender who truly believes, that moment from Jesus a pardon receives." This man is really enjoying his new-found joy. He told me that he looks back over his life now and remembers all the times when someone asked him if he knew the Lord. He would always respond roughly with the comment that he was a Catholic. He said, "Oh, now I wish I had given God my heart long ago."

If you remember a few months ago we told you of an inmate C—— who was saved right out of a severe heroin addiction and has been following the Lord so closely through His Word. A few weeks ago, God gave him a stunning revelation of what still remains in his heart. He came frightfully close to letting the Old Man of sin get back in control and making himself end up in the detention center, and worse by far, back in spiritual Egypt.

God, however, delivered him without incident and he is now really scared of what he saw within. He is really seeking to be delivered from all sin. Please pray for him. God so worked it around that he is now in the facility where we have the Bible study every Friday night and he is so happy about that.

C—— told me the other day that he is spending more time praying and reading God's Word. "Oh, I'm beginning to just see it all so clearly. In the Old Testament God has showed us exactly what kind of a man He wants us to be, and then in the New Testament He tells us that Jesus died to enable us to be that man." I couldn't find much fault with his theology.

Please pray for this man. Oh what it could mean if he can let God finish the work of holiness in his heart.

This need extends beyond just *his* heart. The need is so great for someone to really become a living witness that one of their own number, living right in prison with them, has found this all-important experience. Many of them are beginning to really comprehend what it means to have the old man of sin crucified, to be able to live above all sin within and without. Some still question whether it is possible and others are believing it is. But nothing could be more convincing than for someone of their own number to come up shouting the victory over all sin. C—— testified that this is the first time in his life that he has experienced something where sinning has stopped in his life.

The other Sunday some of the inmates almost got us into trouble. A preacher had followed us up from the previous Sunday and was telling them that there is no way to really live free from all sin. A dear brother stood right up in the service and said, "Chaplain Cawman told us we can!" The other inmates thought the preacher had his desserts, but I cautioned them to back off a little.

I must find room here to tell you of another miracle, inmate S——. Pardon me if I give you a glimpse into this forty-five-year-old man.

He is known to many officers as one of the tough guys. Sometime back in his twenty-year prison career, he suddenly flew off the handle at another man and grabbed an iron pipe and split the man's head open. As his victim fell to the ground, S—— grabbed another iron bar and with super-human might, jammed it right through the man. S—— used so much force that he bent the bar. Pulling it out, he straightened it over his knee and thrust it through the man again. All this time two officers stood watching, so shocked they were helpless to move.

S—— had nothing to do with God or religion, and often declared there was no God. He made a mock of anyone with a Bible; they were sissies—he was a man!

S—— said he wanted to see me. I called him in a few days ago and he sat there and testified to the forgiving, saving grace of God until I felt like shouting for joy. He told me that he had finally come to the bottom of everything and just cried out to God that he needed Him. The man said a sense of forgiveness came until he felt like a load of years was lifted off his shoulders.

This dear soul wants to get out of prison and do all he can to live as hard for God as he did for the devil. He longs to try to help others until they won't enter the same life he lived so long. S—— carries a Bible in his pocket everywhere he goes and does not hesitate to tell others Whom he belongs to now. We enjoyed the visit so much that he asked if he could come back at least every other week. I'll let you guess what I told him.

Let me squeeze in one more story. A request came from the hospital last week for us to see an inmate who is dying and who told the nurse that he didn't feel God loved him. We tried to point him to Jesus and told him to tell all of his sins to Jesus, and ask Him to forgive him.

We went back later and prayed with the inmate again. It is almost impossible to hear him, as he has no strength nor voice left. Last night between services I stopped back to see him again, and as I entered his cell he smiled at me and pointed to the door. There he had someone tape a little paper which said, "Jesus—I shall not die, but live."

I said, "Has Jesus forgiven your sins and come into your heart?" He smiled and shook his head yes. I said, "Do you love Jesus and does He love you?"

He said feebly, "All the time." After we prayed and thanked God for His mercy, he smiled again and struggled to get his hand out from under the blanket for me to shake it.

Small wonder it is that when God condescended to answer the cry of Moses for Him to show him His glory, "the Lord passed by before him, and proclaimed, The Lord, The Lord God, merciful and gracious, longsuffering, and abundant in goodness and truth…" Who is a god like our God?

And now, while we thank God for all He is doing, we are also conscious of such great needs. "He was not willing that **any** should perish." Please pray for those who are still unable to really see God as He is. Many are still in love with some secret sin. Many are bound by Satan's chains and threatened with fear and doubt. Many, oh so many, as yet have no Savior. They take on His lovely name, but they are strangers to the power to live as He desires them to. The plague we face is not the power of heathen darkness, but the crippling tragedy of having been taught that God will love them in their sin. Worse by far than no religion is a religion which slaps Calvary in the face like this. Thank you for continuing to pray.

Once again, yours and theirs in Jesus' Name

William Cawman

May 8, 2000

How quickly a month flies by, and yet no sooner had the last letter gone out than something happened which has blessed my heart ever since.

In the prison hospital there has been an inmate whom I just got to know better in the last few weeks. He was born in Italy and came to this country at a young age. Then for several years he went back and forth between Italy and the United States. Finally the Italian government told him that if he were to continue to come to their country he would have to serve time in the Italian armed forces. So at the age of eighteen he enlisted in the Italian Marines. When his time was expired, he returned to the United States at the age of twenty-one. He is now twenty-nine.

Somehow in the last few years he did something wrong which ended him up in prison. While he was in prison a tumor was discovered on his brain and he was sent to the hospital to have it removed. When he recovered from the surgery, he was entirely paralyzed on the left side of his face and the right side of his body. He has been in a wheelchair ever since because he cannot walk. This man's face is somewhat distorted from the effects of being paralyzed, but he has the use of his hearing, sight and speech. He is a large man and requires an oversize wheelchair, which is difficult to get through door-ways and narrow places.

For several months back, this inmate had regularly attended the services held in the prison and I could sense that he was serious about it, too. He would occasionally ask some very elementary question, but I could see that he really had no living relationship with God.

On Sunday night the second of April, just the day before I wrote the last letter, I was in the prison for a service. It was a good turnout and God really seemed to help many of the men. There were several who spoke to me on the way out and asked if they could have a time to visit. This man was one of them and I could see that he was deeply distressed.

It was the next Thursday, April 6th, before I could get away from the main prison needs to go back over to the hospital. After I visited with several of the inmates there, he came in to see me. He began to tell me his life's story as I have briefly outlined it to you above. Then he went on to tell me with a deep sense of burden on his heart, that for some time he had been trying to find something real in God.

This man had been raised a Roman Catholic, but never found any peace with God in that. He told me that he had been reading his Bible a lot, and that he had been praying a lot, and he had stopped sinning and cursing. "But," he said, "I'm not finding anything."

He poured it out with such deep distress and conviction. I wonder how many other hearts there are in the world that are in the same condition. "Behold how many thousands still are lying, Bound in the darksome prison house of sin, With none to tell them of the Saviour's dying, Or of the life He died for them to win." How many perhaps cry themselves to sleep many a night saying into the black despair of all their efforts, "I'm not finding anything."

My heart went out to this man. How could I help it; I was there once and I know how dark that night is. I said to him, "No, and you won't find anything either, until you stop trusting in what you are doing and trust wholly in the Blood of Jesus. What you are doing is right, but it cannot save you. You must read your Bible and pray; you must stop sinning and cursing, but that won't save you. If you could save yourself, Jesus would not have needed to die for you on the cross of Calvary. You must trust only in the Blood of Jesus.

He looked into my eyes with his open one, and it began to cloud with tears. With a quivering voice he asked, "Could we do that right now?"

I said, "Yes we can, and we will." This dear man did not know how to pray, so I asked him to repeat after me. As I began to pray I felt as if I were the one coming to God. The man fervently repeated every word after me. All I know to say friends, is that when we had come about halfway to the Blood, the Spirit whispered so clearly to my heart, "Don't stop—just bring him right on in."

And soon I was praying, "Jesus, I love You." The inmate responded with deep feeling, "Jesus, I love You so much!"

By now we were both in tears. I said to him, "Do you know that Jesus just took you into the family of God?"

He said, "Yes, I know it; it's so wonderful."

I said, "Jesus just made you happy, didn't He?"

"Yes He did; it feels so good," he replied.

I said, "Do you know what else just happened? You made Jesus happy too. The angels in heaven are rejoicing; a sinner has come home."

"Oh," he said, "I love Him so much."

I made it a point to see this man often for a couple of weeks, and every time he had the same thing to say, "Oh, I just love Jesus so much! I can't tell you how much I love Him." I had his name on my list today to visit and found out that he was suddenly sent home. Pray that he'll keep loving Jesus so much!

I must tell you of another inmate, also in the hospital, but the story is not so bright. I had also seen this inmate in services several times, but he seemed very depressed and unresponsive.

One day I was sent for, the nurse saying that he wanted to see me. I found the inmate nearly dead. I cannot describe in this letter the pitiful shape he was in. He was very infectious and I had to put on gloves and mask to visit with him. I thought to myself, *My dear man, why did you wait till now?*

I asked the man if he felt that his sins were forgiven. He said he wasn't sure. I prayed with him and he said he wanted a Bible. I went over to the prison and got him one, and went back to see him either later that day or the next. The following day when I went to see him they said they had sent him to a hospital in Trenton.

I really didn't think I'd ever see him again. It haunted me, and I prayed for him. Nearly every day I checked the inmate roster and it said he was still in Trenton. After several weeks he suddenly wheeled into the Sunday night service in his wheelchair. He had made an amazing recovery that I never expected to see, nor did anyone else.

But, here is the sad part of the story. He doesn't want me to talk to him now. He knows full well it is only a matter of time until he will go down again, maybe for the last time. But oh, what a cheating liar the devil is.

I finally cornered him in the hall after he evaded visiting with me. I tried to reason with him. I told him that God in mercy spared his life and he ought to do something about getting right with Him before he came to that place again. I told him he had nothing to lose by giving his heart to Jesus.

He said, "Yes, I know," and turned his wheelchair and rode down the hall. Here are two unfathomable mysteries pitted against each other: the marvelous grace of our loving Lord, and the vicious, hellish, bondage of the depths of sin.

I must tell you now that inmate C—— whom we wrote about in the January newsletter is such a blessing to my heart. He continues to grow in grace and in the knowledge of God's Word in such an outstanding way. So often when we get together and begin to talk of the things of God (and we never talk about much of anything else) he will say, "Oh isn't it just wonderful that you are talking to me about this; this is just what God has been telling me."

C—— has taken all the fences down and I cannot see him balking at anything God has to say to him. It is wonderful to see how fast God can lead a person if he really wants to follow.

Today we were talking about how God really expects every part of our lives, inward and outward, to measure up to the standard of His Word. We talked about how clear God's Word is as to how we should live, and look, and talk, and keep the Sabbath, etc. He got so excited as he said, "Oh, this is just wonderful! God has just been showing me the same things."

Wouldn't it be wonderful to have a church full of people who were so led by the Spirit that they were constantly a jump ahead of the preacher? We too often forget that preaching is designed by God to be but a second witness—the Holy Spirit has already been there. I do believe that the reach of C—— for God would snow many longtime church-goers under pretty deeply. I do love the dear man, and I know you would too if you love the Lord.

C——, along with a few others, is really seeing and feeling the need of a pure heart. Please pray fervently as God would lead you for these few. There are two mighty forces working against them. First, the devil does not want them to get it; he really doesn't. And secondly, the undisciplined past of their lives must be brought into obedience to the will of God. In spite of all, pray that it will happen, and happen soon! "Our God Is Enough!"

Once again, thank you each one for your prayers.

In Him,
William Cawman

June 6, 2000

Thank you each one again for your prayers through another month. I don't know how to encourage you enough to keep up the battle. If you could experience some of the reward of your prayers you would need nothing else, and I wish many times that you could. I can only do my best to pass along to you how God is moving in answer to the prayers of His children. It is not His will that we grow weary, but it is certainly the aim of the enemy of our souls. With Jesus, we shall win!

Throughout the month I often jot down a note of something which I want to tell you, but I feel very strongly impressed to come to you with one great need: it is the need of those who are sensing the Spirit leading them on to holiness of heart. I do believe that God honors united, specific prayer, and I feel that this is the greatest need of all others—the cleansing of the heart from all sin. As long as one grain of mustard seed or one drop of leaven is left in the heart, the enemy knows he still has a foothold there. And it is for this very reason he has so successfully cheated many out of the blessing for years.

Some he has made to feel that this blessed work of the Holy Spirit was for some, but not for them; it is just simply out of their reach. Others he has cunningly deceived into thinking they have the experience while down deep inside they know that there are at times unholy stirrings. So many are living here that it is very easy to find sympathy and understanding for such a condition.

The purpose of this letter is not to preach; I only stated those facts to say that we don't need to add a group of prisoners to the number of these who are living short of the fullness of the blessing. We need some prisoners who will die completely to self and sin and the old "me" until they can rise living witnesses to the central purpose of the cross of Calvary. Please, please help us to pray specifically for this; and may the Spirit help our infirmities.

God alone can accomplish this great work; you and I can't, and He has let me know that. I was visiting recently with one inmate who was really walking in the light and reaching for a sanctified heart. As I left him and was walking outside to another part of the prison, my heart was crying out, "Oh that he can get sanctified! Oh that he can really go all the way through!"

All of a sudden God spoke to me very clearly, *Who is it that will sanctify him?* I took the back seat again and rolled him into God's hands and with that I felt like shouting all over the prison, "It is God Who sanctifies!" "Wherefore Jesus also, that He might sanctify the people with His own blood, suffered without the gate."

I would like to tell you of at least three inmates who are really pressing their way on to this precious blessing. One I have mentioned before as one who for many years of incarceration held the reputation of one of the "tough guys" who had better not be interfered with. If you remember, he was the one who thrust an iron bar right through a man twice right in front of two officers who stood shocked into helplessness as he did it.

About two years ago he really repented of his old life and got saved, and has been a changed man ever since. The other day he came to see me and was troubled. He told me again how God had changed him and how his life is so different from what he used to be. He said he didn't even like to think about his old life and all the things he had done. But, he went on to say that for several days one of the officers who had known him for years and a couple of inmates who also knew him well, began to bring up the old "him" and sort of pump him up about it. He said that there is an element in the prisons which admires and respects that type of a "man." They had been telling him that the other prisoners were afraid of him because they had heard of all he had done in the past.

He looked at me and said, "There is something which really bothers me. I gave up that life; I hate it; I don't even like to think about it. If they knew how many times I have cried in the night over my old life and the things I've done, they wouldn't think it was so great. But the thing that bothers me is that I felt something down inside that was a secret love for that type of an image."

Now maybe you think it's strange, but I felt a thrill of excitement. I told him I was really encouraged for him. He couldn't understand why I would say that to him until I began to very simply explain about the old nature of sin which was still living down inside of him. He had no trouble understanding that. I told him that it was God's love for him that was showing him that he had an enemy of God on the inside which He wanted to get rid of. I told him not to ignore anything which he found within his heart which was unlike Jesus, but to drag it to the Cross and ask God to nail it there. He began to see very clearly what was meant by the old "me" that needs to be done away with. Please pray for him that he will let the Spirit do His perfect work in his heart.

Another inmate I want you to pray for is the one we have mentioned before by the name of C———. He is really seeing his heart and his need, and his love for God and His Word is pulling him on. I loaned him the little pamphlet taken from the book *Perfect Love*. He read it and said, "That is just what I need. I can't wait to get there." A few days later he told me that God was really showing him how many things are unlike Him in his heart. He said that he sees it may take a long time to get it all taken care of.

Immediately I recognized the same old devil that had cheated my own heart out of the blessed life of holiness for way too long. I said, "C———, be careful; that's a trick of the devil to keep you from ever getting sanctified. You must be willing to stay at it if it takes you the rest of your life, but you must expect it to happen today." Please pray for him also, that he will escape the snares of the devil. Things like that make me hate the devil more than ever. He has no more right to C——— than he does to you and me. He is no respecter of persons and he is truly just what God's Word says he is: "…your adversary the devil, as a roaring lion, walketh about, seeking whom he may devour."

Let me squeeze in one more. His name is V———. He is a Spanish boy with a tender heart, who truly loves God. In the year or more that I have been visiting with him and preaching to him I have seen a steady growth in his spiritual walk. He is known as a man of God among the other inmates, and incidentally they know who the hypocrites are, too. If the old song is true anywhere, it surely is in prison: "What you are speaks so loud, the world can't hear what you say." For a man to be known as a really genuine Christian among those he cannot get away from and among those who are anything but Christians, takes a little more than many professors possess. He told me not long ago that he used to be like one of those cranes with a huge ball on it for knocking down buildings. He said that was the way he was around anyone who didn't agree with him. He thought he had to bring them into line with the Bible too. But he said God took all that away from him and he just lives for God and remembers the pit from which he was dug.

If there is any characteristic mentioned in II Corinthians 7:11 of a person who has "sorrowed after a godly sort" which is outstanding in V——, it is "what carefulness it wrought in you." V—— walks with God in such carefulness of spirit that God is able to tell him anything He wants to. He has been seeking to be sanctified also, and yet sometimes as I visit with him I wonder if he is sanctified. But then, that's the way really good regeneration victory ought to work, isn't it? The other day we sat together and just spoke of the things God was doing in his life and we could hardly keep the tears back from our eyes. It just felt as if God Himself came down in that little chapel with us and placed His great big warm smile all over him.

The night before I had preached to the men on *Pure Gold:* "I counsel thee to buy of me gold tried in the fire." V—— had listened intently and had thanked me as he went out. The next day as we were visiting, he mentioned it again and said how intensely God was talking to him the same way; that this Christian life is an intensely close walk with God, and that God will invade every area of our lives until we are living according to His Word. He was very specific too, but let me interject something here if I may.

One of the rare rewards of working with these dear men who have not been walking behind light for years is that given the clear teaching of God's Word, they have no problem accepting it as the truth. It burdens one's heart intensely to see young people who have been brought up in holiness churches beginning to re-evaluate and re-interpret the plain teachings of God's Word. It hurts to hear them say, "Oh that's not necessary." I wonder what ever happened to "what carefulness it wrought in you"?

V—— told me that God had spoken tenderly to him and checked him about the often-used expression in today's street language: "Was'up?" Maybe you don't see anything wrong with that—I didn't either, although it wasn't my habit to use it. He said that God told him it was slang and he could leave it alone. He did. He didn't excuse it, or justify it, or say there was nothing wrong with it; he just quit using it. He said, "Now I just greet people with, 'Good morning.' They say, 'What did you say?' And I say, 'Good morning.' They look at me like I'm a stranger. I am. This world is not my home." Oh Apostle Paul, is that what you were talking about? "What carefulness it wrought in you."

Please pray for V—— that he'll never "learn" how to reason with the faithful Holy Spirit. This young man was not raised in a holiness home. He left what home he had at the age of fourteen for the streets, later met his father in a park and beat him up and has not seen him since. He wants so much when he gets out of prison to find his father and ask his forgiveness. This young man sees clearly the difference between those who preach a sinning religion and the real thing. He is literally walking in the light. The incident I just told you of is just one of many; it is the way he lives every day. He is endeavoring to finish his high school work for his GED and God let him know he wasn't really applying himself to his studies as hard as he could. He went right to his teacher and asked her to forgive him and set about to correct the situation. He is truly a man who responds to Him who said, "I will guide thee with Mine eye." Can you see why I go often to visit him? He is worthy of the name *Christian.*

There are others we might sketch to you later, but these I have tried to portray so that you will pray for them and for the greatest need of the hour: a Pentecost. If a few of them can find the pearl of great price they could do more by their testimony than all of our sermons and teaching put together.

Last Friday night in Bible study the men didn't want to spend long in singing or testimonies; they wanted to get right to the Word. The moment we began to speak to them from the fifteenth chapter of John, I sensed an unusual presence of God in the room. It seemed that the Holy Spirit took over the words we were trying to speak and sent them straight to their hearts. I just felt like an empty channel as He spoke directly to them of the need and the possibility of fully living in the Vine. I bowed my head after the service and thanked Him and thanked Him. Would you please thank Him too? And please keep praying. I wish I could express to each of you how sensibly conscious I am again and again of the Arm that is moving in answer to prayer. Several of the men said that night on the way out, "God was really here tonight."

Keep up your courage, praying brothers and sisters. Even that night which cometh when no man can work, is in His hands. Thank you each one again.

Yours and theirs in Him,
William Cawman

3
DEATHBEDS AND BLESSINGS

July 11, 2000

THIS LETTER IS LATER than usual due to our being gone for a revival and a camp meeting. I just returned today to the prison and was warmly greeted by many. I question if any congregation loves their pastor with more feeling than these men.

I was only back a few minutes before a call came that an inmate was dying in the hospital and wanted to see me. I don't know whether it was his idea to send for the chaplain or not. Although he did not object to prayer with him, he evidenced no real concern about his condition. He must know he is dying and is not expected to make it beyond tonight or tomorrow, but he asked nothing about his soul. He asked me to hand him his glass of water, but when I did he shook so violently that he could barely wet his lips. All I could think of was, *There will be no water in hell.*

By the time you receive this letter he will no doubt already be in eternity. I will go see him again before the Bible study this evening; I hope and pray that he will have heeded the words I already tried to speak to him. I have seldom tried to pray with anyone with more of a feeling of emptiness. I hope this man wants God enough to find Him.

There are several men who are dying in the hospital just now. The social worker told me a few minutes ago that she cannot seem to get even their families to care enough to come and see them. What a tragic ending to a tragic life; alone in this life, and forsaken by God in the next—all because of SIN!

I must tell you about the Friday evening Bible study before I left for the revival and camp meeting. We had been studying for several weeks about what it really means to live the Christian life. We had been dwelling in the fifteenth chapter of John where Jesus speaks about abiding in the Vine. Along with it we had been very plain in pointing out that according to God's Word not everything that is called Christian is going to enter the gate of heaven. We had looked carefully at the scriptures saying, "Not every one that sayeth unto me, Lord, Lord, etc." and "And why call ye me Lord, Lord, and do not the things which I say?"

As we came into the study that evening an inmate asked me if he could say something. I sensed it was in order and gave him permission. He stood up before the men and told them how God had been speaking to him through the scriptures we had been studying the last few weeks. He said he felt deeply convicted by the scripture in Luke 6:46 we quoted above. He said he felt he could not go on and say "Lord, Lord" and not do what he knew he should do. He told them how he had struggled to give up smoking, but felt so convicted by that scripture that he asked another brother to pray with him and he gave it up to God. He said that three days had gone by and he felt no desire to smoke. Then he just broke down and began to weep before the men. One after another rose to their feet and began to praise God, and the room was just bathed with the presence and favor of God. By the time I got up to teach there was such liberty and power in the room that it felt as though God was just pouring His truth out upon their hungry hearts. It never fails: when sin is removed, grace flows like a river. I love those times when someone clears the channel for God to come down in power and glory.

Please continue to pray for the inmates who are sensing their need of holiness of heart and are seeking after it. A very heart-warming incident happened the other day in the court yard which I will relate to you as I heard it from both parties.

The incident took place between inmate C—— whom we have told you about, and inmate T—— who was of a radical, Christian-hating sect, and who got saved a little over two years ago and has been loving Jesus violently ever since. C—— has been seeing very clearly his need of getting sanctified and has been seeking it. He was telling T—— about getting sanctified and having the nature of sin removed from the heart. T—— just looked at him as though he was shocked for several minutes and then said, "I see it; I need that; I'm going to call my wife and tell her about it." He did and she confirmed that it was God's will. He came to see me and to tell me all about it, and he said, "I'm going to let God do that for me." I couldn't help relating him to the men whom Paul found at Ephesus who said, "We have not so much as heard whether there be any Holy Ghost." Thank God, understand it fully or not, he wants it just as violently as he has been loving Jesus.

I want to tell you a little more about the first of the three men we told about in the last letter who have been seeking for a pure heart. This is the same man S—— that we told you about some time ago who was such a "tough guy" as to stab another inmate clear through with an iron bar, straightening it out over his knee in between blows.

S—— recently received another stunning revelation of his old man of sin. In the tier below him were two cellmates who were not getting along too well, and one of them had his television set ruined by someone pouring water on it. His cellmate accused S—— of doing it and a sergeant who had known S—— in his former lifestyle believed the accusation and laid the blame on him. S—— came to see me with a broken heart and told me about it. He said, "If they only knew the times I have cried in the night over the way I used to be, they would know I was not about that stuff anymore." But then he told me that the accusation was not what was hurting him the most. It was the fact that when he was accused he felt anger rise in his heart toward the sergeant. He said he did not want that there and was so grieved to feel it. He also said if it had not been for his cellmate he would have bawled all night over what he found in his heart.

I want to share with you what has sent a cry to God from my heart ever since he told me that. What if no one had been there to tell him that there is a "balm in Gilead" which can cleanse the heart of all of that? And, oh God, how many other hearts are crying in the night, "O wretched man that I am! Who shall deliver me from the body of this death?" Dear brothers and sisters of this message of full salvation, the pulpits and airwaves of this present day are filled with the message of a sinning religion. To that heart crying in the night for the ability to live above sin, the message pounds his ears from every direction, "We all know that we can't live the Christian life perfectly. We all sin and are in need of a Savior." If that is the message of Calvary, the Man on the middle cross was a failure. Sin and Satan have won the day; the disease is greater than the cure. May God forgive and awaken us lest as we sleep the tares choke out the tender wheat!

This message of full salvation—holiness of heart and life— is not a message only for the inside of the closed doors of the sanctuary. It is the message the world is dying without.

Someone is crying in the night. No one has told them yet.

A dear friend remarked a few days ago that we must only relate the bright side of prison ministry in our letters. Perhaps we do most of the time. There is plenty of the other side. A few hours ago we stepped into the cell of an inmate who is dying of AIDS. He was sitting in a wheelchair and there was a New Testament lying on his bed. We started to say something about the Testament and he immediately began to curse it violently. We asked him if he would like us to pray with him and he began to curse again with vehemence. We left him, but will return. Oh what a monster is the master of sin. With life nearly gone and nothing but hell ahead, still cursing and damning God, sin claims its victim and death does the same.

Notwithstanding the fact that as Martin Luther said, "On earth is not his equal," God is moving mightily in answer to your prayers, dear friends. This is God's battle for it was His idea. We want to thank each one of you again for your prayers and support. Without it, nothing would be accomplished worth mentioning. Some of these seeking men have asked emphatically that we ask you to pray for them. Just think, one of them might be your neighbor in heaven. The rewards are not all in. Keep up the good work and I'm sure God will do His part.

Yours and theirs because of Calvary,
William Cawman

August 3, 2000

PRAISES BE TO GOD—one of the inmates you have been praying for has gotten sanctified. He is the one we have told you about in previous letters who has been living such a careful life and walking with God so closely. Several times in the last few weeks I have come home from visiting with him and told my wife that I really wondered if he wasn't sanctified. "By their fruits ye shall know them."

Monday morning, the last day of July, he came in to see me and said, "Chaplain Cawman, I just don't know what to think. For some time now, every time I pray and ask God to cleanse my heart and sanctify me I get the same answer— *It's already done!*"

I looked at him and said, "Well, do you think it is time to acknowledge what God is telling you?"

He began to grin and said, "I think it is." He dates back to a Bible study a few months ago when God moved in and changed his whole life on the inside. He has told me about it numbers of times. He said, "That night when God did that for me, a deep peace came into my heart and it has stayed there. One thing I know, from that time I have found no sin in my heart."

This dear man went on to tell me of the precious seasons he has been having in prayer alone in the night. He said there are times when his heart feels so full of God, and as he sits down to read His Word he is so happy that other men pass by his cell and look in and say, "What's the matter with you; you're crazy. How come you're so happy?" Thank you, everyone who has been praying for these men, and may this be the first fruits of a pentecostal revival.

In the last letter I told you about a man I had visited that day in the hospital, and how he cursed and nearly ran us out of his cell. I must tell you the rest of his story which happened after I had sent the letter.

The following day they sent him out to another hospital for evaluation of his condition. He is dying of AIDS. They told him there was nothing they could do for him and that he was soon to die. Hospital personnel sent him back and he was so angry that he tied a cord around his neck and threatened to hang himself. They took him down stairs to the rubber cell and locked him in under close watch. The following day I went back to see him and it was a sight impossible to describe. I could almost wish I could have had a picture of that scene to show to any young man who is about to commit his first sin, or to that young person who is about to yield to the tempting pressure, "Oh come on; everyone is doing it."

As I looked through the food port in the door—they will not allow anyone to enter the cell when an inmate is on watch like that—I saw the wasted body of a former athlete lying on a rubber mat, half leaning on the wall. He is possibly in his thirties or early forties. He had no clothes on for fear of his using them to hurt himself. He turned and looked at me and began to yell at me again. I yelled back at him, "Mr. ——, don't you know that God is love? Don't you know that God can take all that anger and sin out of your heart and give you a new clean heart to take to heaven?" He let out a few more yells and I left him.

That night, Friday, I told the men in the Bible study all about him. I asked them to pray for the man and reminded them that while there is life there is hope. They did pray too.

On Saturday I do not usually go in to the prison, but after lunch I called the officer in the hospital and asked him how the inmate was getting along. He told me they had moved him back up to his cell upstairs and that the nurse might appreciate it if I could come in and see him. I dropped what I was doing and went in.

I went to his cell and looked through the food port. He was lying in bed and I said to him, "Mr. ——, do you remember me?"

"Yes."

I said, "Mr. ——, have you been praying?"

"Yes."

Then I questioned, "Mr. ——, does Jesus forgive your sins?"

"Yes."

"Mr. ——, do you want me to pray with you?"

"Yes."

After I prayed, he looked at me and said, "I thank you, God bless you." That was nearly two weeks ago and he still lingers barely this side of eternity, but every time I go to see him and ask him if Jesus forgives his sin, he shakes his head very definitely "Yes."

The other man whom I told you about also in the last letter who was dying of cancer and made so little response the first time I prayed with him, also made a turn around the following day. I prayed with him and tried to lead him to forgiveness and the following day when I asked him again if he wanted his sins forgiven he said, "Yes, we did that yesterday." The man lived a few more days; the barber came in to shave him and give him a haircut and told him it would make him look better for his funeral, and then he died.

Friends, I leave these men with God. I am just so thankful that Jesus gave us the account of the dying thief. I'm not sure whether I could grasp that degree of mercy were it not for that story. I tell you plainly that the deathbed of a profligate in sin is a horrible spectacle. I pray much that God will allow me to see these men through the eyes of Jesus. They are totally repulsive through mine.

Not all end up with a death bed. One man had come to Bible study many times over the past couple of years but finally ended up bedfast. He too was dying of AIDS and was only in his early forties, I believe. It didn't look good for him and everyone thought he would die very soon.

This inmate called for me and I went to see him. I asked him if he felt his sins were forgiven. He said he wasn't sure of it at all. He wanted a Bible and I took him one and visited with him three times in two days. Then they sent him to Trenton to try and help him. After several weeks he returned in much better shape. But when he returned feeling better, he didn't want to talk to me anymore.

I stopped him in the hall in his wheelchair and talked pretty straight to him. I told him that God had spared his life and that he ought not to wait until he was in that kind of shape again. He said, "I know it." I pressed it a little further and told him he had nothing to lose. He said, "I know it," and turned in his wheel chair and went down the hall. The other day he dropped dead of a heart attack. He never had another death bed to get things right.

I have had several good visits lately with T——, the former adherent to a Christian-hating faith. We leave each other every time feeling like the two did on the way to Emmaus, our hearts burned within us. Oh what a miracle of grace some of these formerly rough characters are. They are no half-hearted Christians, I can assure you. He is another that I would so desire to see get fully sanctified. He is all on fire for God and he has no drawback from whatever God would ask him.

I must ask you to pray, if you will, for a need that I cannot mention for security reasons. The devil is not happy and he is fighting hard. We need God's protection until His cause can go on and His will be done in this prison. He has sent us there for a reason, and He is working mightily; but there is a counter attack going on which could be disastrous unless God intervenes. I know this was His idea to begin with, and He will keep the door open as long as He has work to do, but I would ask you to please pray. Nothing is too hard for Him. Paul said that at Ephesus there was "a great door and effectual…opened…and there are many adversaries." God is answering your prayers and we are depending on them. Again we thank each one of you.

Yours again for needy souls,
William Cawman

+++

September 1, 2000

How OFTEN I AM reminded of the words: "The world's great heart is aching; aching fiercely in the night."

If you could line up the population of the world, each with his hands upon the shoulders of the person if front of him, and then start at the beginning of the line with an automobile going 60 miles per hour, you would not come to the end of the line until five and one-half years later. How many of these have ever heard that the Blood of Calvary reaches deeper than the stain has gone? How many of them have ever met someone who could tell them that there is a full deliverance from ALL sin? I am convinced more every day that there are multitudes of souls whose hearts are aching with sin and they see no way for it to ever be different. How much claim can we think we have to escape from the indictment of him who, knowing his Lord to be an austere man, buried his talent in the earth?

Let me try to tell you in this letter of two of those aching hearts. Looking back in my records I see that I met the first one I'll tell you about on June 11, 1999. He had been recently sent back to prison over drug charges. He has a wife and two small children and she was anxiously awaiting him to be released from prison. When he got out, he said it just seemed like the devil entered into him, and instead of going home to his waiting wife and family, he hit the streets again and within 30 days was sent back to prison with fresh charges.

He was crushed and broken, and so was his wife. She said to him, "All I wanted was for you to come home to me." When I first met him he could not control the sobbing and remorse for what he had done to her. He had lost respect for himself and confidence that he could ever be the man he wanted to be. I could hardly keep from weeping myself as I would listen to him pour out his brokenness over the wages of sin.

As we began to visit and counsel with him, I sensed that there was a real man down inside which had never had a chance. He has become an avid student of the Bible, and really enjoys searching the Scriptures. He has been so humble and teachable, and many times as we would look at a new angle of truth he would say, "Oh my, I've been entirely wrong about that. This is so good." I've watched him as his emotions have been able to find a measure of healing through a steady walk with God. His shattered self confidence has begun to find a new hope, and he has been walking in the light.

A couple of weeks ago I had preached to his group on Sunday night a message of full salvation. I had preached to them before about it. I had talked to this man and tried to point it out to him in God's Word many times. I thought he was seeing it at least in a measure.

A few days after the message I referred to, he sent me a note saying that he needed to see me. He said that message was something he had never heard before and he had some questions about full salvation. As we began to open God's precious Word on the subject of heart holiness, he just shook his head. "Where have I been? I never knew all this. But I see it; it's God's Word." He called his wife and told her about it, but he said he didn't know if she understood it. I told him that he did not need to understand all about it to receive it, but that all he had to do was keep on loving Jesus with all his heart and drag out and turn against anything which was unlike Jesus.

I wish you could have seen his face; he looked like he had just awakened from a long, long night and was dazzled by the dawning light. Please pray for him. I sense no resistance in him; it's just that he had never heard. Forgive me for preaching a little—I fear he has counterparts many!

I will tell you of another inmate for two reasons. One is that you will pray for him, and the other is that after hearing stories such as his over and over, we cannot, as Christians living in a wicked world, be too careful.

Mc—— came to prison in July for the first time in his 57 years. He is a pastor. He has a ministry of compassion to those out on the street. He and his wife have a soup kitchen, a homeless shelter, and even a few beds in their own home for those in need. Some time back he was asked to take in a troubled, underage girl. He and his wife were reluctant, but finally feeling sorry for her, agreed to take her in. They laid down rules for her to go by but before long she began to break them all and do as her wayward heart desired. He and his wife came home one night and found her breaking the rules again and he began to scold her sharply. She flew at him and he says that he must confess that he lost his temper and slapped her in the face. The girl left the house and returned with the police. Two days later, the police came to the door with handcuffs and announced that the pastor was being charged with aggravated sexual assault on a minor.

He went to court and his wife, who had been with him when it happened, stood right by him. Over forty members of his church appeared to bear witness to his character. His attorney told him that if the girl appeared he stood little chance of defeating the accusation. The girl appeared; he was sent to prison with a six flat.

This former pastor began coming to the Bible studies on

Friday nights and to the Sunday services, and after a few weeks asked if he could see me. When we met he told me the above. He said that he feels no bitterness about it and that he has forgiven the girl, but he is hurting. He said his wife and church are going on without him but he misses them so much. He asked if we could get together and talk often and I assured him I would be glad to do that.

The second visit, the man said that he didn't want to dwell on the past, but move on with what God has for him now. He began to open his heart to me. Before long he was in tears as he told me that he was not really satisfied with his own heart relationship to God. He said that he is very familiar with the Calvinistic doctrine but that much of the time his heart is not satisfied. He said that he sees his wife is living a much holier life than he is, and that much of the time he feels a coldness that bothers him. As I began to tell him what God had done for my heart he listened with evident hunger. He said as we left, "I know that God has something better for me than I have had, and I believe He has put you in my life right now to help me find it."

Once again let me say, how many more are just like him; how many more have the same aching lack within—no one has ever told them. Please pray for him and for me as I try to guide him to the One Who came to put away sin.

We lost another inmate who was dying of AIDS. He is one that I have prayed with often in the last few weeks and I trust he made it. The first time I visited him and asked him if he ever prayed, he wrinkled up his face and shook his head "no." A time or two later after we had prayer I asked him if Jesus forgave his sins and he shook his head "yes." A few days before he died he told the Christian nurse that he had peace. He died alone in his cell at two-thirty in the morning.

Now I must tell you that inmate V——, who got sanctified, is growing by leaps and bounds! It is such a blessing to hear him testify and pray. He does not hesitate to put his feet down on Canaan's happy soil.

Friday night we knelt for prayer in the Bible study and after someone else had prayed, he led out in prayer and just exalted and praised God on and on for the power that can cleanse away the old nature we are born with. He is so humble and teachable that God can lead him on without a struggle. He opens up to me about everything and it is thrilling to see that even while he hides nothing there is no trace of the old man of sin left. It is such a reward to help him to "know how to possess his vessel in sanctification and honor."

It is rather interesting that while many holiness people are struggling to find a witness other than the witness of the Spirit, this dear imprisoned man (thirty-one years old), had the witness bright and clear, but yet didn't know how to accept it. All he needed was a little prompting and the light broke all over him. He says that from the moment of acknowledging that witness, it has grown brighter and brighter until the Scriptures which speak of holiness burn like fire in his heart. Praise God!

Thank you again each one for your prayers.

In Him,
William Cawman

4
CLOSE PREACHING/CLOSE LIVING

October 6, 2000

ONCE AGAIN THERE ARE so many things I would like to tell you about. One of the most important is that every where we go Christian brothers and sisters are saying, "We are praying for you." I want to tell you that it is because of your prayers that there is so much to tell of what God is doing. Those of you who are praying are truly as much a part of the ministry here in the prison as anyone else. How it warms and yet humbles my heart to hear of the many who are pulling together in prayer. Someday, dear friends, you are going to meet some dear soul in heaven who is the answer to your prayer. And yet, somehow as I say that I am reminded again of how our loving Heavenly Father allows us to claim that He answers our prayers when in reality they are His prayers which He extends to us.

First I want to tell you about an experience we had recently which will linger with me a long time. We had been in Idaho in the middle of September for a revival, and after the revival we took a few days to drive across northern Washington state and back to Seattle to fly home.

We had come to the top of Washington Pass on the North Cascades Highway and had stopped at a visitor center. Seeing an irresistibly inviting foot trail going on up the mountain from there and not wanting to be gone long from the others in the family, I set off running up the trail. Before long I left the trail and ran on up to the top of the mountain and suddenly came upon a breathtaking panorama of the untouched handiwork of God. Around where I was standing the mountain dropped off into a canyon or gorge, and beyond that were mountain peaks after mountain peaks rising majestically above me.

I stood there in awe for a few minutes, unable to absorb the grandeur of all that was before my eyes, when suddenly I thought of my men back in this prison. In that moment I realized how much I really loved them. There are many men here whom I feel to be just as much my brothers as any of you are, and while I was standing on a mountain surrounded with beauty and majesty which I could not begin to absorb, they were seeing the same four gray walls they had been looking at for months and years.

I felt the tears come to my eyes; I prayed for them up on that mountain. I realized how good God had been to me. What would I be today had I been raised as they were? Oh the seriousness of the words of Jesus, "For unto whomsoever much is given, of him shall be much required…"

As I write this letter another inmate hovers between time and eternity, another victim of that ugly monster—"and sin, when it is finished, bringeth forth death." I pray that I will never become accustomed to the melancholy scene of a man, alone with his last enemy in a ten foot square, windowless cell.

Last evening this man's sisters and father were granted permission to come see him for the last time. I went back to the prison to meet them and escorted them to the hospital and to his cell. The social worker had told him that they were coming. He had rallied a little and was waiting for them, but the exertion of waiting expectantly for them to arrive was just about all he had strength for and he was fighting to stay awake after they arrived.

The family went into the cell and his sister tried to arouse him. After some effort, he rallied his strength and the first thing he told them was that he had talked to the chaplain. I was standing in the door of his cell with one of the officers. The officer said, "He's calling for you."

I went up to his head and spoke to him again. I told him that his father and his sisters were there, wasn't that wonderful. Then I asked his sister, a very beautiful young black woman, if they would like to have prayer together as a family. She said that she would like that, so I told the poor man that we were going to have family prayer. I then prayed for him and asked God that they could all meet each other in heaven. His father and sisters thanked me several times and seemed to appreciate that someone cared about their son and brother. At times during the visit, though, his father could not take it any longer and would go out into the hall and stare off into space. He came back in and stood at the foot of the bed as we prayed together.

I went back in this morning and spent some time alone with him in his cell again. I told him about the love of God, how He loved us as sinners so much that He sent His Son to die on the cross for us. I told him that no matter how much he had sinned, he didn't have to take his sins with him, but that because Jesus died for us we can ask Him to take all our sins away and make us His child. I told the dying man not to be afraid of God, but to just bring him his heart and let Him come in.

He was beyond being able to make much of a response but he certainly tried. I asked him if Jesus had taken all his sins away. The inmate tried to tell me something, but he could not articulate; he just made a deep noise in his throat for several seconds at a time. I asked him if he loved Jesus and if Jesus loved him, and again he tried to respond, but I cannot tell you what he said. I'll just have to leave him in the hands of Him Who does all things well.

I have told you at different times of many of the inmates; now I would like to tell you about my co-worker, my supervisor. For a year and a half after I began working at this prison there was no supervisor of chaplaincy services and there were many areas of the ministry which were lacking on account of someone to organize them.

Let me say that it is a position which I would never desire unless God opened that door, as it so often involves political confrontations with other department heads, appearing at court over inmate accusations, settling differences with other faith groups, etc. God has opened the door for me to give my full time to individual and group ministry and I feel strongly that is where my heart is. However, we were praying very hard that God would send in a man who would have a vision which would not hinder what God was trying to do. It looked very disheartening at one point.

It appeared that we would have to accept a political appointee, a favor from the state governor, who as nearly as we could understand was simply a generic chaplain, possibly not even a Christian. Just within moments, nearly, of his coming on board, it was discovered that he was lacking in the necessary qualifications (by state requirements) for the position. We prayed on and finally a man was selected from one of the county prisons.

The first day the new supervisor came into the prison after being hired, he and I sat down together and immediately there started a bond which has grown without a rift for a year now. He looked at me that first visit and let me know that he appreciated my being there and that he would not hinder one thing that I was doing. He has been true to his word. Many a day we have lunch together, and we talk very openly concerning things which God has done in our lives. Many times the tears have come to his eyes as he has let me know how God is working in his own heart.

The other day the new supervisor told me that he had

been drawing closer to God and that he felt that watching television was not helping him any spiritually. He said he had told God that he was finished watching it. He then related that a few days later he had a wonderful time with God in prayer that morning and God was really helping him to get closer to Him. Again and again he tells me that it just thrills him to hear from the prisoners how much they love me. There seems to be no jealousy in him when he hears something good about another.

One day my supervisor told me that he had asked God before he came to this prison to put someone in his life who could help him and who could bring him closer to God. He said, "I have found that in you." I only tell you this to show you what kind of a man he is. The other day he was placed under a lot of pressure from some of the administration above him and yet I saw no evidence of a wrong spirit. After we had gone home he called me. He knew I was leaving town the next day for a meeting. He told me that he had felt very stressed that day and he asked me to forgive him if he had said or done anything which might have hurt me. I couldn't think of anything to relate it to.

Let me give you second-hand his testimony. The man is in his mid-forties and grew up a hippie. He did everything they did and did it hard. He met a girl and married her, and thank God they are still happily married; but for the first few years of their marriage he drank nearly all the time. Finally a baby girl was born to them and when she was just a day or two old, his wife was feeding her and suddenly the nurse said, "Give me that baby, there's something wrong with her." They rushed her to the X-ray department and the doctor came back and told him that his girl had had a triple brain hemorrhage and would either die or be nothing but a vegetable. The doctor asked permission to pull the plug on her.

Instead of giving an answer, the young father turned and walked out of the hospital. For the first time in years he did not go get drunk or use drugs. He went away to a lonely spot he often visited when he was depressed. He said that one time in his life he had seen on television that there was a man named Jesus Christ who could forgive sins. When he heard it, he said to himself, "I'm going to remember that; I might need Him someday."

The distraught man started to pray. He confessed his sins to Jesus, starting with the first Tasty Cake he had stolen when he was a small boy. After a half hour or so went by he became desperate; he knew that he could never get to an end of all his sins. He threw up his hands and said, "Jesus, I need You." Instantly, everything within him changed.

He then went back to the hospital and tried to tell his wife. She could not understand what he was talking about. Just then the doctor came back to the room and said, "I don't know what has happened, but your baby has made a complete recovery." I've heard him tell this several times but not without tears.

He then went on to find out more about God, attending Bible College, and for his internship acted as a chaplain in a prison. And, he says that from that time, ironically enough, God has kept him right in the place he had always tried to stay out of—prison. Please pray for him. God is using him, and he is hungry for more of God in his own life and in the prison.

Let me close for this month with renewed appreciation for each of you—your prayers and support.

Your Co-Laborer in Christ,
William Cawman

November 1, 2000

WE HAVE BEEN GONE the last couple of weeks in a revival meeting in Ohio. We are back for this week, and then are to go to Guatemala for the week of Nov. 6-13. But here we are in the chaplain's office with another month of news to send to you.

May I say once again that I deeply appreciate and depend on the prayers of each of you, God's children, as we try to bring His truth and grace into the prison. But I also am so thankful for the prayers of my Christian brothers right here in the prison during those times when we have to be absent from them. Many of them tell me, "We prayed for you every day." I treasure that and it warms my heart. And then, they are such a welcoming committee upon returning that I find my heart strings pulled irresistibly.

I must tell you of a real victory which has become such a blessing the last couple of months. My supervisor, the chaplain I told you of in the last newsletter, came to me some time ago and said, "You really ought to find someone of your own faith group to fill in for you in your Friday night Bible studies. The men really see the difference in you and they do not like the volunteers who are being asked to fill in when you are gone."

My supervisor has been holding classes for some time which he calls deacon classes, to try to teach the men responsibility and leadership in spiritual things. In these classes the men are very free to tell him what they like and what they don't. After praying about it, it came to my mind that a dear brother who has been helping in services Sunday nights in the county jail, might just be the right choice for a backup. He readily agreed and was trained and registered as a volunteer. This man has been faithfully coming in on the Friday nights when I am gone to take the two Bible studies, and the men love him. They tell me he has such a sweet spirit, and that he believes just as I do—there is a cure for sin! Praise the Lord!

This is such a blessing and a relief to me, as I was always greatly distressed after teaching a full salvation cure for sin to have someone come in and teach them that there was no such a thing. So please pray for my brother in the Lord as he fills in for these Bible studies.

Now—to those of you who receive this letter by e-mail, I already let you share the good news of another inmate entering into the blessing of perfect love. I will try to describe that wonderful morning, but I know I cannot really do it.

Many of you who have been getting the letters remember the story of the man from a radical Christian-hating faith who for nearly ten years was on a hell-bent mission to destroy himself and others, and how by the mercy of God he had a praying wife who would not give up on him. He had gone out once on a drug dealer raid with all intentions of blowing the drug dealer away and taking his money. God miraculously intervened, however, and didn't let it happen (See chapter one). T——'s wife and her friends were praying for him. He tried escaping by way of drugs, but couldn't get high. With that, he went straight to the church, where his wife and the people of the church were praying for him again. That day he threw up his hands and yielded and God changed his life completely.

When the time came for T—— to go to court, lawyers told him there was no way to hope for less than twenty years behind bars for all of his offences. He began to testify to the officer and tell him what God had done for him. When they asked him what they should do with him, he told them that was up to them. Whatever they did with him was all right, because he had given his life to God. The judge said, "Give him all the credits you can," and he ended up with about three years to serve in prison.

Perhaps I shouldn't make this comparison, but I am reminded of the man named Saul of Tarsus. He persecuted the church of God and wasted it. He breathed out threatenings and slaughter against it. T—— has said that in those years if you were a Christian, you were on his "hit list." Now he worships God just as violently as he one time served the devil. T—— is no quiet, passive "Christian." He is out and out a new man and everybody knows it. Whenever he meets any of those he knew in his former life they fail to recognize him for a while, then they say, "You aren't (his former name from the religious sect) are you?" He says, "Yes that's me, but I'm not that man now."

Well, now to the morning of October 16. For a while it had seemed that every time we visited there was a burning fire kindled as we talked together. He was, however, as ignorant of the doctrine of heart holiness as could be imagined. All he knew was that he loved the Lord with all his heart and he didn't want anything to do with the old life or the old "him." He was so humble and teachable and yet so violently in love with God that as I tried to tell him of the deeper work of the Spirit which cleanses from all the roots of the nature of sin, he just beamed and swallowed it—understand it or not. On that Monday morning as we spoke again of this great work, it seemed to me that it was like the time when Joseph wanted to make himself known to his brethren and asked everyone to leave the room.

I believe the Holy Spirit wanted to make Himself known to T——— that morning, and before long the other chaplain left the room, the secretary left, the officer left, and there we were— the two of us and the blessed Holy Spirit. I felt urged to press into his inner heart a bit. I asked him, "T———, would you say that in the last while you have sensed anything which relates to sin or to the old you, or what you used to be?"

He said, "Oh no. I hate it. I don't ever want that again." I began to speak clearly of that blessed work of the Holy Spirit which cleanses the heart of all sin, and he looked at me with an expression of dawning light and said, "That's what happened to me."

It is said that on the day of Pentecost there was as it were a "rushing mighty wind that filled all the house." That morning as we sat facing each other it seemed that a volcano suddenly erupted between us and a cloud of glory just settled all over us. We both began to cry and praise God and he grabbed my hands in his (I looked down and what a contrast; I mean, black and white, and now blood brothers) and he began to try to pray and thank God for "SANCTIFICATION." He wept; he shouted; he rejoiced, and he did not want to leave the room. He said, "I just don't want to go. I'm not sure where I even am."

Two days later I met T—— and he told me that he had been a different man ever since. He said, "I'm going to testify to 'SANCTIFICATION'." Such a burning, melting presence of the Holy Spirit was there in that room that morning that it felt as real as any other Pentecostal baptism I have ever witnessed.

The following day after this glorious morning, the devil jumped all over me. He attacked me from every angle and tried to make me think it had not really happened. Then God spoke gently to me and said, "T—— might not be able to bear this attack."

I felt so humbled. I felt like laying my heart on the altar afresh and anew and saying, "O God, if I can be of any use in bearing something that someone else is not able to bear, I'll gladly take it for them."

Please remember to pray for T—— as the devil is sure not to leave him alone either. As we said, he has never been tutored in a school of theology. He just knew he loved Jesus with all his heart, and God led him into the blessing.

I believe that after witnessing some of these get through to God, it is very clear what the Scripture means when it speaks of the Three that bear record in heaven and three that bear record on earth. The work of full salvation is not completed until the three that bear record on earth have done so, as well as the Three in heaven. One of these on earth is the water (our testimony). Until this great work of the Holy Spirit is acknowledged and witnessed to, it is not complete. When the Three in heaven have borne witness and then the soul on earth recognizes and bears witness to the divine work, how brightly it bursts forth in the soul.

So as we rejoice with T—— let's not forget to pray for him that the enemy will not trip him up in this new-found way. He cannot wait to be released to throw his life into witnessing for God and His great work, and yet he is willing to stay as long as God sees fit. He says it is all the same; he's just living for Jesus wherever he is, and wherever God puts him that's where he wants to be.

Please pray that others will also soon be led into this blessed experience and that many others will be clearly saved. This is the whole purpose of our prayers and ministry. It is amazing how some who have long been schooled in a church background are much slower to accept the message of full salvation than others who have never known anything at all. But then, that is nothing new.

Please pray also for the special holidays coming up. Christmas especially is a very hard time of year for the prisoners. Cell blocks see many tears on Christmas day. We want to do something special for them for Thanksgiving and Christmas.

Thank you to each one for your prayers and support which is definitely felt again and again.

Trusting in Him,
William Cawman

December 1, 2000

In Sunday School last week we sang the song which contained these words: "In tenderness He sought us, From depths of sin He brought us, The way of life then taught us, To Him give thanks." Sometimes we who have been bred and born in the church struggle the most over all that we know about the way of life. I wish you could sit and visit with the dear brother who we told you in the last letter got sanctified. His hungry heart pulled him in and now he is learning the way of life.

Perhaps Mrs. C.H. Morris has the way of redemption straighter in her song than we often do in our experiences. Dear T—— was so excited at our last visit, he was just pumping both arms like a steam locomotive as he said, "Ever since this sanctification process..." and then went on to tell how wonderful it is.

Could I make a request? If any of you would happen to have a copy of the book *Bible Doctrines*, by Smith, and you would be willing to part with it, I can tell you where it would be most welcome. The men in the prison consider it a gold mine. I loaned my only copy to an inmate nearly a year ago, and I will probably never have it back. It is not that he would not give it back, but too many want to read it. Right now it is in the possession of T—— and he loves it so much that he is copying the whole book by hand so that he will have it. If anyone knows of an available copy, I would be so glad to get a few more.

Inmate C—— who was saved out of steady heroin use a year ago last August, is steadily growing spiritually and seeking a pure heart. I recently got him enrolled in college Bible studies and when he got his first course of study in the mail, he just got down on his knees and cried. I'm trying to arrange a place for him to study with a desk and typewriter, because he has no place to study and write except the edge of his bunk. This position is very painful to him at times. He suffers a lot from joint pains that have resulted from his long years of drug usage at such an early age. He is doing exceptionally well with his studies and just can't wait for what's coming next. He told me this week that the more he studies, the more he feels his need of full heart cleansing. He said that he feels so humbled when God lets His Word become so real to him. Please remember him in prayer.

Many inmates who have not yet been transformed by the grace of God struggle immensely with others on their cell block. If another inmate holds a different view of some Scripture than they do, their old street "manners" rise up to set him straight. After all, he must know the truth straight. And then many of them struggle so hard over really acting the part of a Christian when another steps on their rights. By and large, one would have to assess the majority of them as a pretty rough bunch.

Last Sunday night I asked a group of them if they really meant business about living the Christian life. Oh yes, of course, they did. So I told them I was not going to take them up among the stars but behind the closed doors of their cell block.

I took my text from the words of Jesus in Jn. 15:13: "Greater love hath no man than this, that a man lay down his life for his friends." I asked them how many of them knew someone in their life that they thought enough of that they would step in front of a bullet to save their life if necessary. All hands went up. Then I pointed out to them that the keeping of this Scripture was not always that heroic. It was speaking of a willingness to lay down our pleasures, our preferences, our way of doing things, our time, our comfort, for the sake of winning that ugliest rascal in our life to Jesus.

I got really close to where they live with such things as being willing for a cell mate to use their belongings, and eat up the food they had purchased from canteen, and leaving all the dirty work for them to pick up. They began to throw knowing looks around the room. I heard a few forms of *ouch*. Some were grinning with raised eyebrows. One good brother who has a Christian roommate, responded with, "That's a hard saying," and looked across at his roommate. They began to laugh together.

I knew I wasn't dishing out much sugar with the meal as I pressed it to them with Paul's words in Romans 12:17-21, but I just left the truth as raw as Paul wrote it. Many of them told me afterwards, "We really needed that." I doubt if these men are the only ones who need to quit playing religion.

I would like to request special prayer for the dear man I wrote about in September, Mc———. He is the one who was a pastor and was sent to prison over a false accusation from a girl he was trying to help. As we visit together I sense a longstanding hunger for more of God than he has experienced in his life. He readily confesses that he has long struggled with insufficient victory in his inner heart. He said he really hungers to know God in a fuller way.

Mc——— is open to light and as we talk together I sense a reach in him that pulls deeply on my heart. He is just my age;

why has God been so good to me? Oh that God can help me to share His grace in such a way that others can see the God Who delivered me. I feel with Charles Wesley: "The arms of love that compass me, would all mankind embrace."

The other day as I went back over my own life very openly with him and told him of the years of my own spiritual struggles and of my up and down inward life, he listened intently. He said, "I know exactly what you are talking about. My heart is longing to be free of that and to be able to live the victorious life." Well, praise God! That's exactly the reason Jesus died on the Cross of Calvary. So please add to your prayers your faith for this man's full cleansing in the Blood of the Lamb.

Thank God for another victory from the hospital. I found another inmate dying alone in a cell. I asked him if his sins were forgiven and he instantly said, "Yes sir, they are. Praise God, I know they are all forgiven." A few more days and he was gone.

And then, let me tell you of another heart-warming victory. W—— is a tall, thin, black man who was in the very first service I held in the prison, and he has been there faithfully ever since. He is a very happy man, a very sincere man, and a very humble man. I have watched his life for nearly three years without seeing a blemish to a Christian testimony. Many times when others were tempted to quarrel over some personal viewpoint, I would notice him with his face turned heavenward, just enjoying the presence of God.

Once in a while he would get up and testify briefly and I remember his saying several times that he was saved and sanctified and filled with the Spirit. I do not know why nearly three years have gone by without it really dawning on me where he was really living.

This week W—— asked to visit me. He was beaming with happiness and as we began to talk, he again said in such a humble, non-boasting way, "I know I'm saved and sanctified."

I stopped and began to probe a little further. I said, "Bro., as you look back across your Christian life, can you recognize two definite epochs of God's grace in your experience with Him? Can you remember a time when you were forgiven of your sins and made a new creature in Christ and then a definite time when God cleansed away all of the original sin nature out of your heart?"

He looked me in the face with a great big smile. "Oh yes, I sure can. All through that two-and-a-half year Bible study you did on the heart life, I knew exactly what you were talking about. That's what God has done for me. I know my heart is pure."

I asked him to tell me more about how it happened. He said that when he was in the county jail in 1996, God saved him and forgave all his sins. He said that for two or three months after that his heart cried to God continually, "Oh God, please deliver me from this mess in my heart." And he said, "God did it." He said from that time there has been not one bit of sin in his heart or life. He said it is so good that many times at work he gets so happy that the tears run down his face. The men ask him what is the matter with him and he tells them it's all right; they are just tears of joy. Well, how often where we may not even realize it "The Holy Spirit hour by hour, exerts His sanctifying power—under the precious Blood."

Thank you once again for listening, and thank you most of all for praying. Some day, through the gift of His infinite grace, some day, when prayers and labors are done, some day, oh glorious day, you will meet these dear ones whom God loves no less because of what they one time were.

Yours for every single needy soul,
William Cawman

5
PUNISHMENT AND REWARDS

January 1, 2001

A S WE LOOK BACK across another year which has slipped by so quickly, we see so much for which to be thankful and to give praise to our precious Redeemer. We have just celebrated His simple birth. Where would we be had it not been for a Savior? We have witnessed cases enough in the last year to remind us of the depths to which man can fall without the grace of God. Let me tell you of a couple of them before I go on.

Just a few days before Christmas I was visiting with an inmate on the cell block. When an inmate leaves his cell his door electronically locks behind him and he must wait at his door until the control officer sees him and opens it for him. I saw another inmate go to his cell door across the hall from where we were visiting and look in the little window. Immediately he went ballistic. I didn't know what had possessed him. He began to kick the door, jump at it, scream and wave his arms, until an officer ran down to him. The officer looked in the window and immediately called for a lockdown and a clearing of the floor. The man's cellmate was committing suicide. Fortunately they caught him just in time and I noticed he was moving as they transported him to the hospital. Oh the horrible, horrible wages of sin. I will try to visit him as soon as I can. Please pray for him.

As I knew that there would be no more visiting on that cell block for a while as they photographed the room, etc., I moved to the tier next door to see another inmate. After I had visited with him I was intending to go home for the day, but on my way out another inmate stopped me and asked if he could see me.

We stepped into an office at the end of the cell block and he said, "Do you have a few minutes?" I told him to sit down and I would stay with him. He began to open up his heart to me. The stains of sin had become unbearable and he could not live with them any longer. As he began to unlock his horrible past life he began to sense he could trust me.

He took two hours to go back over his whole life and unload the terrible crimes that were haunting him. He had been forced into one of the most violent gangs in the country and was personally acquainted with the big mob bosses in the Mafia. As he narrated the hair-raising events of his life he stopped for a minute and said, "Oh it feels so much better to get this out of my chest. I have nightmares over my crimes every night." It seemed he could not get relief until he had vividly gone back over every detail of the murders he had committed and just how it was done. After one of them, he looked around and shivered and said he felt cold chills all over him. It was a story I would not even think of writing in this letter, it was so ghastly and horrible.

He told me he feared for his life if he ever got out of prison. He said he knows that there is a God and that he is going to hell unless he gets right with God. He told me that he has never told anyone the things he told me, and that no one yet knows who it was that committed the crimes. I assured him that the things he had told me I would keep in trust and that I knew if he really wants to be a different man, God could forgive the past and make him all over. But oh the scars of sin; some memories will no doubt haunt him as long as he lives. Please pray for him as I try to help him find a new life in the forgiveness and changing power of God.

Again, I can't help thinking of the song which says, "Praise God, Christ changed all that might have been." Dear friends, don't forget at the close of another year of mercy to thank God for changing what might have been.

I need to go back to the last newsletter. Dear Bro. W—— whom I wrote about must have an update. The night after Thanksgiving, I took my wife and two daughters into the prison for the Bible studies that night. They sang a number of songs and made it a special time of praise. In the middle of the service, I told the men of the things which Bro. W—— had told me while we were visiting, and asked him to come up front and share with everyone his testimony of a sanctified heart. When I did so, I noticed that there was a universal applause from those who know him best. I'll have to confess, I rather liked that. I believe that is a good spiritual thermometer. He humbly came to the front and testified very clearly to two definite works of grace and to grace that works. By the time he finished men were getting up all over the room to come up and hug him. God still witnesses to His own work.

One Friday night recently I was exhorting them from the last part of the first chapter of Romans and was sparing no words on the nature of sin which causes the condition spoken of. I looked down at W—— and his face was aglow; he was certainly not looking for any cover; he had faced his sin and come clear on it and it showed all over him.

God has been sending a revival in the group where we are having the Friday night Bible studies. There has been a real move of the Spirit among the men; the attendance is increasing, and there is such a hunger for the Word. Recently they came to me before the study and said that they would like to eliminate the singing and just go right into the Bible. What a blessing it is to minister to hearts who are so open and eager to hear God's Word. We are starting into a study on the Book of Romans and I told them we are not there to argue doctrinal differences but we are there to study with a desire to get as close to God as we can and as far away from sin and sinning as we can.

I must tell you that I recently reaped a reward for being among these dear men. For several years I have been bothered by a herniated disc in my neck which at times radiates a pain and numbness down my arm. For nearly four months it had been really bothering me and I had been to a neurosurgeon who had scheduled me for surgery on it.

The Friday night before I was scheduled for the surgery I told the men in Bible study about it and after the class W——— asked me to come over to him. He gathered several others around and they laid their hands on me and prayed. The following morning the pain was gone. When I went in for the surgery, there had been a misunderstanding regarding the payment for it and they told me they would have to reschedule the surgery. I haven't rescheduled. The pain has not returned. I believe I'll leave it in the hands of the Great Physician.

I have had the hands of trusted brethren laid on me several times for various things in my life, but I do not believe I was ever so melted as when those dear men, some of them from every pathway of sin you can imagine, gathered around me so tight that I could not have gotten away, every one of them wanting to get their hands on me in prayer. Forget what they one time were—God has. Grace and love was pouring through them that night to a brother they love, and who loves them back.

In my last letter I asked if anyone had a copy of *Bible Doctrines* by Smith. Several responded with a copy, but one dear man who is in prison ministry in Ohio called and asked how many copies I wanted. He had reprinted them. I told him I could use 30 to start with. He boxed up 62 copies (a special edition for T——— who was copying it by hand) and said if we needed more he would get a larger box. Praise the Lord, and thank you dear brother. T—— was so delighted with his copy that he pressed it to his lips and kissed it.

For Christmas this year we had several smaller services instead of one large one as we did in other years. We had two services on Friday night before Christmas, two on Christmas Eve, and two last night, New Year's Eve. As the young people sang to them so sweetly many of the inmates were struggling to keep back the tears. Some did not succeed. At the last song on New Year's Eve, "Into My Heart," the men stood and raised their hands and I believe conviction was doing its work in many of them. Others were rejoicing that He had come into their hearts. They were so grateful for those who came and ministered to them. One man said, "I have never seen such godly young people. It just shone all over them."

We want to thank everyone who prayed for these services, and also everyone who has faithfully prayed for us this past year. If Jesus tarries we are looking forward to laboring together with Him and with you for these dear ones whom Jesus loves when no one else does.

My burning desire is to be faithful to Him; my only regret that I have so little to offer Him. In the shadow of Calvary there is no choice but to lay our all at His blessed feet.

With all on the altar for a new year in Him,

William Cawman

February 1, 2001

IT IS MONDAY MORNING, January 29, 2001. I have come into the chapel to fill in this morning for my supervisor chaplain in his deacons' class. It is a class which he has been holding for a year now in each facility, and which has been blessed of God in training these men into responsible Christians. My heart is melted by the opening prayer poured out of the heart of one of their number:

"Dear Lord, we come to you this morning a scruffy bunch

of men, the offscouring of the earth, but so thankful that You cared enough to send Your Son to die on the Cross that we might be lifted out of our sin and into Your presence. We were nothing before You found us. We're not here about us, but about You, and we want to learn all of You that we can. We thank You, dear Lord, for our dear chaplain who has come here this morning, who You have called to come and feed us with the Bread of Life. Continue to use him and fill Him with Your Holy Spirit as he ministers to us. We're not here to promote our individual minds about You, but to hear what You have to say to us. We love You, dear Lord, we love You. Amen."

Many of you would remember the inmate V—— who got sanctified last July 31 and who was walking so tenderly and carefully with God. A few months ago he was sent out to a rehab program as a mandatory part of his sentence. During that time he was corresponding with one of the men in the church and seemed to be doing well. Then a few weeks ago his mail began returning with the notification that he had been sent back to the clearing center. That is where they examine and balance the original sentence, the nature of the crime, the programs already completed, the time remaining on the sentence, etc., and then the inmates are sent either to a halfway house or out on parole or back to prison.

V—— was hoping of course to be sent out on parole, but when they reviewed his case and saw the amount of time remaining on his sentence, the officer told him they could not send him out; he would have to go back to prison. He asked V—— if he would prefer to go to some other prison than he was in, and V—— told him that it would be just fine to send him back here.

Friday morning I had gone to new inmate orientation and as I sat there waiting my turn to introduce the chaplaincy department I saw a hand wave at me. I looked, and there was V——. Of course I did not know why he was back, and was a little concerned about it, so that afternoon I called him out for a visit. He told me the whole story and then with a beaming face began to tell me all that God had been doing in his heart. I quickly sensed that he had been growing not only in grace, but in his sensitivity to the Blessed Holy Spirit. It was a wonderful reunion, and such a blessing to see that when God does His work in the heart, it keeps the soul regardless of the circumstances.

V—— said he was disappointed for a few minutes about being sent back, but he said, "It's just fine; I belong to God; whatever He wants for me, I want." He told me how wonderfully God is leading him in the place of prayer. He then looked at me and said, "What were you doing on Jan. 5?" I told him I was right there in the prison all day and all evening. He looked a little puzzled and said, "Did you feel all right?" He said that God had laid me on his heart that day in a special way. I thanked him for being faithful and told him that it might not be until we get to heaven that we'll know why he prayed that day. It may take all eternity to thank God and others for those things which are hidden from us here.

Early in January an inmate who has been in Bible study for a long time and who has really been a sincere student of the Word came to me and asked if he and his cell mate could come and visit with me together. His cell mate has also been coming to Bible study for a long time and both of them have come a long way in letting God work on them.

Some time back the second one I mentioned had asked if he could bunk with the other Christian so that they could study and grow together. The officer was friendly enough to them to allow them to do it. Previously they had lived one above the other and would study back and forth through the register hole. They were so glad to get together and praised God for it in the Bible study. After several months went by, I began to notice just a few signs of something between them, although they continued to get along. But now they wanted to talk to me about something.

They came into the room and both sat down. The one who had requested the interview asked if he could pray first. He asked that all that would be said and done that day would be for the good of them both and for the glory of God. Then he began to point out some "faults" in his brother. The other man just listened until he was finished, then he calmly pointed out a few in return. (I said to myself, "Oh God, how did this familiar enemy get inside this prison? The last time I saw him he was sitting snugly on the church pew.")

After a few rounds while I just kept my mouth shut and listened, the one who had called for the interview said to his brother, "I see what you are doing now; you have just turned this thing right around on me."

With that I stopped them and said, "Brethren, I see something neither of you are looking at while you are looking at each other. I see right between you an ugly head and the name on it is 'The Accuser of the Brethren.'" I reminded them what a privilege God had given them of living together to grow in the Word and in grace, and how much the enemy didn't like that. So now he was driving a wedge between them over their mutual faults. I pointed out to them that both had a point in what they were offended at in their brother, and then I asked them to bow their heads. I took them to the throne of God. I just sort of confessed out for both of them and I really felt the unusual help of God while praying for them. I asked God to rebuke the "Accuser of the Brethren" and lift up a standard against him in cell #——. When I finished, they both stood up and threw their arms around each other. The one who had asked to come see me looked at me and said, "Chaplain, if it had not been for that prayer, there might have been an argument when we got back to the cell. But in that prayer God showed me that I need to be worked on. I'm at fault." Both of them agreed they were going to humble themselves and help each other.

I hate the devil! He acts the same, smells the same, looks the same everywhere he shows his ugly head. But, praise God, John says that he "heard a loud voice saying in heaven, Now is come salvation, and strength, and the kingdom of our God, and the power of His Christ: for the accuser of our brethren is cast down, which accused them before our God day and night."

I ask you to remember in prayer the inmate I mentioned in the last letter who had been unburdening his awful past to me. I fear for him. He is literally living in hell on earth. I wonder that he can retain any sanity at all. The atrocious chain of blood and organized crime that he has lived with for years haunts him like a living nightmare. He cannot get any response from anyone in his family and fears that they may have already been "taken out" by the undercover gangs with which he was involved. The man has only a few more months to serve in this state after which he must be turned over to the state in which he is wanted, and he has every reason to fear that as soon as he enters the prisons of that state he will be killed.

Yet for all this, he does not know God. And because he does not know Him he sees too much risk in trusting Him. He still has faint hope that he can come out on top. I confess, I don't know where to go next except to pray. Only God can reveal Himself to a man in the measure he needs. He has never trusted anyone from the time he was seven years old, at which time such unthinkable trauma tore his little heart apart that he has never recovered. He seems unable to really weigh things in the light of eternity when his entire emotional and psycho-logical capacity is totally occupied with the living hell in which he lives. My brothers and sisters who know Jesus, if you really believe that the Blood reaches deeper than the stain has gone, please remember this lost soul in prayer.

I also ask you to pray for the officers in the prison. Many of them make some claim to Christianity and are very sup-portive and helpful. Some are otherwise. Many of them would thank you for your prayers; the others need them just the same.

I am conscious that the world is so needy. Everywhere one turns there are souls by the masses on their way to either heaven or hell. Pray however God leads you to pray. He knows where the trembling soul is. I feel more and more that no matter what or where the ministry is, prayer is our greatest hope. It is deeply more than words when I say, "Thank you for praying."

His and His alone,
William Cawman

✝✝✝

March 1, 2001

PAUL THANKED GOD for the Roman believers and rejoiced "that your faith is spoken of throughout the whole world." Isn't it interesting that the faith, not of some prodigy of ecclesiastical pedigree, but of sinners such as society has thrown away should be used to bless hearts around the world? Such is the grace of our God. And such also is the divine estimate of human worth. He came not to call the righteous, but sinners to repentance.

Last September and again in December I wrote about a pastor who had been incarcerated over what I have every reason to believe was a false charge. I told you how God has been helping him to see a deeper need of God in his life. He has been earnestly searching his heart and eagerly reading all the books I could give him on full redemption through the Blood of Jesus. The light has been dawning clearer and clearer that there is such a thing as a second work of grace whereby God fully cleanses away not only the acts of sin but the nature of sin. He has been seeking after it, and as we have visited together often I have sensed a really sincere hunger for this cleansing of his heart. Many of you know how clearly the Spirit witnesses when a soul is really on the trail after God.

Well, on Sunday night, Feb. 11, this former pastor got up and said he needed to testify. He began by thanking God for "second blessing holiness." He spoke with such positive assurance that he was finding the old motions of sin within to be gone, and in their place the fruits of the Spirit. On the way out of service he was beaming as he shook my hand and said, "I can't wait to talk to you."

A few days later we had a chance to sit down together and he began to tell me that everything was changed on the inside. He had encountered a blast of bad news from someone on the outside who had been responsible for his being in prison, but said he felt nothing of the old reactions he used to have. He felt nothing but love for the person who had harmed him.

He then said, "But I need to ask you something about sanctification which is not clear to me. What is it that a person receives that is different when he is sanctified? Doesn't the Holy Spirit come to live with him when he is born again?"

I explained to him that in the first work of grace the heart is born again; a new life is born within and yes, the Holy Spirit comes to live with that heart. But in the second work of grace there is a death; the old nature of sin is cleansed out of the heart. It is not a different Holy Spirit that enters, but with sin purged out, the Holy Spirit possesses his whole heart and so he feels so much more of His presence.

His face lit up and he gestured as if he were driving a nail as he said with satisfaction, "That's it! I see it now. I just wanted to know how to tell others what had really happened to me." Once again, blessed are those whose hearts teach their heads. Grace works so much better that way.

On Friday, Feb. 23, we again sat down for a few minutes to visit. I had a few books on holiness that I wanted to give him to read, and after we had looked them over we came right to the subject of what God was doing for him.

He said, "Oh it is just all becoming so clear to me now. I look back and see that for a number of years my heart was hungry for this but I did not know I could have it. I remember reading Psalm 51 over and over and praying with David, 'Create in me a clean heart, O God; and renew a right spirit within me.' I knew I needed that but I didn't know how to get it. I heard of holiness, but I thought it was just a set of rules. I heard of the gift of the Holy Spirit, but I thought it must be accompanied with the gift of tongues. Then God led me to this prison to meet you to show me the way to a satisfied heart. Oh, it's wonderful! I feel like I'd like to get up and run around this room." Do continue to pray for him that he will continue to walk in the light as God gives it to him. I do believe he has a good start in that direction.

The other Friday night I was passing out of the main prison to hold a Bible study in the minimum unit and I met a posse of officers all dressed in riot gear bringing a man back in a wheelchair from the hospital to lock him up again. As I looked at the poor man I thought of the extremes in life that a man can live in. I thought of my own life, so happy and contented in the sweet will of God, with so much to look forward to in both this life and the next. Then I thought what it must feel like to be locked up in prison and still be so unhappy on the inside that a fight would break up his body and put him in a wheelchair surrounded by riot gear.

I couldn't help but wonder how deep man's capacity is for trouble and sorrow. What takes place on the inside of a man who was created by a loving God to be happy and contented, that can cause him to go right on smashing his head into a brick wall and go back for more? What a bleak existence, and what a dark future. And all the time, he is just a heart cry from a merciful, loving Savior.

God is continuing to move in real revival power in the Bible studies in Facility III. The first Friday night of each month we take a few moments for observing the sacraments of the Lord's Supper.

The first Friday night of February we had just taken of the elements and I was speaking to them of the fact that Jesus told us to "do this in remembrance of Me." I asked them to go back in their memory to the darkest hour of their life; the moment they felt the farthest from God and heaven and the closest to hell they would ever want to be. I heard some groans and sighs. I said, "Men, what if in that hour there had been no way back, no shed Blood, no redemption from sin." Some began to pray, some began to cry, and some began to shout out praise to God, and for some time such a weight of God's presence settled down that we could not go on with anything else, nor did we want to. That Presence lingered on through the whole Bible study. It is that Presence and that alone which makes the men so hungry for more. And I believe that God's presence comes because there are hearts who are wanting Him and because you are praying. Please, please continue to pray! God answers prayer.

I haven't had room in the last couple of letters to tell you of a dear man who went to his reward on New Year's day. He was an intelligent, educated man in his early forties who was in the Minimum Camp outside the prison walls. He was being used there as a teacher's aid in the education department and had only four months left before his release.

Last October this inmate began to feel unwell and thought he had a cold, then he got a pain in his back and finally asked to see a doctor. They sent him over to the hospital and tried for a few weeks to determine what was wrong with him. He got worse and worse; the pain became severe and soon he noticed a lump forming on his neck. Next he found lumps breaking out other places and when they sent him for an x-ray they found a lump on his lung. By this time it was mid-December and he was sure he was full of cancer.

It was about this time that I first met up with him and we began to visit. He expressed with floods of tears his fears that he would die in prison and never get to see the day of his release. He also felt pain over the fact that his mother who lived in the south could not afford to come see him, and he might never see her again. He said he had been asking God why He would allow this to happen to him only four months from his release. I felt so sorry for him—filled with excruciating pain, terrible anxiety, and worst of all, resentment against God. I asked him if he felt any sense of forgiveness from God. He said that he had known that in the past, but he did not feel very good about it now. I tried to tell him that he could not be forgiven by God unless he was willing to forgive God.

I said, "You have a lot of unforgiveness in your heart toward God for allowing you to be in this condition, don't you?"

He said, "Yes, I do, and I know that God can't forgive me until I'm willing to forgive." I tried to point out to him that he had nothing to lose. I faced him with the fact that without God he would die and be lost forever; if he gave his heart to God and died he would go straight to heaven.

He could not hold back the tears as he told me he was going to forgive God. A few days later he met me in the hall and told me he had given it all to God and that a peace had come into his heart.

We visited several times after that and he said that everything was right with God. I never knew a man could go downhill so fast. He suffered so intensely toward the end that pain medications had little effect, and that not for long. The last time I saw him he said, "I want to thank you for all you have done for me. I love you." On New Year's day he passed from this life into the next, and I believe he passed into a better world. I'll have to confess, I loved him too, and I hope to meet him someday, beyond the reach of pain and tears.

Once more I mention the needy man I've written about in the last letters. Several of you have written that you have taken him on your hearts in prayer. I mentioned that to him and he said he wanted to thank you. Please continue to pray for him. And please ask God that you may pray in faith. It might be your prayer which will reach the throne and "save a soul from death" — death now and hereafter.

I am trying to help this man grasp just a glimpse of who God is, but where does one start? How can a heart conceive of God as a loving Father when he has never known the least thing about an earthly father? From the age of seven years and up, every single thing in life has robbed him a little deeper of the ability to trust — the only way he can ever know God.

I did have a profitable visit with this dear soul last Friday.

The week before he had told me that he did want God to help him, but there was one thing that he did not know about in the near future. I would not want to reveal what it was that he told me. He said if certain events turned out to be as he feared, he would have to tell God to wait because he would have to take revenge into his own hands. I told him we would talk about that the next time we met. I did not feel I could tackle that without time to pray about it first.

The next week I started by saying to him, "Do you remember what you told me about what you would have to do in such and such a situation?" He did. I told him that I wanted to help him in any way I could, and that I really wanted to see him happy in God. But I told him I would have to be honest with him and tell him that God would never take him on those terms. I said, "God will not come into your life until you are willing to give him that key to your life."

He said, "I've been thinking about that all week; I'm willing to give that to God. I promise I won't revenge myself." Pray that he will enable God to reveal Himself to him, just as He did for you and me.

I cannot thank you enough for your interest and prayers; I firmly believe they are our only life-line. God is a covenant keeping God—He will, if we will.

Yours in His Service,
William Cawman

6
SIN'S PAYDAY

April 1, 2001

I MUST SAY THAT the written Word of God takes on very plain and stark reality when one leaves the security of the church pew for the raw environment of prison life. When God's Word declares that "the wages of sin is death," no interpretation of that fact can be more glaringly obvious than where those wages are being meted out. Along with the thrill of witnessing hearts turn from sin to God, there is the ever-present reality that sin has a payback. One can choose to enjoy the pleasures of sin, but when payday comes there is no control over the wages.

Just the other day it seemed that I had listened all day long to broken men pouring out, in essence, this distressing dilemma: "I know I have sinned; I know I deserved to be punished; but I never did anything to merit all this. Everything is going from bad to worse; now my family is falling apart, the men on the tier are accusing me, the officer wrote me up for something that wasn't my fault and now I'm losing comp time, etc. Why do I have to suffer like this?"

Cain also cried out, "My punishment is greater than I can

bear." But no one ever seems to stop to reckon with the dire fact that the pleasure of sin is costly, very costly. When the payback starts there is no stopping; the cruel master of the sinning business loves no one. The heart cries out, "It's enough! It's enough! Stop! Stop!" But the merciless tidal wave of the wages of sin rolls on and on, bringing death with every billow.

I left the prison that day with such an abhorrence of sin, such a filled-up cup of listening to its merciless tyranny, that as I drove away my heart cried out to God, "Oh God, I want to get as far away from sin as I can get. I don't want to play with even the appearance of evil. It's cruel; it's hateful; it's horrible! Yet as I write these words, men are still hugging it to their bosoms with passionate addiction. Even the Catholic chaplain said to me the other day, "Wouldn't this world be a wonderful place if it were without sin?" Yes, it would. But until then, "My soul be on thy guard!"

Again I find several dying inmates in the hospital. The majority die of AIDS, and it is an awful sight to witness. I thank God that there are several very helpful Christian officers who work in the hospital, and they are more than ready for us to minister to these needy souls. The other day I went to the second floor and a female officer told me there were a number who really needed me to see them. Some of them are infectious, and though I take every precaution to be safe, I cannot turn them down. After all, in those moments just a word, a prayer, might make the difference between heaven or hell for all eternity.

I went to the first cell where there was a white, forty-year-old man who knows he is dying of AIDS. He is not allowed out of his cell nor is anyone allowed in, so I visited with him through the food port. To give you the picture—I am kneeling in the hall on one side of the door; he is kneeling on the other side. The first thing he tells me is that he knows he is dying. The tears begin to flow freely. He tells me that he is all alone; his family, even his mother, will have nothing to do with him anymore. He has been raised in a Christian home; he has three uncles who are ministers. His grandfather was a circuit-riding preacher, but this grandson has drifted away, far away. The officer slips up behind me and hands me a mask and a list of cell numbers and names that need help when I'm finished with him. She sees that I need some time with this man.

The inmate goes on to say that nine years ago he was infected with AIDS and the person responsible did not tell him they had the disease. He went on to infect others, and now he says he cannot forgive the person who did it to him.

I feel in times like this I cannot be anything but starkly honest, even though my heart bleeds for him. I tried to point out to him that he is responsible for his condition; he was sinning when it happened to him. He knows that; he knows that he cannot be forgiven unless he forgives, and yet he says he can't forgive. He says he wants to; he is willing to; but he can't. He says that he believes this is the only thing which is keeping him alive, and yet he shakes his head, "I just can't forgive." I tried to point to Jesus hanging on the cross; He was not being punished for His own sin; He did not even have to endure the punishment. He could have called for help from heaven and He would have been rescued in a moment, and yet He looked down from the cross and said, "Father, forgive them." I told him to ask for that forgiveness.

I came home and sent out an urgent prayer request which many of you received. Now let me tell you the outcome. I took his need before the Bible study group on Friday night. They prayed for him until I felt they broke a hole clear through to heaven. We felt the witness that God had heard and what a weight of His presence lingered after it.

I went back on Sunday and told the dying man that I believed God was going to answer prayer for him and that there were many praying. He was so thankful and humbled and asked that we keep on praying. I visited him very often and on Monday afternoon, Mar. 26, as I walked up to his cell window I could see his face was different. He said, "Chaplain, I was just thinking about you; I said, 'where's the chaplain?'" And then he told me that between 7:30 and 8:00 Friday evening, one week after the men had prayed through for him, God forgave his heart. He kept saying, "Oh it's so peaceful now."

We had a prayer of thanksgiving for the abundant mercy of a loving God. Isn't God wonderful? Thank you each one who prayed for this man. He is now a child of the King. Praise God.

Now I must tell you of something which warms my heart immensely. I am observing with delight that God does not give an inferior or second-rate or infantile grace to those whose theology may not be really advanced as yet. I am witnessing before my eyes that God's great grace works! I am melted again and again in the presence of those whom God has sanctified here in the prison as I watch them grow and walk in the light and not stumble. I find that one does not need to understand the fruits of the Spirit for them to operate.

One dear man who got sanctified a few months ago and has been walking so carefully in the light and enjoying unbroken communion with God, has taken it on his heart to pray for another chaplain. He gets up for a while nearly every night and prays for him. The other day he had an opportunity to talk to this chaplain and he witnessed very clearly to the man how God had cleansed his heart from all sin. He said the chaplain lowered his head and listened and his face got red. But later that chaplain said to me, "He's a good man." The inmate witnessed so humbly and with grace that I believe it must have spoken to the chaplain.

The dear pastor that I wrote about in the last letter who was sanctified recently and has been "catching up" in his mind as to what took place in his hungry heart, came to me glowing with the reality of what was happening within him, but with some questions he was grappling with in his mind. He had been reading one of the little booklets a dear chaplain in Ohio had sent to me, John Wesley's *Plain Account of Christian Perfection*.

This sanctified inmate was finding some degree of conflict with his lifelong teaching that a man cannot fall from grace. He said with great feeling, "My main concern is, I don't ever want to lose this. I don't ever want to grieve God again in my life." As we looked together at the plain teaching of God's Word, he saw that the healthy fear of grieving God was his greatest assurance that he would not do it. He saw that God had made such abundant provision for him not to fall that he need not stake his security on the belief that he couldn't fall.

As I looked into his face and saw light dawning upon his mind, I couldn't help but thank God for a man more in love with Jesus than with his theology. I hope I am!

The next Friday night in Bible study I was speaking to them from the Scriptures which show that we can indeed lose God out of our hearts and backslide after we have been saved and sanctified, but that the abundant grace of God is so sufficient that we need not, nor do we want to sin and fail. I saw him sitting near the back with his eyes closed in deep thought; occasionally I saw him stroke his little goatee and look up at the ceiling. I wondered how it was all going down with him. At the close of the Bible study he came up and as he neared me his face broke into a full moon. He grasped my hand and said explosively, "I feel like I could turn cartwheels!" Oh the wonderful grace of Jesus! As the song says, "It saves and keeps and satisfies the soul."

May the same great grace which has become so precious to some of these dear men reward you who have labored in prayer for their souls. Thank you!

Only through Him,
William Cawman

May 1, 2001

I MUST CONTINUE with more of the same testimony I left off with last month. After all, haven't you found this great salvation to grow better and richer every day?

The pastor mentioned continues to grow in grace, and as he brings up different questions about the life of holiness, I explain to him that the work of sanctification is both an instantaneous and a progressive work. All self and sin is cleansed at once from the heart by the fire of the Holy Spirit, but the human vessel with all of its infirmities and shortcomings and mindsets undergoes a continuous operation of the indwelling Spirit as He enables us to become more like Himself. He understands with evident satisfaction and replies, "The real miracle of all this is that anything God comes to work on in or about me, I find absolutely no resistance left within to Him doing it." He goes on to say, "I just can't get over the change within; I mean, just look around me, nothing has changed here—I'm still in prison, my family is out there pining for me and I'm in here doing the same thing—but I have found what I always craved; it is 'joy unspeakable and full of glory.'"

I wish each of you could meet him and see the glow of grace. Many times I wish I could share with each of you who are praying so faithfully, the joy of sitting with a dear man who has never had the chance you and I have had, and sensing the Holy Spirit in the room with us, guiding him into all truth, just as He promised He would. I cannot think of any greater joy than watching a street urchin grow into a saint, but such is the grace of our Lord!

And then there are the amusing moments as well. One dear brother who has been walking so carefully and closely to the Lord, never knew how to read until he learned so that he could read his Bible. He loves his Bible and sometimes adopts some of its language when he speaks of God talking to him. He told me he was lying on his bunk the other day and God spoke to him so gently and said, *"Thou talks too much."* He knew just what the Lord meant, and is walking in the light.

Another dear man who had heard some phraseology that he adopted, was waxing eloquent in prayer. After praying for the various needs in the room, he began to pray very lovingly for his chaplain. "Lord, bless our dear chaplain; bless his shortcomings and his longcomings." (My computer just told me that last one is not a word). Please answer prayer, Lord, anyway.

Many of you will remember that we have written several times of inmate T——, the former radical Christian-hater. Recently, he had been feeling unwell and was just taking extra medicine and pushing on with his job in the boiler room. Well, he suddenly went down with a heart attack and had to be rushed to the hospital. They found two badly clogged arteries and opened them up, and now he says he feels like a new man.

T—— told me afterwards that in those moments when he thought he was dying and everyone else did too, he felt a deep sense of peace sweep over him, and he thought he was going home. What a wonderful testimony! I never visit with him but what I feel I've been in the holy presence of God. He is one of my dearest brothers—a blood brother. We are black and white, made one in the Blood of Christ.

The dear man that I wrote about in the last letter, who was dying of AIDS, is also so different. In fact, he seems better physically, so much so that others around him are noticing it. He was testifying to me last night at great length and so eagerly from inside of his cell. He told how he now looks back over his life and feels so bad over it all. He said he left home in a huff at the age of seventeen and lived for the devil until now. His parents always made him go to church even if they didn't go. He would slip in the back door and grab a bulletin to show he'd been there, and then run away. Now he can't wait to go to church.

This inmate said that for 23 years he gave all he had to the devil and self and he said, "What did I get in return? A prison cell, a broken body, a wasted income, and an outcast from home." But now he says that is all forgiven, and he never wants a bit of it again. He is so eager to get out of prison and go home and be with his family that he has hurt and missed for 23 years. He told me that he is happier to-day than he was in all of those 23 years. He says that if God had not allowed him to be sent to prison he knows he would have been dead by now. Oh what a change comes with the grace of God.

Last night was such a precious time again in the Bible study. I have never been in such a "church" where there is so much real hunger and thirst for the Word of God. The men worship for a few minutes and then announce, "Now it is time for the real meat," meaning they are ready for the study.

We are studying the book of Romans, and what a book it is. I have preached in many holiness churches, but the grace of holiness shines most brightly when explained the most simply — isn't that amazing? Some men have been in the class now for over three years and are more eager for truth than ever. One dear man who has been there for over a year now came to me with beaming face at the close of the study last night and said, " I am finally seeing it very clearly now and it's wonderful." Pray that he will not only see, but plunge in all the way.

I am convinced that the sly old devil performed one of his master strokes in spreading so far and wide the teaching of a religion that allows one to excuse sin in his life. No matter what form that is done in, it is the most dangerous doctrine on earth. The teachings of atheism in our colleges and universities are nothing in comparison with the havoc of having been taught that there is no real solution for the sinning business but to be chronically forgiven and to sin again. Oh how these men are rejoicing to hear that there is a way to be rid of that nature of sin. Perhaps this is due in part at least to the observation of Ps. 36:2, "For he flattereth himself in his own eyes, until his iniquity be found to be hateful." When a man finds the load and nature of sin too heavy to bear, he is glad to know that there is a cure.

On my way out of the chapel after such a good time together in God, the Westminster Chime sounded out over the prison system—another dear soul had just passed from time into eternity.

Last Sunday evening I had slipped over to the hospital before the evening service and the officer told me that they were in 911, waiting for an ambulance to take away an inmate. I asked if the inmate would want to see a chaplain. He said, "I don't know; go ahead and poke your head in the door." I went down the hall to the cell and immediately recognized the inmate as one I'd often seen in services. He seemed to be feeling terrible, but I didn't find out what was really wrong with him. The officers were getting him ready to be transported on the stretcher to the city hospital. They handcuffed him and leg cuffed him, and then snapped a black box between the handcuffs and hooked a chain into it and wrapped the chain around his waist and back into the black box. This, together with his IV tubes and oxygen hoses, fitted him out for the trip. At that point the officer told me to go ahead and talk to him. He was glad to see me and welcomed a time for prayer before he left. Once again it was so starkly obvious that "the way of the transgressor is hard."

That evening I preached to a group of one hundred men from Ex. 15:26, "I am the Lord that healeth thee." As I laid out very plainly areas of their lives that God was longing to heal (their guilt, their depravity, their memories, their past, their marriages, etc.), they would grow intense in listening and then burst out clapping and then listen intently again.

The next day many of them seemed deeply moved. They came and said in essence, "How did you know that we were struggling with those very things?" They said they looked at each other in disbelief that I had read their minds. I didn't know, but God did. I hadn't even planned to preach on that until a couple of days previous when I felt God so strongly impressed me with it. I told you that to say this: God is hearing their cry for help, and I believe He again and again lays their cry on some of your hearts and as you pray, God gives guidance. I cannot express how often I know without a doubt that the enabling to say a word, or quote a Scripture, or preach a message has come in answer to someone's prayer. Could I plead, please keep praying!

Do you remember the man I've been writing about who has such a horrible history which haunts him? I told him yesterday that many of God's children around the world were praying for him. I could sense he was deeply overwhelmed. "Really?" You may be the first ones who ever cared for him. He wants to thank you. I do too!

In His love,
William Cawman

††††

June 1, 2001

THANK YOU SO MUCH ONCE AGAIN for your faithful prayers during another month. It is so encouraging to meet God's children around the country or receive a letter from them saying, "We are praying for the work in the prison." It melts my heart every time I hear it, but it does far more than that; God is moving in answer to those prayers.

Of all the things I could tell you in this letter, let me first highlight or feature one particularly needy man. I see looking back, that I have mentioned him in every letter this year except the one for April. He is the man who has had such a horrible background from his earliest years and has had awful nightmares about his past and all that he has done and seen. Several of you have written to me at different times and told me that you are praying for him. I want to say that God is really working on his heart.

Let me go back and tell you a little more about this man so that you can understand how to pray for him (that is, if it is possible for any of us to know how to pray for him).

At the age of seven or before, his profligate mother would use him to gratify her lusts until his body and mind were all torn apart. When his schoolteacher noticed that he was having trouble, she sent him to the school nurse and doctor who then called in his mother and threatened her. The state department came and took the children away from her, but they were so scared that they jumped out of the car and ran back home. These things infuriated his uncle, who was living with his mother. He took the boy into the back yard, threw gasoline all over him and tossed his cigarette at him. Of course, the boy burst into flames. From that time on, his brothers would take him down to the drug houses and he very soon learned the life of the underworld.

By the time this soul was a young man, he had been led into such atrocious company that he was forced to join one of the nation's worst gangs or be killed by them. He joined. From there life became a living nightmare of murder scenes, criminal gangs, death in every conceivable and inconceivable form, and all that goes with it. The scenes he witnessed and took part in would make a person's blood run cold just to hear about, let alone be involved with. As I have listened for hours to him pour out the awful scenes of the past and the things he can no longer keep sequestered in his bosom, I have been staggered at the capacity of the depravity of the wicked heart. I tell you, sin is a cruel taskmaster.

I could go on and on, but I have not and could not tell anyone even the beginning of the awfulness of it all. But there is something he has told me which moves my heart to tears. Back through all the years of his tumultuous life, he would steal away whenever the load became too heavy to bear, to a quiet garden where there was a huge crucifix, and there he would huddle at its base—the only refuge he knew about in his life's stormy sea. I can't help but wish I could have found him there. Oh the hearts that are aching in the night of sin. To look into their faces we might recoil and withdraw ourselves from them, but what if I had been the little boy born into his "home"?

For weeks it seemed there was little breakthrough with him. I told God it was the hardest assignment He had ever given me, but I didn't feel clear to leave him alone. The young man would tell me story after story of the most atrocious blood-baths imaginable. I would try to help him to see that he could find a refuge in the loving arms of a heavenly Father who could heal the deep scars that he could no longer bear. He would seem to get a glimmer of hope, or at least of wishing, and then, like a rabbit pursued by a blood-thirsty hound, he would look over his shoulder and slip back into one of the scenes from the past that he hated but couldn't escape from.

One day as we were visiting, the young man looked at me and said, "When I get out of here, I'm going to look you up. I know how to find you." I knew he did too; and I knew that he had all the underworld knowledge that could easily remove a man and his family from the earth without a trace of investigation to follow it up. I pondered it for a split second and then felt a rush of love for the "man" (or perhaps child) within this man. I looked him straight in the eye and said, "C———, I don't take that as a threat; I want you to look me up; I want to be your friend."

I cannot forget the look on his face as he put out his hand and grasped mine. It seemed I saw years of broken trust—inability to trust which was not his fault—crumble in his eyes. "That's a deal," he said.

From then on it seems that there has been a change coming over him. He seems to be gaining confidence that he really can become a new man. He knows he is not yet saved, but he believes it is coming. Although he cannot read well at all, he is reading his New Testament as well as he can, and each verse that he understands he puts beside it a star. If he doesn't feel he understands it, he doesn't put a star because he wants to read it all and know what it says. All I can say about him at this point is this: Oh the goodness of God which leads to repentance. I have been melted to see the hand of God, in answer to your prayers, so gently wooing him back to be able to trust Him as the Father he never knew. He is so overwhelmed that you care enough about him to be praying for him. I want to ask you if you will please pray earnestly and believingly that this victim of Satan's dominion will lay down his heavy burden and become a child of God. Remember, His Blood reaches deeper than the stain has gone!

The dear man in the hospital who was dying of AIDS and is now forgiven, continues to exhibit a genuine miracle of prayer-answering, miracle-working conversion. He told me that if he sees an advertisement for beer on the television he feels like throwing up. He says, "I don't need that anymore, ever."

I told you that he seems better even physically since God forgave him. Well, recently he saw the doctor and they ran some tests on him which showed his T-cells up 200 points and his viral load down from 1000 to 79; and he was twice told by the doctors to set things in order because he was on his way out. Maybe God isn't finished with him yet. If you feel led to pray that God will heal him completely, don't be afraid to do it. He said God is still working on him and sometimes He has to thump him on the head, but it feels good.

I also wanted to tell you something so precious about dear V——, the Spanish boy who got sanctified last summer and hasn't missed a beat since. He told me the other day that he had ordered a little radio from commissary. When they passed out the commissary, he was out on a work detail and did not get his things. He told it to the officer in charge and the officer told him to see him the next day and he would see if he could get it out for him.

The next day V—— saw the officer in the hall and started to go ask him, when he remembered that it was Sunday, the Lord's Day. He went back to his cell and sat on the edge of his bunk and thought about it. He wasn't really buying it on the Lord's Day. As he sat there meditating on his feelings, God spoke to him so sweetly and said, *If ye love Me, keep My commandments.*

Instantly his heart melted and he looked up and said, "Lord, I do love Thee! I don't need the radio, but I need You." He said his heart was so filled with love and peace that he just told the

Lord he was going to fast all day just because he loved Him. Later that day another inmate brought him a cup of coffee. He said he loves coffee, but he set the cup on the window sill until the inmate was gone and then poured it down the toilet—he loved Jesus more than that too. I guess you can understand why I feel rather excited about fulfilling his request that I baptize him when he gets out of prison.

Once again last Friday night the Bible study was charged with God's presence as we dwelt on the words from Romans 3:21, 22: "the righteousness of God." I cannot describe it to you. One man sat quietly on the front seat wiping tears constantly. Others were beaming; one looked miserably under conviction, and another just got so excited he could not keep his seat. He finally stood up, turned clear around and sat back down again, pumping his fists in the air. It pulls one's heart clear out to minister to hunger and response like that. I'll confess, it might have a profound tendency to spoil a preacher until he would find it necessary to employ conscious charity on a complacent crowd. These Bible studies have been a wellspring of blessing to my own heart. Oh the power of the Word of God. After all, didn't even His enemies say, "Never man spake like this man"?

My page is up even though there are other things to tell you. Thank you, dear friends, for all you are doing.

In His great love,
William Cawman

7
TRAILING THE HOUND OF HEAVEN

July 1, 2001

PRAISE GOD FROM WHOM all blessings flow. He is still bestowing those blessings wherever hearts will open the door to Him. He is still standing at the door, knocking, and I believe nothing brings greater pleasure to His heart than to be able still to say to the Father as He did in John 17:8, "I have given unto them the words which Thou gavest Me: and they have received them." If the angels in heaven rejoice over one sinner that repents, shouldn't we also?

In the last newsletter, I gave you a sketch of a dear man and asked you to pray. Later that week those of you who receive the letter by email heard that your prayers were answered in a wonderful way. To those who didn't receive the note, it will be enclosed with this mailing. As we rejoice together over God's wonderful power, I want to follow up the miracle with a few observations.

Someone wrote to me asking about the thought of God scaring people into His grace or into heaven, without any fruits of repentance. I really appreciate this sound thinking and will explain his state more fully as I feel God has revealed it to me.

This man was not running from God, or thoughtless about Him, and then suddenly scared into making amends with his Maker because of being caught in a corner. He had been earnestly seeking God's help and had told me over and over that he really wanted to trust God with his life and become a new man. I had been praying definitely that God would somehow reveal Himself to C—— as only He can, because the poor man had never, ever in his life been able to trust anybody. I believe that is exactly what God did. He revealed to C—— that He is real and that He is powerful, and that He cares about him. I believe what really happened is that God broke the chains of all that had been his past and gave him, perhaps for the first time in his life, one good chance to choose the right way.

I am amazed at how God works. The man had developed over the years a hatred for blacks, and when he went down on the cell floor with a heart attack, the first person to his rescue was the black he hated the most. He said right there he lost his hatred for black people. Then God showed C—— that His power was able to work a miracle, and He broke the chains of C——'s inability to trust Him. Then, I really believe God wiped the slate of his past clean, much of which he was dragged into before he had any power to choose those things, clean except for memory. He told me, "The past is gone; it's gone!"

Now, let me tell you how it has gone. The next Sunday night I went up to his cell in the hospital to see him. I found that he was all worked up because he had experienced a little pain again in his chest and asked the officer if he could see a nurse. The officer told him "no" and he felt he was being mistreated. I felt so terrible for him. I went into his cell, sat down on the bed with him and began to talk to him. I told him that God had saved his life and his soul, and that now he was going to have to choose to let the life of Jesus work in him and not his old way of doing things. As he listened he grew calmer, and we ended up going out to the officer's desk to make an apology.

I went home that night under a real burden for C——, and

went out to the garage to pray for him. As I brought his case before God, I felt God began to talk to me about him more than I was talking to God about him. I realized that here was a man who had never known what it was to resist a single temptation in his life. He had never even tried to control his reactions. He had just simply and habitually let the devil run his life as if he had no power to choose. And then my heart burst into pieces as God allowed me to share the heart of Paul for the Galatians, "My little children, of whom I travail in birth again until Christ be formed in you." Yes, thank God for the broken chains, but oh that Christ can be allowed to be formed in him.

Since that night I have been working closely with this new brother in Christ, trying to show him what it means to be a Christian, within and without. And, I am so glad to tell you that God is not giving up on him. C—— is open and teachable and is really trying to live differently. When he got back to his cell in the prison, he went to the officers and told them that he knew they had gotten off to a wrong start, but he wanted to be different and he would respect them. He was put in a four-man cell, which is really difficult, but he told the other men that he was trying to live a different life and he would really appreciate it if they would not use dirty language around him. C—— got up in church and told the men what had happened to him and asked them to help him and pray for him. So now, would you please pray with me that Christ may be formed in him?

Many of us grew up with a knowledge of what a Christian should act like. We knew that we should not give in to temptations to react carnally. Does he? Oh God, I pray, let me see this man through Your eyes until I can lead him just as clearly and yet as gently as You would.

I must tell you of a victory in the life of V——. He is such a precious young man and lives inwardly and outwardly the life of holiness. He walks so carefully with God and is so sensitive to His every direction. I have told you many things about him before. Recently he told me that for some time God had been dealing with him about things which bothered him when he watched television. He said he narrowed down his viewing, but still he couldn't dodge all that made him feel bad. Finally he said, "God, I believe You would be pleased if I quit watching it altogether. You said in Your Word, 'I will set no wicked thing before mine eyes.' Every time I look at it there is something wicked." So he said he just pulled the plug and God drew so close to him that he has no intentions of ever plugging it back in.

V—— said he really had a blessed time the other day witnessing to one of the other chaplains about how God had cleansed his heart from all sin. He said he didn't really intend to say all that he did, but he just kept feeling God's hand behind his back telling him to say it all. Another inmate was present who is earnestly seeking the blessing, and he told the chaplain that what V—— was saying was true; he told him that he was a witness that V—— was living without sin in his life.

I want to squeeze in two or three more things and I see my page is running out. The other night in Bible study, I felt suddenly an urge to ask W—— to give his testimony again. It had been a while since I had heard him do it and he immediately and very humbly came forward and began at the very beginning of his Christian life a few years ago in the county jail where he had repented of his sins and then gone right on asking God to take "that nasty thing out of his heart," and He did it. He told it so clearly and simply and then just began to exhort the men. The further he went the more of God's Spirit attended his words until the atmosphere was just charged with the presence of God. The men have no question about him; he lives what he preaches.

The man whom I have told you about who was dying of AIDS but is now a happy child of God, is soon to go home. His charges have been dropped. He said he can't wait to go to a church and begin a new life. Even though he is in prison over a false charge which has now been dropped, he says he is happier in that cell than he ever was out on the devil's pathway. He wants no part of his old life back again. Please pray for him as he leaves and goes to his mother's home half way across the country. I expect to hear from him again sometime.

Here is one more request for prayer. For probably a couple of years now I have watched and worked with an inmate who was an army ranger. He fully understands the factors which can so easily produce a Timothy McVey. The nation trains its own worst enemies. God has really helped him and I have watched him come through some really rough spiritual and emotional territory. But recently he has come to realize that his spiritual life is stalled and becoming stagnant. He wanted to talk to me about it, and he just broke down and sobbed over his lack. I began to point out to him from God's Word that to fail to go on to holiness and have the nature of sin removed from the heart can only result in spiritual backsliding and failure. He owned right up to it and the following Sunday night as he came into church he was just vibrant with emotion. He said that V—— had been talking to him about the experience in Romans chapter six, and he said, "I need to talk to you about it." I told him I couldn't wait, and what a visit we had. Will you please pray that he will not fail to find the fullness of God he is hungry for?

Again, words cannot thank you enough for your prayers. May God be praised.

Thanking Him and you,
William Cawman

August 1, 2001

How great is our God! Moses heard Him proclaimed as "The Lord, The Lord God, merciful and gracious, longsuffering, and abundant in goodness and truth…" And truly He is Who He says He is.

Let me start by telling you how wonderful He really is. The dear man that you have prayed and are praying for is such a marvel of the patience and goodness of God. As we told you in the last letter, he has known absolutely nothing of the fruits of grace nor even of basic principles and ethics. But oh, how patient God is being with him.

I was gone for a couple of weeks in camp meeting and I kept lifting him up in prayer lest Satan should get an advantage of him, for I knew he could be such an easy prey. But when I returned and met him again I felt like exalting our God with highest praises. Surely He knows how to do His own work better than you or I. The dear man had spent the time really putting off his old self, and asking God to help him, and he had come a long way. He is learning to love His Bible, even though he reads painfully slow. He sat with me the other day as I was trying to help him see how he could let the love of God move in his life where sin used to have its way, and the phone rang. After I had answered the phone, he pointed to what he had been reading while I was on the phone. It was Hebrews 13:17, "Remember them which have the rule over you, who have spoken unto you the word of God: whose faith follow, considering the end of their conversation." He seemed thrilled with what he had read as he said, "Is Somebody talking to me, or what?"

I knew that ever since he had come back to the tier from the hospital he had been in a four-man cell. He was really suffering from the others as they made it so hard for him there. He would get up early in the morning to read his Bible and stay up late after they had gone to bed to read again. They had threatened him and mistreated him, but thank God, I believe hearts were praying for him, and God restrained him from reacting like his old self. C—— told me that while I was gone, every time the devil would try to get him to act like he always had, he could see my face right in front of him. (Pray that God will be able to wean him to a better Face).

I felt that perhaps it would only be right to try to remove

him from such a continuous trial, so I asked the superintendent of his facility if he could be moved to a two-man cell.
They did, and he is really thanking God for it. His new cell
mate does not profess to be of any religion at all and is just as
much a heathen as he was, but they are talking together and
looking into the Bible and are getting along really well. He
said he got down on his knees to pray before going to bed and
he could tell the other man leaned over the edge of the bunk
above and watched him, but he said that was just all right.
Pray for this man, too.

Let me tell you a little more if I can without running out of
room. I really want you to know how to pray for this man
until Christ can be formed in him. He told me today that he
sees other "Christian" inmates hiding their Bibles under their
arms or behind their backs. He said he was not going to do
that. He never hid what he used to do behind his back and he
won't hide his new walk either. He said that he went after the
devil's way with everything he had and he's going to do the
same thing about God's way. Well, bless God!

Dear inmate V——, whom we have written about many
times, is approaching his first anniversary, July 31, of the coming of the Blessed Holy Spirit into his heart. He is so excited
about his "first birthday." He came up really close to me and
just like a child, grinning with delight, he said softly, "How
did you feel on your first birthday?"

What a year of growing in grace! This week he and I and
another inmate who is seeking to be sanctified were visiting
together in the chapel and we had a wonderful time of it. I
was speaking to them of some areas where God desires to balance us up after He fills us with Himself and after about an
hour V—— wanted to pray together. We got on our knees and
he cut loose with no fear of anyone hearing him pray and just
told God all that was in his heart.

Part of it was too good to not share with you. Because of the
things we had just been speaking of, he prayed; "Now Lord,
when You sanctified me You took my heart through ahead of

my head. But now, Lord, I need some wisdom along with it. Oh Lord, help my head to come along too." After he had poured out his whole heart to God and had prayed for the other inmate (the former Army Ranger we spoke of in the last letter), he got up as happy as he could be, and the ranger did too.

I had given V—— the book *R.G. Finch, The Man and His Mission.* He has read it over more than once and just loves it. He always refers to Bro. Finch as "Old Finch," but he says it so endearingly. On the way down the stairs from the chapel he said, "You know, I read that Old Finch said that is what happened to him; his heart went through before his head." Well, pray for V——'s head. I guess I would have to say that his head is certainly not standing in his way of walking in the light, so I don't think God is going to have any trouble with it.

The inmate who was dying of AIDS is still here awaiting his release, but he is so much better. And he is so happy in God. I went to his cell the other day and he sprang up from where he was sitting on the edge of his bunk and said, "Oh Chaplain, I have something I need to show you." He then took from the windowsill his book called *Chicken Soup,* in which he has written all kinds of quotes that he has found and likes. He looked and looked until he found the quote he wanted to share with me. Here it is: "A God you can understand has to be smaller than yourself." Maybe you and I ought to think about that a little too.

This happy inmate then went on to tell me again how glad he is that God brought him into this prison. He said he can't wait to go home, but he thanks God he is here. He said he used to have it all, and went on to enumerate what it was, but he said it didn't work. What he has now, works! He says he doesn't want and doesn't need anything else; God is all he needs.

Now, I would like to share an urgent prayer request with you. Quite recently a few inmates have perhaps had a little more zeal than wisdom and the devil is taking advantage of it.

Some of them felt so full of the good news of full salvation and deliverance from sin in practice and in being, that they came on pretty straight in services with other chaplains who believe it not possible to live above and without sin. It began to create a little tension in some of the services until it was brought to my attention. I asked one of the other chaplains what he perceived the disturbance to be about and he said, "Well it seems to be over the idea of sinlessness." I smiled inwardly only.

I felt it necessary to address the good brothers with a little common sense and prudence and told them I appreciated their zeal, but that they might need to add a little wisdom. I pointed out to them that they were in a peculiar situation being a captive audience. If they were at home they could choose what they put on their plate, but in prison the plate was handed to them. If there was something they didn't like it would be best to just leave it on the plate. I explained to them that if they were sitting in a service where truth was being preached that they could fully agree with, and someone got up and started contesting that truth and claiming it to be false, such action would be anything but edifying to the church. Just so, it would not be wise to confront what they considered to be less than truth, but to just get all the good they could and leave the rest to God.

Thank God, they just immediately hugged up to the admonition and saw their mistake and God really blessed the service. But I did sense that behind it all is the sly old devil doing his dirty worst to shut up the message of full salvation. Please help us pray that God will cover His own Word with the Blood of Christ and not allow the animosity of those who love not the truth to prevail against it.

Several new inmates have started coming in to talk about their lives and their needs. If this is "Christian America," where have these men been? Some of them have never read the Bible, have never prayed, and have not the cloudiest clue about God or salvation. I don't mean to be caustic, but give me a few of these men any day in place of a congregation of well-tutored professors who are walking behind light and yet could preach the message back to you as well as you to them. I tell you God's truth and God's way is so clear and simple, and I don't believe He wants it any other way. Sin, salvation, God and holiness shine the brightest when told the simplest. No wonder Jesus said, "Except ye become as little children..."

I am so conscious of your support in prayer, my friends. Thank you, and please, I beg again, keep praying. You are a vital part of God's work.

Encouraged in Him,
W. Cawman

✝✝✝

September 1, 2001

HERE IS ONE of those times when I wish I could let each of you who are praying for us, join us and reap this priceless reward. It is 2:30 on Monday afternoon, August 20, 2001. I am in the chaplain's office with two precious men who, although they are labeled criminals, are nonetheless my brothers in the Lord. Both of them, after some time in coming to the Bible studies, have let God purify their hearts by faith, and are not only professing to be sanctified, but are living beyond all question marks. I sit and listen to them as they share their hearts, and as they speak of the things God has done for them and of all they are discovering of His great work within them, my heart burns with theirs.

One of them confesses the following: he had told me often that for many years he would read Psalm 51 and long to know what David was pleading for, "Create in me a clean heart, O God." He always told me even though he longed for that, he didn't think he could find it. He said, "God has showed me that is not really true. The reason I couldn't find it is because I was not really ready or willing to separate from my sin. As soon as I was willing to put away sin, I knew I could find it."

Oh what rivers of grace flow into the perfectly honest heart.

As these two men just shared their walk with God and all that He was revealing to them, I felt rewarded beyond any power to describe to you. It is these times I wish I could even relate, let alone share. I have met many people who dearly love the Lord, and I have again and again felt my heart burn with theirs, but I cannot say the truth and not tell you that these men are not the least of them.

The Bible studies on Friday nights are another high feast of the week. The men come in so eager for the Word of God that they spend very little time in preliminaries and then say, "Now we're ready for the real meat." They do not go to sleep on the preacher. They do not sit on him until he cannot get his breath. They do not look at him with a blank stare. They are as excited as eager school children on the first day of school. They want untarnished truth. They are hungry for the genuine. They so pull the "preach" out of one that even at the end of a twelve-hour day, it is totally inspiring to feed them on the Word of Life.

In case you don't know it, I love these men. I cannot tell you that every man in the group is of this quality, but those who are set the tone until one can hardly be conscious of any dragging of feet or of any disinterest. These are a group of men who believe in salvation and holiness of heart and do not want any lesser doctrine. They do not all have all the grace they need yet, but they want it. This steady group usually runs between forty and sixty men, and some of them have been with us now for over three years. I thank God for calling me to minister to these men. I wouldn't trade them for any church in the whole world.

The dear man that I have written so much about, who had such a terrible background and then had the four heart attacks, and God raised him up right at death's door and gave him another chance, really needs your prayers. I fear he has allowed the evil spirits to re-enter him and it has gotten him in a lot of trouble. He was sent to detention for something he did, and he has allowed anger and resentment to flood back into his heart. When I first visited him there, he was so wrought up that I had to tell him if he wanted me to help him he would have to be quiet and listen. He did, and the poor man really wants help, but the habits of sin are gripping him just like a demon.

I explained to this new Christian that God had given him one good chance to let the life of Christ overthrow the old nature he had exercised all his life, but that he is letting the devil rob him of that chance by feeding into his thoughts like he is. He acknowledged that and grew quiet as I talked to him about where the two paths were going to lead him and where they would end up. God alone can rescue this man from the awful grip of sin. I long to see him turn his back on sin forever and really let God come into his heart, but I can't do it for him. Oh the blindness of sin! Please pray for him if God would lay him on your heart.

An exciting event is coming up. Inmate V——, who was sanctified a year ago on July 31, and of whom I have written much in past letters, is scheduled to be released from prison. I will tell you in the next letter how it all turns out. We plan to have a dear brother from the church pick him up at the prison and bring him right to the church where several of us will gather and have a time of prayer with him. We will plan to lay our hands on him and dedicate him to God, and then the following Sunday morning we plan to have an early morning baptismal service for him. He plans to bring his family for the baptismal service.

Please pray for this young man that he will never waver or falter in his walk with God. He has lived for the past year without a mark against him or his character, and he lives so close to God that not one little area of his life is withheld from obedience to the God he loves. He is so tender and teachable and yet at the same time so dead set to obey God with all his heart. I do believe God has much in store for him.

V—— says he has work to do when he gets out. There are

several of his family members he wants to look up and ask their forgiveness. He wants to get everything in order so that he can have full custody of his children (he's never been married). He then wants to move closer to where he can worship with us and join with us in reaching others. Please do pray for him as he makes this momentous transition in his life. I have taken a lot of time to try to speak with him about things which will either help him or hinder him in his walk after he gets out. Without fail, the Holy Spirit has already been there speaking to him before I ever get there. I fully expect to have more to tell you about him in the next letter.

Another inmate of whom I have written before, inmate T——, the former member of a radical Christian-hating sect, came to me at a recent Sunday night service and whispered that he wanted to see me as he was getting out of prison the next week. I scheduled him for Friday morning and he didn't appear. I called his housing unit and they said he had been sent to a pre-parole class and from there would be sent on to parole so would not be back on his unit until around 11:00.

At 12:30 I was going into his housing unit to see him when another inmate stopped me and told me that T—— had received bad news; his parole date had been postponed. I went on in and as we stepped into the room together T—— broke out with a huge smile and threw his arms around me as he said, "Chaplain Cawman, God is so good."

He then related that when he got to the parole hearing they had not gotten his paper work in order so they could not process him as yet. He said for a moment he was disappointed, and just then such a Hand of love came down over him that he felt baptized with submission. He said he knows God has everything under control and that this is for his good. We had such a good visit together as usual, and once again I looked down at two pairs of hands clasped together in brotherly love— one pair white and one pair black.

Some people dream of a new home or a new car or a

vacation to some lovely spot. I'd have to say that I dream of someday walking beside this man through the streets of Philadelphia and Camden and listen to him tell the love of Jesus to men who are where he once was and are doing what he once did. I can almost hear him now, all in Ebonics of course! Of this I dream; would you feel led to pray that dream into reality?

I must also tell you about inmate C——. I have written about him at different times and how God delivered him from a steady heroin addiction two years ago this month. He has never had one desire to return to his old life, and he is seeking to be sanctified. C—— has an insatiable thirst for the knowledge of God and has been taking accredited studies in theology and Bible in which we helped him get enrolled. Several dear friends have aided him in making this possible and I wish that they, as well as others, could know what these studies mean to him.

C—— is right now taking a course in Pentateuch. He has come to me several times and told me that the course is driving him to his knees. As the course binds the book of Leviticus to the book of Hebrews he is so moved he just bursts into tears and has to lay it aside and go to prayer. God is using it to show him his own heart and his need of full cleansing. He said that he completed one lesson and it was so overwhelming that even though he knew he did well on it, he was going to lay aside his studies for a day and just go to prayer and then go do the whole lesson over again. Pray that God will soon give him the desire of his heart. He told me today, "I do believe it's coming."

Thank you each one. My paper runs out before the news.

In Him,
William Cawman

8
SET FREE

October 1, 2001

L ET ME TAKE YOU with us to a few precious moments on Sunday morning, September 16. It is 7:00 in the morning; the sun is just peeping over the eastern horizon. It is chilly but a lovely morning, as some Christian friends gather by the side of a lake for the baptismal service of former inmate V——.

The evening before, I had accompanied another brother from the church to the home of this newly-released prisoner. As we approached his house, we could see the plume of smoke still arising from the rubble of the Twin Towers across the river in New York.

After visiting a few moments with the family who are so happy with the change in V——'s life, we started on the two-hour ride home. I have had many precious visits with this dear man in the last two years, but none were more sacred than that two-hour ride. We were oblivious to the passing scenery; we were lost in the wonders of God's keeping power.

Let me relate a little of it to you. As V—— spoke of how God has been so faithfully leading him, he said, "I will not lie to you; the old tempter has been around. But I looked him right in the face and said, 'Old devil, I told you when I was in prison that you could go to hell by yourself, and it hasn't changed now.'" Oh thank God for such grace as this! What is it the old song says? "O how it saves!"

V——— told me that shortly after he got out an old friend came to see him and offered to help him out. The friend said he would be willing to give V——— a thousand dollars if he needed it. V——— thought it over after he was gone, and the idea occurred to him that he didn't have any suitable clothes for his baptism, but he really didn't want to beg from the man. V——— called the man and asked if he could just borrow fifty dollars to get some clothes. The man was very willing to give it to him, but as soon as V——— hung up the phone he felt a cloud begin to come over him. God spoke to him and reminded him that He wanted to supply all his needs. So, he called the man back and told him to forget it, that he would be all right without it. Immediately he felt the peace of God again.

Right after that his sister came and offered to take him shopping, and she bought him a lovely new black suit. He is so happy. He said he isn't looking for things to entertain him; he just wants to be with his family and with his God. V——— walked into the kitchen where his mother was cooking and put his arms around her and said, "Oh Mom, I'm so happy with what God has done for me." His mother told us that she knows the change is real. Both he and his mother would like to move down closer to the church, but he feels he needs to stay for a little while in the area in which he was raised in order to straighten up as much of his past life as he can.

V——— said it is amazing how God is bringing about circumstances so that he can straighten things up. He had said some very ugly things about his brother-in-law several years back, and he felt he needed to make it right with him. He told his sister that he wanted to meet the brother-in-law to make things right that he had said. She told him that her husband knew nothing about it. V——— replied, "God knows about it."

He met his sister's husband and told him he had said things about him and that he wanted the man to forgive him. He said, "Now, let's just start all over. Welcome to the family; my name is —— ——."

But back to the baptism. We sang a couple of songs, one of which was "There's a new name written down in glory; and it's mine!" V—— had never heard it before, and when we finished, he looked at me with a smile and said, "That's a good one." The pastor read some Scripture; another brother prayed, and then V—— testified. Every man there came and gave him a hug, and then we went into the water.

We related that wonderful day a little over a year ago, when sitting together with him in the prison, the witness came through bright and clear that the Holy Spirit had cleansed his heart from all sin. I can honestly say that I have not observed nor felt a single flicker of anything but pure love to God and a life above sin from that day to this. It was therefore a sacred privilege and an honor to baptize this dear child of God in the name of the Father, Son, and Holy Spirit, all of whom he has learned to love so well. As you rejoice with him and love him, please don't forget to continue to pray for him and for his family. And, before I leave him, he asked me to try to thank all those who had prayed for him. He loves his new family with obvious feeling.

I would like to ask you to pray especially for those inmates who are becoming extremely conscious of their need of full cleansing from all sin. Just as in many churches, the numbers are not large, but thank God for the few.

It is almost universal in prison settings in this area of the country that roughly ten percent of inmates are regular attenders at the Christian services. Perhaps half of these are serious enough to regularly attend a Bible study, and that may depend largely on what is being taught. But out of these numbers there are a few who are dead in earnest, and are hungering for a real walk with God. Even though I have felt warned of God over and over that we are to sow beside all waters, and that it is not mine to select candidates for God to operate on, yet I will freely confess that these few who are hungering and thirsting for more of God pull my heart nearly out of me.

Six of these dear men asked the other day if they could meet together with me for a time of heart-to-heart talk. We met together for two hours and it was hard to stop. They want to do it on a regular basis. They expressed the fact that they are well aware of the many who are only half in earnest, but said, "We have work that needs to be done in us; we need to be sanctified."

Two of these I really believe to have entered into full salva- tion, and their lives are a real witness to those earnestly seek- ing it. The others did not hesitate to bear witness that these who profess to have found it are living it, and everyone around them knows it. How precious is God's provision that those to whom He has called us to minister can minister back to us.

Some of these dear men have caused my own heart to grow in grace. One of these is the falsely accused preacher that I have written about before. The other day we were together and I asked him to pray about a need I was facing. I wish I could have recorded that prayer. It was not the eloquence, but the "in-tune-ness" with God that brought God so near as he prayed. He began, "Oh God, Your mercies are new every morning…" Truly they are, and God answered prayer before the day was over.

Besides this little group, let me request prayer for a couple of others. In previous letters we have mentioned an ex-Army Ranger who has been really seeking for God. We told you how he had gotten caught up in trying to help others for a good while and had neglected his own spiritual need, and then had come back, broken and humbled, realizing that he was stalled spiritually. Since then, he has really been seek- ing God for a pure heart, and he has been letting God show him the real nature that is within him. He is reading some good holiness booklets and I believe he really means to go all the way through with God. He is settling every issue God brings to him in the light of God's Word and has settled it to remain single if his wife does not want to come back to him. He does not want to risk losing heaven for anything in the world. Please pray for him.

Then, there is a man from Puerto Rico who is very Americanized and has had a lifelong background of emotional religions. He has recently looked very seriously into his whole life and has seen the error of emotional religion while living in sin. He said he is done with it and has asked God to forgive him of it all, and says he is experiencing a real live communion with God.

When I introduced to this inmate the fullness of God's cleansing provision for sin, he embraced it eagerly. I gave him some books to read and he says he really wants to find that in his own heart. God has been so good to him, and since he has been in prison and getting his life in order, his relationship with his wife has grown stronger than ever it was before. He desires to get all God has for him and then go out to work among his own people. He too, needs your prayers.

I pray that God will continue to reward each of you who often let me know that you are praying for us. And should this be the last letter we ever write to you (some day there will be the last one), may you find it not a small part of your reward for being faithful, to be able to meet some of these dear souls among the great family of God in heaven. Thank you again for your prayers.

Working, for the night is coming;

Your fellow-laborer,
William Cawman

November 1, 2001

I CANNOT START by any other means than by thanking each of you who are praying and our great, wonderful God Who is answering.

How should I decide which victory to tell you of first? There is a command with a promise in Ecclesiastes 11:1, which reads, "Cast thy bread upon the waters: for thou shalt find it after many days."

The other Sunday night as I arrived home about 9:30, the phone was ringing. A voice and name I had not heard from since the man left the prison over two years ago, began at once to testify. He told how he had stumbled for a time after he had been released from prison. Then he related, "I couldn't forget those things you had told me about deliverance from sin and holiness of heart." He said God had brought him back and that now he was earnestly seeking to get sanctified.

For the next 45 minutes or so my heart burned as he told me how God was dealing with him in every area of his heart life. He said God was showing him how jealous he was when someone else received more attention than himself, but then God showed him that at the core of that was a deep self-centeredness about everything he did or said. My heart was saying a big "amen" as he went on talking about seeking the fullness of God for his life. Oh what a reward are things like this. Please pray for him that he will not stop until his heart is completely made whole in the Blood of Christ.

Inmate C—— who is so thrilled about his Bible courses that he is taking, is still seeking to be sanctified, and he told me today that he is getting excitingly close. He has been talking to another young man on his unit who has been coming out of a terribly traumatic background. The young man committed an atrocious double murder when only 17 years of age. One of the victims was his own grandfather, who lay on the floor under his attack and looked into his face saying, "I hate you." This young man has now been in prison for nine of 30 years. Until recently he was continuing his evil life right in prison, doing and selling drugs and beating his head against the system. A few months back, however, he began to really seek God.

He came to see me for the first time last week, and I never

would have guessed his past life by his carriage and person. He began to tell me how God was helping him and I knew he was genuine about it to the core. He had had enough of sin and was dead in earnest to find God. He told me that C—— had been telling him about holiness of heart, and he said, "I really want to find that. I see exactly what it is and I want it, but I am not really sure whether I am saved yet." He said he thought he had gotten saved a while before, but that he had kept right on sinning.

He then mentioned several things he had in his room which he was wondering whether he should get rid of, as he knew they were not going to help him spiritually. He has access to all the money he needs and had formerly used it freely to buy drugs and cigarettes. The man had turned himself into a garbage can for any drug available. But a few weeks ago, God delivered him instantaneously from all desire for drugs and a little later from the cigarettes. God also delivered him from cursing and now he was trying to come to a decision as to whether to sell the things in his room (a big collection of Dungeon & Dragons which were worth about $1500), or whether he should pitch them in the trash.

It's interesting how, when a person confesses openly where he is hung up, clear direction comes through in a moment. He told me he thought maybe it would be wrong to sell them if they were wrong for him. I smiled at him and he went straight to his room and trashed the whole lot. Along with it, he and C—— had been coming to a decision that their television sets were hindering their getting close to God, so they cut the cords off and trashed them.

Now, the wonderful part. Today this young man came in to see me with a smile all over his face. He told me how he had gotten rid of everything bothering him, and then he said that last night he and C—— talked and prayed for a long time and that he asked God once more to forgive all the sins of the past. He then went to his room and sat up for a long time reading and communing with God.

He looked me in the eye with a bright smile and said, "I know now that I am saved." And let me tell you it was one of those confessions that rang the bell with a clear tone. I grabbed his hand and his heart at the same time.

Now the path is clear for him to get that holiness he so wants to have. Oh how wonderfully true to His Word is our God. Clean out the channel and watch Him come in! Take all the professions of accepting Christ as your personal Savior when the heart is still full of sin and throw them back at the author of them, but give me a heart who will turn his back on sin and clean every questionable thing out of his life, and his testimony will ring clear and true.

This inmate has a lot of questions. He is just a baby in Christ, and he is ravenous. He asked what to do in various circumstances and I gave him some advice. Then I told him to just follow the voice of the Shepherd that would bring him into the greatest light in every decision. I told him he didn't need to settle for clouds in the sky, but that he could rise above them at whatever the cost, into clear upper air. I told him just to live above every question mark and he would walk right into holiness and that very soon. Please pray much for him; I really believe he means to go through.

Oh dear, my page is running out so fast. Let me condense two more victories. One is the continuing victory of V——. I wish every holiness church had a few of him. Until he can get enough clear time from his parole officer to get away to the church he loves, he has tried a few in his area. One of them is a small Pentecostal church, and he said that in the first service he went to, they got his two children to come forward and accept Christ. He was glad that they would want to do it, but then he was disappointed that there was no real change in their lives. A few services later he sat at the back and as the preacher turned up the volume to a lot of bass, he said to himself, "What's all this about? This just doesn't sound like the Shepherd's voice I've heard."

After the service he noticed they were going to serve breakfast @ $4.00 per head. Someone invited him, saying they would pay for him. He excused himself and on the way home, his 13-year-old son said, "Dad, in the Bible didn't Jesus drive out those that were selling things in the temple? Is it right for them to do that?" Nathan told him it was not right; it was totally wrong. Nathan said he then went home and got in his closet and had such a good time in prayer it was hard to leave. Keep praying for this dear man. God knows what He is doing, and when He has tried him, he too will come forth as gold.

Here is both a victory and a special prayer request. The group of six men that I told you about in the last letter are enough to make any pastor's heart throb with excitement. As we met together for the second time, there was such a presence of God that it was hard to know whether to weep or to shout. I can't express the sheer joy of sitting with six hungry, honest, open men who literally pull truth out of one side of your heart, while God pours it in the other side. It just seemed that for two hours, God led us from one truth to another, each more on fire than the last.

We are not meeting for the primary reason of teaching theology, nor doctrines, nor standards of living, nor church creeds; we are there to get as close to the heart of Jesus as His drawing power can get us. The passionate desire of my heart is to bring them to Jesus. Whatever they need to know of the way to heaven will become plain and clear when they have been in His presence.

We spoke together of our desire to come out from the lukewarm religious atmosphere all around us and be sure that we are "Found in Him." I told them that as we draw closer to the heart of God and really take on the mind of Christ, every one of us, including myself, would very likely be drawn into agonizing revelations of personal shortcomings. They echoed back emphatically that they were hungry for just that.

Do you wonder that I feel my primary calling is to men like this? I've preached in many atmospheres—frogs in a hailstorm; spiritual indigestion; sleepy self-satisfaction; comfortable complacency—but not often to those who will in turn make one feel like pulling up stakes and running for heaven. To be with these men makes one feel it will be worth anything to shake loose from the Laodicean church and hear that One Who stands at the door, and knocks. Oh that it can be said of these men that "These are they which follow the Lamb withersoever He goeth."

C——, having heard of this group in Facility III, immediately formed a group of five in Facility II. Our motto is simply this: "That I may win Christ, and be found in Him."

All because He first loved us,
William Cawman

††

December 1, 2001

Do you remember the parable of the sower, and in it the fact that some seed fell upon good ground, thank God, but other seed fell upon stony ground, some among thorns, and some by the wayside? How easy it would be for any of us to become selective in the division of our time and attention were it not for the clear teaching of this warning of Jesus. To explain this in reference to the ministry in a prison, let me give you a glimpse into two different types of soil.

The first is a man in his fifties, rather dumpy looking, quite bald on top, and having been in prison long enough to lose much of his concern about his personal appearance. He has an ugly charge, which subjects him to much harassment and even threats upon his life from other inmates. Due to this he has requested special protection, so is holed up in solitary confinement in a small room in the prison hospital.

For over three years I have again and again exhausted every avenue I can think of to help him to find a real, living relationship with God. He was raised in a church-going family and is very knowledgeable in the Bible, but oh the struggles he has been through trying to find real salvation.

I sit once more before the little food port in his door as he kneels on a pillow inside. There is nothing that would naturally attract me to this man. The stale smell of food and body odor wafts from the hole in the door in overwhelming repulsiveness. His bunk is littered with dirty tissues, mingled with all of the paper work he has accumulated through his years in prison. He hasn't shaved for several days, and his clothes are just as wrinkled as they came out of the dryer too many days ago. But for all that, the dear man has a soul that is as precious to Jesus as yours and mine.

This particular day he is almost in desperation that he cannot seem to find God's conscious forgiveness. He has studied his Bible and has struggled with every sin he is conscious of in his life, but it seems he is no better. Even though I have tried to get through to him that he must trust alone in the Blood of Christ, he cannot seem to let go of his own fruitless efforts to merit the grace of God.

He hands me no less than six pages on which he has written in every available space how he feels about everything in his life. He has written it in the form of a prayer and as I read it I can hardly hold back the tears of compassion. There are gut-wrenching confessions, deeply-felt longings, heart cries which show the bleeding state of his inmost heart. He asks me to read it and tell him what can possibly be missing that is keeping him from finding the favor of God. I try to tell him there is nothing missing in the prayer, but the prayer will never save him; he must throw himself upon the mercy and forgiveness of God. The tears fall freely and as he tries to wipe his eyes and nose with the only thing available, cheap toilet tissue, the tissue breaks and rolls up in little balls in his unshaved stubble, as on and on he weeps. Is this stony ground? Are there thorns? Is he too far over on the wayside? Why, Lord? Why does this man go on and on like this?

Then there is the dear man who was raised in a church where there was a lot of emotion and excitement, but by the faithfulness of the Holy Spirit he was enabled to look around and realize that in spite of all the religious excitement, there were no changed lives; people were still living in sin. He cried out to God and found forgiveness for his sins and at once began to look for something better in God. Oh what good ground! His heart is so hungry and open for more of God that when I begin to tell him what it really means to be cleansed of all sin and filled with the Holy Spirit, he just drinks it in. I gave him several little booklets telling of the blessed work of God in holiness of heart, and just the other day he told me that he was lying on his bunk reading them and suddenly he jumped right up off of the bed crying, "I want it, I want it!" I find it easy to go back to him again.

But, they both have a precious soul; both need the good seed.

A few days ago I came once more into stark reality over the end of the pathway of sin. I stood again over a little hole in the lonely little cemetery of those whom no one on earth wants anymore. I held a little box in my hands in which was all that remained of whatever his life had been. I did not know this man; at least I did not recognize him by the name on his death certificate. And so, in the most vivid sense of the word "unwanted", he is now all alone in this world, and terribly, terribly alone in all the next. Not a relative, not a friend, not a flower, not a song; the life of sin is done. Its promises have faded; its bubbles have burst; its fun is over. He is now to be placed in the cold bosom of the earth by the hands of one who doesn't even know him.

I bowed my head for a moment, and then realized I was at a loss. It would do no good to pray for what was in the box. There was no one among the living who had come to be prayed for. I never felt more helpless in my life. I simply said "Amen" and placed the little box in the little hole. Good bye, sinner; how awfully sad. But that, friends, is how much the devil cares about his own. What a tragic difference to what might have been if he could have known, "What a friend we have in Jesus."

Many of you will remember the dear man who was struggling with such an awful background of atrocious memories and how God brought him back from death on the operating table and gave him a new chance to turn to Him. He has had some struggles and the devil has been determined not to let him go. He began to react to some situations in his surroundings and to listen to the old habits and temptations again. He felt anger rising up in him and thought perhaps he could get help by talking to a mental health counselor. He expressed himself to the counselor, and the counselor had him placed in detention. I went over to see him and he was nearly beside himself. He felt he had been betrayed, and he told me that if he ever met that counselor again he would get even with him. He threatened the counselor's life and was really feeding back into the devil's trap.

I tried to talk to him and finally got him somewhat quieted down, but I knew I had to report the threat he had made. I immediately called in the threat and had to fill out a written report on it. The dear man received for it a loss of time and a year in solitary confinement. He was a little angry with me at first, but I explained to him that I had told him when he first began to see me that if he ever threatened anyone I would have to report it. He then seemed to see that it was his own fault and we were able to begin talking again about how much he needed to really come clean of his old way of doing things and let God come into his heart again and help him to react rightly as Jesus would.

Shortly after that, this inmate was removed to a northern prison to put in his confinement time. Just the other day I received a letter from him which really touched and melted my heart. He wanted to tell me how much I had meant to him and said he was really sorry for how he had acted. He wanted me to ask the counselor to forgive him also. He said, "I really want to be the man you want me to be and the man God wants me to be, and God is really helping me again."

Please don't give up for this dear soul. After all, he hasn't had the opportunities and privileges you and I have had. As a matter of fact, he hasn't had anything but a living hell from the day he was born until now. He really needs someone to pray for him that prayer he may be unable to pray for himself. Yes, I'll be the first to admit that he looks like one of those impossible cases, but that is exactly why Jesus "went a little farther," yes, even "went a third time."

Thank you for your prayers for inmate C———. He and the young man I wrote about in the last letter, who are eagerly seeking to be sanctified, came into the last Sunday night service all aglow with excitement. They came right over to me and C——— said with evident anticipation, "Oh my, we're getting awfully close to receiving the blessing!" If there is anything wrong with getting excited with anticipation over the infilling of the Holy Spirit, I cannot conceive why. I feel not a little excited about it myself.

I would like to share a special request with you as I feel it really needs to be covered with prayer. In the recent state elections there was a shift of power, and time only will tell just what impact that will have in all departments. At the same time of the election changes, the man who has been the coordinator of chaplaincy services for the state was promoted to another position. This man was very evangelical and had come down and talked to me a number of times, expressing his appreciation for those who would really preach the truth in the prison. He has done all he could to promote the right thrust in the chaplaincy department, but has not had a lot of cooperation.

Now with his post open to be filled, God only knows (and God can control) who will fill it, and what their mindset could be. Along with that, the supervisor of chaplaincy in this prison is also very evangelical and wants the door kept open for us to minister the truth, but there are many chaplains throughout the state who are eyeing his position as supervisor of the largest, most modern facility in the state, and would love to have his spot. Many of them are as totally void of grace and the fruits of the Spirit as the devil himself, and would spare no means to pull political wires to advance themselves. My supervisor's attitude is: God knows all this and is in control of it, but we need to cover it with prayer.

Many who know how the atmosphere is in state prisons, marvel at the open door God has given us here and the freedom we have to preach uncensored truth. But all that could change over night through a few political moves. So I would really ask you to please pray that God will keep His hand on every detail and I believe He will in answer to prayer. When God opens a door, "no man can shut it" until God sees fit. I will confess that I was burdened over all this the other day, when suddenly God spoke so clearly and with such peace and assurance, "Whose idea was this anyway?" I gladly laid it all back on the altar and in a moment knew I was all His. Oh that we could do more while the day lasts, for truly "the night cometh, when no man can work."

Once again I must tell you that your prayers are such a vital part of all that God is doing and wants to do. I thank you each one from the bottom of my heart.

With our hands in His,
William Cawman

9
FROM SHADES OF NIGHT

January 1, 2002

WE WISH EACH OF YOU a very blessed New Year. Oh to be more like Jesus this year; to know Him better; to enter more fully into His blessed heart and desire. Yes, let this be our whole ambition, that every moment be lived for Him.

To look back over the blessings and mercies of the past year only gives a deeper appetite for more of Him Who gave all for us. "Perish every fond ambition, all I've sought, and hoped and known; yet how rich is my condition, God and heaven are still my own!" It has been joy unspeakable and full of glory to serve Him, and Him alone.

Lest we leave an unrealistic picture of this corner of God's harvest field, there have been disappointments and trials also. Not all are willing to leave the false hopes, the pride of self sufficiency, and the battered wreck of their past life to accept the offer of such free and amazing grace. It is not easy to experience nor to tell such scenes as a dear young man lying on a prison hospital bed, dying of the disease of his sinful life; bloody mucous oozing onto the pillow case, and hardly strength to lift his head. But harder still to ask him if he would like you to pray for him, and the only answer is, "No." But, to brighter scenes.

Several weeks ago I was visiting bedsides in the hospital and came into the room of a man I had not met before. He was possibly in his late thirties, dark haired except for a few gray strands. I could immediately recognize another victim of the death reaper, AIDS. He also had other things wrong with him as he had large sore lumps breaking out on his stomach. His face was gaunt. I began to speak to him and he informed me that he was Jewish. I told him that was no reason we could not talk about God. He agreed and we visited for awhile. I asked him if he would like me to pray with him. He looked into my face for a moment and then said, "Sure, I guess it can't hurt." I didn't think it would either. I prayed with him, but would have to say that I sensed no particular liberty nor help.

But, oh the gracious God of mercy—let me finish the story. Possibly a couple weeks later I visited him again along with a man who was with me for two weeks as part of his ministerial internship. It was not hard to see that the inmate with AIDS could not last much longer. While his shoulders, face and arms were wasted away to bones, his abdomen was distended like a huge balloon. As I walked up to his bed I asked him if he remembered me. He looked up and studied me but couldn't seem to remember. The intern started to speak to him and was very shortly talking about God's ability and willingness to forgive our sins.

After a while the intern asked him if he would like to have prayer. The Jewish man said, "A while back there was a minister in here, and he was a different religion than I am, but he had prayer with me and it was really cool. It was nice; it was really cool." He began to show some excitement and about then turned his head and saw my face. "There he is; that's the minister that prayed with me; that's him, right there." We had prayer again.

A week later we returned. The Jewish inmate said, "The Rabbi was here, but when you and I had prayer together we (he searched around for words), we got close to God." Then he looked up and said, "I want to meet you in heaven." Tears welled up in his eyes and fell to the pillow. We held his hands and prayed again. Last week after the intern was gone I visited him again. The first thing he said was, "When we held hands and prayed, it was really good. It's still good." He still lingers. Please pray for him. God's Word says, "And they also, if they abide not still in unbelief, shall be grafted in: for God is able to graft them in again" (Rom. 11:23).

We move on to another cell. A middle-aged man stands in the middle of his cell and as we begin speaking to him he acknowledges that he is a sinner in need of God's help. On his little narrow window sill is a picture of a young man and another of a young woman. I ask him if that is his son; his eyes fill with tears. "Yes, and that is my daughter." He is broken because he has disappointed his children and disgraced them. He is evidently proud of them, but so ashamed of himself. We are reminded again of the tragic selfishness of sinful pleasure. But we are reminded again also that one can choose sin, but he cannot choose the wages that result from it. And sometimes those wages roll on and on while the heart cries out as Cain, "My punishment is greater than I can bear." Our heart goes out to these, but the heart of the paymaster of sin does not; he just continues to extract his demands without mercy, without justice.

In another cell we find a man sitting on the edge of the bed. It is obvious that he has had recent brain surgery. We soon discover that he is totally blind. His story is that in October he was, for whatever reason, in the path of a bullet which passed in one temple and out the other, taking his sight from both eyes at once. He freely admits that it was a wakeup call to his sinful life, and that he needs to start down a new pathway. We saw him only once; where he went I don't know.

Some of you will remember the man who was dying of AIDS

and could not forgive, and how the men prayed for him in Bible study, and God forgave him. He has been different ever since. I lost touch with him for a while and thought he had been sent home as he was expecting to be, but one day I found him again in the hospital and he said that his paper work is so tangled up that he was sent back. He longs to go home, but he constantly reminds himself that had it not been that he was sent here, he would have been dead without a doubt; not only physically, but spiritually as well. He says that whatever God's will is, that is all right, but naturally he longs to go home to his mother and begin a new life. I'm sure God has a reason for holding him here and I would love to see him fully cleansed of sin before he leaves.

I want to tell you of a few men who are not in the hospital as well. Recently, a sixty-year-old man began to visit me. He is an Italian man who was very successful as a corporate advisor and was very well off. He was also a very dedicated family man who loves his children dearly. He claims he is in prison with a false charge and that he has never done anything but good in his community. He has been battling with thoughts against God and man for being here, but he is also willing to look at things sensibly. He admits that while life was going along just like peaches and cream, he was on his way to hell as fast as he could go. He is a very broken man. I had watched him in public and group settings for some time, but when we were all alone he broke down and could not hold back the tears. He has begged me to stand by him and help him to find a real relationship with God. This man's family is suffering, and because of the affluent life style they had lived, they are fast running out of resources. But even though he is struggling with these things which could produce bitterness and anger, his hungry heart is telling him that so all-important truth, "For what shall it profit a man, if he shall gain the whole world, and lose his own soul?" (Mark 8:36) As he sits and opens his heart for help and confesses that he needs to turn the control of his life over fully to God, his eyes brim with tears with hardly a letup. Whether good or bad, it is definitely a Hand of loving mercy that stops the wheels of life and reminds a man that there is something more important than this life only. Please remember him too in prayer.

The dear pastor that I have written about several times continues to be such a blessing to my own heart. He recently came in with such a smile on his face and said, "My brother, you have to read something; I was just reading this morning the Christmas story in Luke's Gospel, and look what it says about Zacharias and Elisabeth." It said, "And they were both righteous before God, walking in all the commandments and ordinances of the Lord blameless." He said with a beaming face, "And that was before Pentecost! It is possible to live a sinless life; oh it's wonderful; it really works!"

This former pastor went on to tell me that all through those years when he had embraced a doctrine which taught that we could not live without sin, he really, down deep inside, did not believe it. He admits that he was just not ready to face truth. He really hesitates anymore to place any degree of ignorance on his past failures to live a pure life. Oh what a testimony to the faithfulness of the Holy Spirit Whom Jesus promised would guide us into all truth.

I must confess that something really draws me to this dear man, just my age, and it's something more than that, too. I have met very few men who are so willing to be so absolutely honest about themselves, without one effort at pretense, or self-image. He is totally in love with the grace of God and with the focal objective of the Sacrifice of Calvary—the cleansing of the heart from all sin. And just as honestly as he declares everything else about himself, he says with beaming countenance, and that while living in a hell hole of a prison, that this life of holiness is gloriously possible, and he is finding it to be so. That which his heart had longed for years as he read Psalm. 51, "Create in me a clean heart, O God..," he says he has found, and I cannot feel any reason to doubt it. He is humble; he is sweet; he is teachable; he is in love with God; he has settled it to go through with God.

And then, before I run out of paper, I want to update you on the continuing miracle of grace, ex-prisoner V——. I trust he does not find this letter because I would not say this to his face; but I guess it's permissible to say something good behind a person's back.

To be really honest I would have to say something that some might not consider too charitable, but former inmate V—— is living beyond where many are who have grown up in the holiness movement. Many of us know how we should live; we know how to buy and sell and how to speak to others and how to do our job at work. This man lives and breathes with a heart searching for God's will in everything. "God gave me the green light; God checked me," are frequent comments of his. He has not yet learned the comfortable, complacent art of being a "holiness" person. He is living a holy life. He listens for the still small Voice in every act of life, and God is pouring grace into his heart. He feasts on the Word of God and often has to call and share some nugget of gold he has found. He had to look up in the dictionary the word, "betroth," because God said he had done that to him forever. V—— found that really exciting. His family sees such a change in him that his mother and children are feeling deeply moved on. And he just smiles and chuckles and says if he can stay out of the way, God will get them in. Pray that God will keep him blind to all but the face of Jesus, and deaf to any voice but His.

Thank you each one for your prayers through another year of the mercies of God. Please continue as God leads you. God answers prayer!

All I have and am for Jesus,
William Cawman

February 1, 2002

THIS REALLY IS the February newsletter, so you can wait till then to read it if you care to. My wife and I will be leaving January 3rd to spend two weeks in Guatemala and then three weeks in Bolivia, so please pray for us. I will not plan to send another letter until March 1st.

In case you are wondering about our being gone so long, three families from the church are now trained as volunteers and will fill in the service times while we are gone. The daily visitations one-on-one will have to wait until we return, however. Please pray a little extra if you can and by doing so, you can be the one to minister to them by way of the throne of grace.

There is another reason for writing this letter now instead of waiting. I want to take this space and opportunity to lay before you a special request for prayer and at the same time an answer to prayer,and the following story is both the answer and the request.

Some of you have expressed to me at various times a concern that these dear men whom God has touched would be able to find continuing help when they are released from prison, and not just be thrust out into the dragnet religious program of today's society. I want to say to you that I deeply appreciate your carrying this burden; I have certainly shared it with you.

One of the most distressing situations I have faced numbers of times over the past few years has been to sit with a dear struggling, hungry soul about to be released from prison, and have them ask, "I'm being released and I'm going to whatever town; can you tell me where I can go to church to find the help I need?"

I feel torn apart to tell them, "I don't know." But the fact remains, I don't. I cannot conscientiously recommend a man to a church that I don't know anything about and then have him find some sinning preacher who will do him more harm than his former companions ever did. And so as you have prayed, I too have prayed that God would somehow open another door.

Along with this burden, I have sensed a great drawing for several years to the spiritually-neglected area of Philadelphia. This past summer I spent quite a bit of time in that city whenever I was not working in the prison. It seemed the more I looked, the more open doors there were, needy hearts everywhere asking for help. There are many homeless shelters for men, women and children, scattered over the city. Every one we visited begged us to come and asked us to come back. Women, broken by sin and neglect, wiped tears from their eyes; some of the men nearly clung to us, asking how they could contact us again. As we were leaving one of these shelters one hot summer day, we looked up from the faces marred by sin and abuse and asked one question: "Oh God, is this really where You want us to come?" Instantly our eyes were filled with tears as He answered from His own Word; *They that be whole need not a physician, but they that are sick.*

Just on this side of the river from Philadelphia lies the notoriously corrupt city of Camden, New Jersey. Many of the men who leave the prison, perhaps a majority of them, go back to this city. There are many halfway houses and programs there to try to help them get back on their feet. For a long time I have prayed that God would give some direction concerning this burden we have shared, that there could be a place for these men to find help when they come out of prison and also that they could then become the ones to go back into their own neighborhoods to tell others that there is a God Who can save from all sin.

During the month of December, we had the wonderful privilege of having a young couple in our home for the purpose of fulfilling part of his ministerial internship. He grew up in north Philadelphia and although his mother and grandmother belonged to a holiness church, he wandered out to the ways of Philadelphia's street life and became familiar with the game played there. But thank God, he couldn't get away from his early training, and God miraculously rescued him from going too far in that lifestyle, and sent him to Bible school to prepare for the work He had for him to do. John has felt for some time a drawing to go back to the city of Philadelphia to minister. And so, not only was he with us to gain ministerial experience by working in services and pastoral counseling sessions in the prison, but also to know whether God was really opening a door for him in the area of Philadelphia, or if it was just his desire.

It was one of the most blessed experiences I have enjoyed in seeking the will of God. The men in the prison bonded with him instantly. They sensed his heart and love for them, and they are begging for him to come back. On the days we were not in the prison, we spent our time up in Philadelphia. Together we felt the great need and the great drawing to that need. But the intern kept saying that he sensed a leading to explore Camden, that perhaps that area would be the kingpin to the whole need. Many of the men coming out of prison would not be able yet to leave the state to go to Philadelphia, and many of them would go to Camden. Camden is nearly within walking distance of the needy heart of Philadelphia.

On Saturday morning, December 8th, we knelt in family worship. All four of us prayed specifically that God would direct our steps that day and give us clear leadership. We planned to go up to Camden and look it over. Although I am very familiar with south Philadelphia, neither of us knew a thing about Camden.

We were delayed in getting off to Camden, and were bothered some about it as we figured we needed all the time the day held for our mission. We drove up the expressway and without a clue where to get off, took the last exit before the Ben Franklin Bridge. We found ourselves in the middle of Rutgers University Campus, so went a few blocks further and found ourselves on a street lined with row homes on both sides. We noticed there were a number of shelters and programs in the houses and then noticed a sign on one of the houses regarding available housing.

We pulled to the curb and while he was writing down the information, a van pulled in front of us and parked. A woman got out and went up on the porch to unlock the door. I jumped out and went up to her, and here she was secretary for the men who knew everything that was going on in Camden. All the information we felt would take up our day to obtain, fell into our hands in a moment of time. And that moment was perfectly timed by the God of the whole universe. That office is not open on Saturdays and that woman does not work on Saturdays, but she had a little extra work to do and had come in just then. Had we been a moment sooner she would have been inside and we would not have known it. Had she been a moment later, we would have been gone.

We got back in the truck and looked at each other. It would have been sheer presumption and unbelief to have asked, "Has God answered prayer?"

In a little while we realized that we were driving around and around the same little area of town and hardly knew what we were doing. It just seemed that the same star that led the wise men to Bethlehem was hanging over the area with a warm glow of God's presence. Suddenly we noticed on the corner of two streets what appeared to be an abandoned church and parsonage. I said to the intern, "Look, there's your church, and there's your parsonage." We had in mind to try to find perhaps a row home that could be used for home and Bible studies and…well that's as far as our plans could get. We looked it over well and then drove around and around some more.

Every time we went by that church it just seemed it had to be the right place. It is within walking distance of another state prison, the halfway house so many men are sent to, and the bridge to Philadelphia. After a while, we decided we probably didn't need to drive around it anymore and suggested we also go look at south Camden. As soon as we crossed under the bridge into south Camden, all sense of direction, of warmth and of leadership lifted just as quickly as it had settled on us a little while before. We didn't say anything about it to each other until later, but both felt it keenly.

The next chance we had, we went back to the city hall in Camden and spent several hours trying to find out who was the owner of the church. We finally found out the information in the tax records and noticed that the appraisal on the church was around $56,000. Next question: where would $56,000 come from, plus the parsonage? Well, we found out that the church is not abandoned, but is used by a small black congregation on Sunday mornings. We contacted the pastor and he invited us to come up the next Saturday morning and meet with him.

Now that I have told you how God is answering prayer, here is the prayer request. As the intern so aptly stated it, it seems that God is opening a peculiar door. The little group, from what we have learned so far, is very open and even excited about having a young couple move into the vacant parsonage and use their church for a missionary outreach. But there are as yet many unanswered questions that we are holding before God. We cannot doubt His clear direction to this church and this area, and yet just how it will work out to use someone else's facility and to what extent they would want to be involved, we don't know.

We have talked to them several times and can appreciate the fact that even though they are very open and excited about the proposal, they are wanting to know all about us too. I told them I respect that about them and that we would not really be looking for a united ministry when we don't know much about each other. They seemed very understanding and want me to contact them again to meet with their board, as soon as we get back from South America.

This is the newsletter for February, and perhaps it contains more need for prayer than any former one. I do believe that God has not opened one door without the ability to open another. Could I ask you each one to join us in

fervent prayer as God lays it on your heart that His perfect
will be done in all of this?

With that, I say once again from my heart, Thank You!

Yours in Him,
William Cawman

†††

March 1, 2002

RETURNING AFTER FIVE WEEKS in Central and South America, what
a warm and loving welcome we received from these dear men,
many of whom followed us in their prayers every day. My
heart goes out to them as Paul's did to the Philippian Christians, "I thank my God upon every remembrance of you."
And what a joy to find many of them learning to find God all
sufficient for their lives.

First let me tell you of a wonderful victory. I have been raised
within the holiness movement and have heard testimonies all
of my life which declared that God undertook the hardest case
when He took on theirs. I learned that language and used it
myself at times, until…. About three o'clock one afternoon I
was getting ready to leave a cell block to go home. I was stopped
by a man and for the next two hours entered a battle that for
the next several months challenged me and my little faith to
the point of almost shutting my mouth that I had been the
hardest case. Laying all false modesty aside and just telling the
raw-boned truth, I said to God at times, "Oh Lord, this is the
hardest challenge You have ever faced me with."

Those of you who have followed some of these hearts
through the letters will remember that we presented his need
a number of times with an urgent plea. He is the one who
nearly died of a heart attack on the operating table and promised God that if He would give him another chance, he would
give his heart to Him. God miraculously answered and immediately his pulse came back to normal. He was ecstatic for a
short time with what God had done for him, but then began

to feed back into the temptations of the devil and give in to his old ways and mindsets until in a fit of anger he threatened the life of another staff member in my presence. I was obligated to report it to special investigations and as a result he was placed in administrative custody in a northern prison for a year. Before he left for that prison, I talked with him several times, and he saw that I could not have done otherwise and that it was his own fault for acting like he did. He forgave me and said he would never turn against me.

After this inmate arrived and settled into the other prison he wrote to me and told me that he was so sorry for the way he had acted and that he wanted me to forgive him and ask the other staff member to forgive him. T—— said that he really wanted to be the man that God wanted him to be. Well, praise God! Now another letter has come which has the clear ring of a forgiven child of God. It sounds so good that I will share a little of it with you.

He writes: "Brother I feel the comfort of God in my heart and I'm at peace. I really feel that God is right next to me and I'm always thinking of the light that I seen and God's hand on my head. I felt God's hand on me and no one can ever change my thought of that because I know it was real. I put my trust in God; this made me a believer more than ever in the Word of God. When I pass away I know that God is coming for me again. I belong to Him. I feel in my heart that God is testing me to see if I will turn from sin to be with Him and I want to be with Him because I seen and felt His power. Brother, I am not the same person I was in my past. My heart has changed a lot over the years. The year 2001 changed my life for ever. I will be a man of God for ever. What ever God's plan is for me I will find it because I'm looking for it now. God will lead me to it in His way. In a way I fear what God will do to me if I don't turn from all of my sins, and the sins that I did do in my past I'm very sorry for. I wish that I never sinned, ever. I just pray that my life for God will come together where I can do a lot of good for God and others. Brother, when I get out of prison I'm going to a church and really pray and thank God for the change in my life."

Perhaps those of us who prayed for him should stop right now and thank God too for such a change in such a life. Let's continue to pray that "Where sin abounded, grace [will] much more abound."

Let me share another great victory with you. There is a man we've been trying to help for several years now. He had a terrible drug problem. After he was in prison for several years he was released and should have gone right home to his dear wife and two little girls, but instead he said the devil entered into him and he went to the street for 30 days and landed right back in prison for another seven years on a fresh charge.

His wife was broken hearted. She said, "All I wanted was for you to come home to me." She was so hurt that her affection for him began to wane and after a year or two she got divorced from him. It doesn't seem she wanted the divorce because of another interest, but only because she was so hurt by him. This inmate struggled with such pain and remorse for what he had done that he was nearly suicidal at times. They pronounced him as bi-polar and were treating him with all types of drugs to try to level out his personality. He would swing from the depths of despair to overconfident highs. At times the medications would tear him up until he couldn't keep from weeping as we would talk together. All this time he kept right on seeking after God and wanting Him to make him what he ought to be.

Yesterday I visited with him again and just marveled at what God is doing in his life. He said he feels so wonderfully happy in God. He held on in prayer and determination until he is now entirely free of all medications. He feels he belongs to God without a doubt, and he says everything he has and is, has been given to God to never take it back. His older daughter has been wanting to visit him and then the younger daughter started crying the other day. Her mother asked her what was the matter and she said, "What happened to my daddy?"

148 Voices from Prison Walls: William Cawman

This weekend his ex-wife is planning to bring the two girls down to visit with him. Please pray that she will allow God to also heal this part of the dear man's life.

If you will remember, in the January letter I told you of a young Jewish man who had been responding so touchingly to prayer. The day after I visited him last and sent you the news about him, he died in his cell. I trust to see him in heaven.

Yesterday the inmates were visibly upset. The afternoon before, a sixty-year-old man hung himself in his cell. Inmate C—— lived right next door to him and was one of the first to find him. Another one came in and told me, "I feel terrible about it. I tried to do the same thing a few years ago, but God didn't let it work. I know He had a reason for it." Then he poured out his deep inner lack with unchecked tears running down his face. He begged me to pray for him; will you help me?

And then there is the dear Spanish man who was so tangled up in Pentecostalism but faced the truth that all the emotionalism around him wasn't changing any lives. He is such a seeker after God. He was so glad that we got back after our trip and said he really missed being able to visit with us until God spoke to him and reminded him that he had His Word. He said, "I began to read it more, telling God that I wanted that cleansing of heart you had told me about."

This Spanish inmate said that while I was gone, his wife came home from work one night and as she entered the door of her house, a man slipped up behind her and beat her up pretty severely. He said that he really felt an awful lot of hurt about it, but he feels no anger nor bitterness toward the man and his wife doesn't either. He said he knows that is so much different than the way he used to be and he doesn't ever want those things back in his heart. Pray that he will not stop until his heart is perfectly cleansed by the Blood of Christ.

Another continuing victory is the pastor that we have written about several times. What a marvel of the grace of God! He leaves no room for any doubt that the Blood of Christ cleanses from all sin. When I visit with him I find instead of the pastor or counselor relationship that is necessary with so many, a brother-to-brother relationship. I get as much from our visits as he does, I'm very sure. He radiates the grace of God where ever he moves about the prison.

I try to put myself in this man's place, for he is just my age, and I could have been the victim of a false accusation just as well as he. So I try to imagine how I would feel if I were suddenly jerked out of my home, away from my loving wife and family, away from all that I enjoy so much, and shut away in a prison cell while the wheels of life stop short. But, dear friends, this precious child of God comes in to see me with a peaceful serenity all over his face and begins to say, "I can honestly tell you, that while my situation hurts and hurts deeply, nothing matters; I'm God's and He is mine. He fills my life. All I see is Christ. I have no complaint; I'm happy in Him." Oh the Blood of Jesus; what healing for the soul, what rest from the storms of life. What joy became ours when Jesus prayed, "that they might have My joy fulfilled in themselves." Perhaps it is only in the depths of some unsolicited valley that the fullness of the prayer of Jesus is ever completely answered. There are no limits, no boundaries, and really no ability within us to fathom the extent of those words, "I pray for them."

Way down in southern Bolivia, a dear woman came to me and said, "I'm praying every day for that man in the prison." Thank you for praying too.

All for Jesus' sake,
William Cawman

10
To Plains of Light

April 1, 2002

H OW OFTEN WE HAVE sung: "In loving kindness Jesus came My soul in mercy to reclaim, And from the depths of sin and shame, Thro' grace He lifted me.

From sinking sand He lifted me, With tender hand He lifted me, From shades of night to plains of light, O praise His name, He lifted me!"

But stop right here a moment—how great is that distance between those *shades of night,* and those *plains of light?*

Sunday morning we had been in a convention in the hills of Pennsylvania in one of the most precious services we have witnessed in this country in several years. Heaven and earth became all mixed up together as the redeemed through Jesus' Blood rejoiced and worshiped together. Our hearts were melted and bonded and made one in Christ. That hallowed Presence lingered all day long and finally we parted earthly ways at about eleven that night. We needed to be in the prison the following day, so made the three-hour drive home that night and went to bed around three in the morning.

By nine o'clock that morning we were sitting with a dear

black man who recently came to the prison. He is forty-two years of age and forty-two years in "shades of night." He hadn't talked long before tears were falling like rain and his heart was breaking under the heavy load he could hardly bear. He never knew a father; his mother always stood up for him when he got into trouble, telling the judge over and over, "That's not my boy; he wouldn't do that." His brother is in prison for a long time and has a bad case of AIDS. His nephew was shot and killed. His mother is now in the hospital along with his grand-mother. The man's brain is obviously slowed down by long drug use. He himself has been diagnosed as HIV-positive and now has been diagnosed with Hepatitis C. His health is start-ing to break down. He has no friends and everyone dislikes him. He is in prison for homicide.

His question: "Do you think God can forgive me?" Friends, would you please pray for this shattered soul, that "from shades of night" he might through the forgiving grace of Jesus be lifted to "plains of light?" But stop! Perhaps even before you pray for him or read the rest of this letter, you had better look up and thank our Jesus for what you have been *saved from* in that moment when "He lifted me!"

Let me tell you a miracle of the goodness and love of God. My supervisor often checks the inmate reports and if he sees that any inmate has had a death in the family he gives me his name so that I can go visit him. Of course this elicits all types of reactions, but is often also an opening of a door.

Recently, the supervisor gave me a Spanish name and I went to the cell block and called out the name. The inmate is a man in his mid forties who had recently lost his mother. As I ex-pressed my condolences to him he asked if we could sit down and talk. He began to tell me some of his life and how filled with sin and shame it had been, but he said that a short while back, he had asked God to forgive all of his past. He began to tell of the peace and rest it had brought to him, and how much love he felt to Jesus. He said that he had never gone to school much at all either in the United States or in Puerto Rico and consequently had never learned to read or write. After God forgave his sins he wanted to be able to read the Bible but knew he couldn't. He got a Spanish New Testament and then asked God if He would please help him to be able to read it.

He said, "I don't know how it happened, but I can read it!" He said he still can't read much of anything else, but he can read his Bible. He wanted a whole Bible and asked me what the difference was between the Old and New Testaments. He thought perhaps the New was just a later version of the Old. I gladly gave him a Bible and he began to read it right at the beginning. He came and told me, "It's wonderful. I have read about Abraham and Noah and the ark. Oh that is so wonderful; no one ever told me about how all those things happened. It just makes me love Jesus so much." Then he looked at me with a deep sense of longing in his eyes and said with his hands out in front of him, "How can I be—well, just be all God's? I don't ever want to lose this that I feel in my heart." Well bless the Lord, in cases like this I am quick to tell how; I just tell them to keep loving "Him." God is so able to finish what He has started. Isn't He wonderful?

Here's another story. Without looking back in my records, I would guess that I first started working with this man about two or three years ago. He was very bright and responsive and began to really listen in Bible study and then come to talk to me. He was hearing for the first time in his life that God could really not only forgive committed sins, but also cleanse out the very nature of sin from the heart. As light would dawn on him, his face would light up and he would say, "I'm beginning to see." But then he backed away for several months and I did not see much of him except at church services.

Recently I visited the inmate and this time he really began to open up his heart. I knew that somewhere he was living behind a false façade, but of course I didn't know what it all was. He just broke down one day and began to spill out his inmost heart and all the mess that sin had gotten him into. I knew he was finally getting at the root of his trouble. I tried to help him to look to Jesus for a complete healing of the scars that sin had embedded so deeply in his mind and heart, and he really began to move into new territory with God.

Then recently the same man came in and with tears and deep gratitude told me that God had delivered him from smoking. But listen to his story: he had known for a long time that he was hung up in getting any farther with God because he was not giving up his smoking; he knew that God didn't want him to smoke. He said he tried to quit and then would start again, tried to quit and started again, until he said that he became addicted to quitting and starting.

At that point in his story I took a deep breath. I looked back into my own life and saw the same addiction, although not to smoking. Even as he spoke of this, I could sense a deep revenge in his heart turning him against the whole thing. He said that one night he had been crying to God in his seeming helplessness to break the chains of that bondage, and after he fell asleep he had a dream. In his dream he saw a flock of birds which began to fly away from him until they became like little specks in the distance and finally disappeared. He said God spoke to him in his dream and told him that the smoking was gone. From that moment he had no more desire to smoke again. But what is even more wonderful is that as soon as that stumbling block was out of the way, all kinds of other problems he had been struggling with began to go out the door until he felt God was just cleansing him through and through. I told him that is why he saw a *flock* of birds and not just one. Pray that he will not stop until he is completely cleansed within.

I have mentioned before the Spanish inmate who was raised in the charismatic movements until he looked it in the face and asked why all the emotion and no changed lives. God is really working in his heart. He and his wife have such a precious relationship and she is so thrilled with what God is doing in his life. She came to visit him and as he went to exit the visiting hall the officer stopped him and took the little gold chain and cross from his neck and accused him of getting it from his wife. He told the officer that he had had it ever since he came into the prison and that she had not given it to him. They buffeted him around a little and he told them they could check his property slip from when he came into the prison and they would find that he had it then. They went and checked and came back and apologized but said they were keeping it anyway.

He said just then a great peace came up into his heart and he said to the officers, "It's all right; you can take anything you want to; I have peace in my heart. Here, do you want to take my wedding ring too?" He said he went back to his cell and later his wife called him and asked him if he wanted her to complain about their taking it. He told her not to do a thing; he was happy with God and they couldn't take Him away, so just forget it.

This dear Spanish inmate said he was so happy about the change in his heart from the way it used to be, but he also realized that he still felt the old nature of sin trying to rise up again under that pressure. He knows that there are two natures at work in his heart and wants to be cleansed fully of all sin. I began to tell him how absolutely wonderful it is when all of those big and little areas of our heart which are inhabited by the nature of sin are cleansed by the fire of the Holy Ghost and how then that same fire becomes the abiding Presence of the New Nature. Lord, hasten the hour.

The other Sunday night I was preaching about Agrippa's answer to Paul that he was almost persuaded to be a Christian. I was pressing the point to them that the almost Christian is no Christian at all. I began to get right down into their cell blocks and asked them if they come to church and sing and praise the Lord and then go back to their tier and accept something from someone that they know that person had stolen out of the kitchen.

The following day, one inmate after another told me how it had cornered them. One dear man said, "Chaplain

Cawman, you nailed us all with that one." He said he loves apple pie and he really likes it with cinnamon on it, and he had a little cinnamon in his room that he knew hadn't come to him rightly. He said he went home and threw it in the trash, and he would from now on eat his apple pie without the cinnamon. Bless his heart—I just love people who are willing to walk in the light.

One dear man, however, who has lived a consistent sanctified life for several years now, met me the next day and threw his arms around me with a huge grin and said, "Altogether." I didn't get it for a moment until he said, "Not almost; altogether."

I must tell you an amusing incident about our dear brother, former inmate V——. He had been diagnosed with a physical problem before he left the prison, but wanted to wait until he got out to correct it. After he got out a doctor told him he didn't have the problem. He continued to have trouble and finally they confirmed that he did have the problem and would have to have minor surgery. He said immediately the old devil jumped on his shoulders and started to shout, "Now's your chance; malpractice!"

He turned to the devil and said, "You're the malpractice!"

Please help me pray for a series of special classes I will be starting soon in each of the three facilities. The classes will be "Christian Living in Today's World." The inmates are excited about it and I am too.

Thank you again for your prayers, I know Jesus thanks you too.

In His love,
William Cawman

May 1, 2002

YES, THERE IS A REASON why I keep on addressing these letters to you as "praying friends." Jesus said, "Greater love hath no man than this, that a man lay down his life for his friends." Every time you lay aside moments you could have spent for something else, and pray for these "friends," you have shown love greater than all else. And oh, how I wish I could adequately convey to you what those prayers have done. It matters nothing to God that you may not be able to place a name on whom you are praying for; He hears the prayers of His children.

I want to tell you about a man who is at the same time an answer to someone's prayer and an urgent request for prayer. Several weeks ago a man turned in a request to see a chaplain about getting materials to practice Taoism (a Chinese meditation ritual). I went to see him and could tell immediately that I was listening to a desperately needy, hungry young man, but one who was also very damaged in his concepts of God. He was extremely reserved and reluctant to reveal much about himself until he began to sense that I was not there to pounce upon him with a cloak of sectarian conformity. He then began to tell me that he had just come through a long and painful separation from the Mormon cult (his own words). He was a third-generation Mormon and because he had begun to listen to the faithful Voice within, drawing him to know the truth, had been chastised severely and thrown out. This man had gone the Mormon route to the limit, even going as a missionary to Brazil for a couple of years as a very young man. But the thing that began to disillusion him was that he could see his own father putting on a front that he was not living at home.

This honest soul said that he dared to look Mormonism in the face and recognize how wrong it was and that with it came a craving to know truth. He set out on a quest for truth at any cost (also his own words) and it cost him everything. He lost his wife and child and ended in prison. I didn't confront his ideas about the value of Taoism, I just began to focus on that craving he felt for truth. How important in cases like this is the example of Christ: "A bruised reed shall he not break, and smoking flax shall he not quench…"

I've now had several visits with this disillusioned man, and even though at first he was reluctant to open up because his trust had been shattered in what he had been taught all his life, little by little he now looks forward to the visits and is opening his heart, many times amid tears. The last time I visited him he came in the room saying, "I want to tell you first of all that you don't know how much it meant to me when I came in to see you and you gave me a hug. I haven't had a hug for two years."

He began to relate to me the struggle he was having to sort out truth from error. He said that his conscience has been manipulated all his life until if he would drink a cup of coffee or drink a Coke he would have an attack of his conscience for days, whereas other things which should bother his conscience he has always been told were all right. He said he feels like a formatted disk; and he wants to be careful what he allows to be placed on it. He then went on to say that he had been reading the Bible a lot, and he said, "I find that the words of Jesus really speak to my heart. I just know somehow that those are spiritual truths which I can trust, and I'm separating those from all the other things I don't understand yet." But then he went on to say that as he looks at mainline Christianity he finds it so different in many ways than what he reads in the Bible.

I looked him straight in the eye and said, "You might be surprised at what you're going to hear from a Christian chaplain, but there is much about mainline Christianity that I don't agree with either. But I can tell you that the Voice that is drawing on your heart, I am acquainted with, and that Voice has answered every need of my heart."

He almost melted in relief as he said, "I'm so relieved to hear you say that; I'm not ready to just say, 'All right, now that I'm not a Mormon I'll be a Lutheran', etc." I could easily see what he meant, but I would really like to ask that you pray for light for him and for wisdom for me to know how to tenderly lead him to the God he is seeking.

The dear man from Puerto Rico who couldn't read, but

God helped him to read the Bible, continues to grow in the love of Jesus. He is trying to understand why things are so different in his heart. He asked me, "Why do things I see on the television bother me when they never used to? Why does it make me feel so bad on the inside when I hear someone curse when it never used to?" He said, "I never felt like this before. I feel God all the time telling me, 'Don't say that,' etc., and it feels so good. I really love Him. He's very real to me, and I find in the Bible that God is love. I want to learn all about Him I can." Then later he said, "I love this heart God has given me," and then he broke down in tears and could not say any more. What was that Jesus said about "except ye become as little children..."?

And then what a continuing miracle is the preacher who has entered the rest that remains to the people of God. He comes in with a radiance of peace and joy saying, "It's just wonderful. I'm finding it so easy to live without sin. You know—I always struggled to try to live this Christian life; and I really needed Romans chapter seven to sort of cover for me. But now I see it all so clearly, but—why did it take me so long?"

There is a man who lives next to the preacher's cell who is next of kin to the devil himself. He constantly, for an hour or so at a time, will keep up a steady barrage of torment through the heat vent. There is no question who it is aimed at and it comes every day in relentless waves. But the preacher says that God is helping him to learn patience and that even though the persecution becomes almost unbearable, he finds his own heart without condemnation when it is over. He is such a blessing to the inmates around him, who see him as a father to them.

The other man from Puerto Rico that I told about last month who is really growing in grace, has really been seeking to be cleansed from all sin and filled with the Holy Spirit. One Monday recently, after I had preached the night before about the "Empowered Life," he told me, "Oh Chaplain, that was so powerful; I just stayed up until three o'clock this morning praying and seeking that cleansing for my heart." A few days later he said, "Chaplain, God is so wonderful to me; for the last two or three days I haven't even known whether or not I was in this prison; I'm just lost in the presence of God. Nothing else matters anymore."

Another man came in after him and said, "Oh my, Chaplain, what you preached last night was just exactly what God had been talking to me about. It was just a second witness to His voice. And then a third man came in and said the same thing. Isn't the Holy Spirit so faithful to hearts? Beyond what we see and are ever conscious of, the Holy Spirit is doing His work in every heart that will listen to Him.

I will tell you a little more about this third man. He has been in prison for a number of years and still has a good number to go. His parents died when he was young and he quit going to church after they died. He then went into military service and afterward became a police officer. He had a very unhappy marriage and ended it by murdering his wife. This former officer tried to hide the evidence and lied about it, but was apprehended anyway and placed in the county jail. As soon as he entered the jail he realized the terrible place sin had brought him to. He got on his knees and really prayed through to pardon with God.

Immediately this inmate knew he had to confess his wrong and so went before the court and owned his crime. He has really walked with God with a sincere heart but has never known anything except the Calvinistic teaching that there is no real deliverance from sin. Understandably, he was greatly apprehensive when I was moved to his facility for Bible studies because he had heard that I didn't teach a straight theology. Well, as he began to listen, his face lit up and he began to drink in the truth. He began to come to me and say, "I'm thrilled; I believe what you are teaching; I believe there is such a deliverance from sin."

As we went further he told me that he realizes this is exactly what his heart has wanted and what God has tried to show him, but he said he was unable to see it until God sent someone to show him clearly the way. I would have to say that it pulls my heart out to talk with him; he is so genuinely in love with the Lord and so hungry for all of God he can get. With a few men like this sitting in Bible study, can you see why I'd rather be there than just about any place in the whole world? The hour slips by so quickly each week and they can't wait until the next week.

I must squeeze in one more story. Several weeks ago I was visiting the cells upstairs in the hospital. I came into one room and found a middle-aged black man sitting on the bed with the obvious marks of recent brain surgery. He told me that on Oct. 14 he had been shot right through the head with a bullet. It went in one temple and out the other, and instantly took the sight from both of his eyes. He has not been able to see a thing since. As he sat there he told me that he knew it was a wake-up call for him as he hadn't been living right. He asked for prayer, so I had prayer with him.

On Easter Sunday night I had taken a small group of volunteers in for some special Easter music and the blind inmate came to the service. I went to him and put my arm around him and told him I was glad he was following that wake-up call. Again he wanted prayer. The following week I was back in the hospital again on Sunday night and as we began singing he put his head down in his hands and the other inmates began to notice him. After the songs I went over to him and asked the inmates to gather around him and we began to pray. Oh my, I would rather pray with a soul that's getting to Jesus than anything else in the world. It just seemed that heaven came down in that little assembly room and it was easy to bring him to Jesus. We all felt the precious presence that comes with the forgiveness of sins, and soon his face brightened up.

I started to ask him this question: "If I could offer you back your eyesight right now and you could see for the rest of your life, would you choose that or choose to have Jesus without your eyesight for the rest of your life?"

He hardly let me finish before he said, "I've already made that choice. I thank God for letting this happen to me."

Again, I say, "Thank you, praying friends." Every moment you lay aside for these, falls into God's ear as "Greater love hath no man than this..."

Together for Him and them,
William Cawman

┼┼┼

June 1, 2002

It is late Monday morning, Memorial Day, and also the 32nd anniversary of the most wonderful relationship in my life except for my relationship with Jesus Christ. My precious wife and I will celebrate that this evening, but with the many daily needs in the prison, I am somewhat behind with things in my office (one of those things the writing of this letter), so I set aside the day to come in and get caught up. My day is not going as I planned, and I confess that to be uncomfortable to the organized "me." But I don't belong to "me" anymore, and I'm overjoyed that it is that way.

I preached last night to a record number of men in the minimum camp and felt the need to stop in there this morning on my way to my office "for just a few minutes." I really wanted to visit briefly with inmate C——, and I will tell you about that in a moment, but I sat there visiting longer than I intended, because God was ordering every moment of it. As we visited, other men began lining up at the chapel door, each with a heart of need just as important to them as my little agenda was to me. I soon sensed a measure of what Jesus must have felt as "He saw the multitudes, [and] He was moved with compassion on them, because they fainted, and were scattered abroad, as sheep having no shepherd."

I laid the "me" on the altar for something far more important to the heart of Jesus. And, dear friends, I do not hesitate to lay my personal heart wide open and humbly confess that in obeying the compelling call of God to lay myself aside for others, God is saving my own soul from the deadly snares of Laodicean complacency. I thank you that in praying for these men, you have also prayed for me. God has so answered your prayers that a few of these men are making me scratch and dig to keep up with them. I'm asking God that as they pass me up, I won't be left behind.

These men are not living in the bondage of mere conformity to a sectarian culture, but in the liberty of those who "walk in the light as He is in the light." One of the most priceless jewels of ministering in a prison is that it does not work to appeal for authority to what your church or my church believes, but instead, one is driven deep into the Word of God. And oh what a gold mine! No wonder a saint of old cried out "Oh give me that Book!"

But now, back to C——. I haven't said much about him for a number of months, and I've been burdened for him. He is the one who three years ago this coming August was delivered so miraculously from the chains of heroin, and then walked so carefully with God for quite a while, seeking to be sanctified. He has studied all about it with great enthusiasm, has preached it to many others, convincing them of the truth of it, and has been fully persuaded that it was God's way to heaven. But for all that, he has been back-peddling for some time.

He wasn't admitting it, but I could sense the lack of progress and was burdened for him. He is very intelligent, and is used in the system as a paralegal to help inmates with their cases. Several of his friends have died while in prison because of what he sees as a failure to supply the proper but very expensive medication to treat Hepatitis C. He felt it was his duty to write up a legal case, thus bringing this to action by the state to prevent others from dying in the same way. He put a lot into it; hours of work, as well as a lot of his attention.

Last week I stopped to see him and he told me that he had

begun to realize he had lost his first love. I urged him to seek it again without any delay, and then visited him again on Thursday. As we talked, he began to confess how the legal case had caused him to put his spiritual life on the back burner, but that he felt it was so right that he win the case.

I began to face him with God's Word that says, "For what is a man profited, if he shall gain the whole world, and lose his own soul? Or what shall a man give in exchange for his soul"? I tried to show him how the enemy was working; that seeing he could not ensnare him any longer in drugs, etc., he was trapping him in a "good thing" that was taking him aside from the way of the Cross.

As we spoke, I suddenly saw a look of almost panic come over his face. God was showing him the error of his way. He said, "Chaplain, I see it. I'm going back to my room right now and get down before God and get things straight." Just previously someone had sent us a number of copies of *Pilgrim's Progress,* and he picked up a copy of that and headed to his room. He began to read it and God, as he says, struck him right between the eyes with such conviction that he dropped to his knees and vowed to God that everything else would stop and that he would seek God until he found his need fully met.

I had preached last night from Ephesians 5:18, and C—— said he left so convicted that he is letting God search his whole heart through the book of Ephesians. The atmosphere was so different about him this morning. In fact I found him sitting alone in the chapel reading his Bible. He had already spent a long time there on his knees. He was so surprised to see me walk in and we had such a precious time together. He asked me to tell all of you who had been praying for him to forgive him and to pray for him. He wants you to know that he has quit his back-peddling and is heading for the kingdom. He told me that when I spoke last night about Jesus' command that we were to "tarry until," and had said that the disciples waited there ten days before God for the Holy Spirit, he prayed desperately to God that he would not have to wait ten days. Pray that he won't.

The former Mormon I have written about before is continuing to draw closer to God's presence. He says that the Bible really speaks to his heart, especially the words of Jesus, and that he feels a warm, inviting and secure Presence about him when he reads the Bible and opens his heart to God. But he says that between those times a fear grips him because he was always taught that it was wrong to seek out truth for one's self. He was raised to believe that his whole responsibility was to serve "the system", and that if he felt any insecurity in his life it was because he was failing to be a good enough Mormon.

This young man was always taught that the words of Jesus in Matthew 6:33 meant that if all these (temporal) things were not being added unto you, it was because you were not seeking first the welfare of the kingdom of God, which was the Mormon church. But down deep inside, the faithful Holy Spirit kept ringing the alarm, "Something's wrong." Sometimes when I encourage him to just keep listening to that warm Presence that is drawing him, his eyes suddenly well up with tears and he says, "You can't imagine how comforting it is to hear you tell me that; that is so opposite to what I was always told." What a wounded soul! But such are those to whom His stripes bring healing.

The dear Puerto Rican man who asked God to help him read the Bible is such a wonderful Biblical picture of a baby in Christ. The other day when we were visiting, he was telling me how precious the love of Jesus has become to him. He said with great feeling, "I received a date to go home in six months — I just don't want Jesus to ever leave me." And with that he broke down in tears. I assured him that Jesus had no desire to ever leave him; that if either one left the relationship it would be him. He said emphatically, "I won't do it."

A very vibrant, bright young man who labels his past life as being "a messed up kid," is another really bright spot lately.

He has been really in love with Jesus and has been throwing things out of his life that are not pleasing to God with that violence characteristic of old-time salvation.

He told me he has really struggled to give up smoking, but that he knew it was wrong and he just had to quit. I didn't pamper his weakness, but told him to take it to the Lord in prayer and then "cut off the right hand." Shortly after that, he came to me at the close of a Sunday night service with a beaming face and said, "I'm eight days clean." I encouraged him that God could see him all the way through, but oh how I hate the dirty devil.

A few days later he came in to see me and I knew right away that he was frustrated and discouraged. He said that he had gone without smoking for nineteen days and had even gotten beyond the craving for it, but he went over to medical and stepped on the scale and had gained twelve pounds. He is already overweight for his age and height, and it so disgusted him to think that he would leave the prison in a few months weighing 250 pounds that he reacted and smoked two cigarettes. I told him that was not the answer; that was just a trick of the devil. I suggested he use some strict discipline with his appetite and start to exercise regularly. He said, "Chaplain, you're right; I see what I did and it wasn't the answer. I'm so glad you called me in before it went any further. I'll do the right thing about it." Do pray for him. I believe he is sincere about letting God take complete control of his life. He told me he is so hungry to have what I've been preaching to them about the infilling, abiding Holy Spirit.

And then, my dear preacher man. Oh what a blessing he is to me. A few days ago he came in to see me and was just radiating the sweet presence of the Comforter within. I just love to watch the fruits of the Spirit working within a man who does not even yet understand why they are there. That is so much more glorious than to see someone who knows what the fruits of the Spirit should be and accordingly tries to produce them by conscious efforts.

He said, "Chaplain, I don't know why this is happening to me, but I find I have lost all desire to get up in front and try to teach others. I just have no appetite any more to be seen or heard; all I desire is to absorb more and more of the love of God. I don't understand what God is doing with me, but I feel like He's just breaking and breaking me in every part of my life, and I tell you it feels so good; it's just so precious." By this time he was choked with tears. You and I understand it, perhaps, but I wonder sometimes if that hinders us from bearing as genuine a fruit. You see, he is entirely free from having to measure up to anyone's expectations of him; he is just lost in God. At the same time that he has lost all desire to get up and teach others, his life is bearing spotless testimony to the other men everywhere he goes.

Have you ever heard it said that "God is good"? Listen to this. The Puerto Rican man I have told you about who saw the sham of the Charismatic movements he was raised in and really got saved, has been walking close to God and seeking to be cleansed from all sin and be filled with the Spirit. His wife is thrilled with what is happening to him and she has been concerned about where they live in a very rough neighborhood in north Philadelphia. She was recently mugged on her doorstep as she came home from work at night, and she doesn't want him to come home to that neighborhood anyway. She told him she would really like to move to a different area, but he told her he didn't see how it was possible as they didn't have the money to move. She works at Jefferson Hospital and saw a house on the board that one of the doctors was selling. She went to see him and he told her it was his mother's house in a very nice neighborhood, and she had recently died. When he heard this woman's story, he told her that he would sell her the house for just what his mother paid for it 25 years ago. They will be able to sell their row house and move to this single family home without going into debt. I guess "God is good," isn't He?

I would like to ask you to pray for the class that I am preparing to teach throughout the prison on "Christian Living in Today's World." I will be teaching it soon in each facility once a week for a two-year period. Please pray that just the right ones will enroll and that it will be fruitful in bringing many more to understand what it really means to be a Christian.

Yours once more through His mercies

which are new every morning,

William Cawman

11
MENTORING "MY BOYS"

July 1, 2002

YES, GOD DOES answer prayer! Many of you who have been following the letters will remember some time back an inmate who had stopped me one afternoon on the cell floor, wanting to talk. For two hours that afternoon he poured out his story of a life-long tragedy, which I still can hardly fathom a human mind and heart being able to stand up under.

For several months I tried to help this inmate, but it seemed just about the time I would think we were gaining some ground he would slip back into the awful guilt and trauma of his past: all the murders he had witnessed and been involved in, the gangs, the drugs, the nightmares, the cold sweats, the anxieties which caused him many times to even look around and shudder as we talked.

One day after he had told me more than perhaps he had ever told anyone else, he suddenly got a strange look on his face and looked at me and said, "Chaplain, when I get out of this prison I'm going to look you up." I could tell he felt the need to protect himself as he always had by trying to intimidate me because of all I knew about him. Suddenly I felt such a pity for this broken, wounded man. After all, what chance had he ever had in life? His profligate mother had subjected him to sinning with her long before he could have had any choice for his behavior. His life had been lived in a literal hell from his earliest childhood. I looked him in the eye and said, "——, I don't take that as a threat, I want you to look me up; I want to be your friend." Instantly I saw the fear and the anxiety melt from his eyes and I never met that in him again.

Shortly after that is when, as you remember, he had four heart attacks in a row and was taken to the hospital. While lying on the operating table having his arteries opened up he suddenly started going under. The doctor leaned over his face and said, "Son, do you know anything about Jesus?" When he said he did, the doctor said, "You better start talking to Him; you're about to meet him." He looked up and promised God that if He would let him live he would give his life to Him. Immediately his pulse came back and he quickly recovered. This inmate was so happy, almost beside himself when he next met me.

Just what his relationship to God was during this time, I really don't know, but he did say that he really wanted to forsake the old life and live for Jesus. As usual the devil was mad and soon attacked him from all angles. The dear undisciplined, untutored victim of the pits of sin soon fell under the onslaught, perhaps more from habit than from willful sin. He became angry at a staff member and was placed in detention. I went to see him and he was very angry and threatened the staff member in a very serious way. I immediately reported the threat to Special Investigations and he was told he would be sent to a northern solitary confinement prison for one year. Before he left, he forgave me because he knew I had only done what I had to do, and he said he would never turn against me.

After he arrived at the other prison he began to seriously seek God and has been writing to me ever since. The letters have gotten better and better until my heart is melted to tears to see what God is doing in this poor victim of sin and hell. He just had heart surgery again and that is what he is referring to in the letter below which I am now quoting. You too can rejoice that God is answering many of your prayers for this dear soul for whom Christ died just as much as for you and me.

He writes:

> Hello, I received your letter today and it touched my heart. The Holy Spirit is speaking to me right now. If there was any way possible, I would like for you to thank the dear old lady in Idaho for me. Tell her my heart surgery went well and I feel like I'm 18 years old again, and if I could I would run to Idaho to thank her in person, and I'll be praying for her as well. God bless her heart. I also thank you and the church for all of your prayers. I can see the power of God at work and it's a wonderful feeling in my heart. The Lord is filling my heart with so much love for people; for sure we are a loving family together in Christ. I'm so sorry it took me so long to understand the love of Christ. I cry with joy in my heart. I never felt the way I do now. God is covering me with so much Christian love, joy, and peace. I know in my heart that I must honor him in every way. Nothing makes the heart as happy as the Holy Spirit Who would come to those who put their trust in Him. I feel very different inside. I know that the only life worth living is through Christ. I will not let Satan drag me down ever again. Romans 5:9; Ephesians 2:5,8.

(This man could barely read when I first met him.)

Now I have another prayer request. A few days ago one of the social workers called me and said he was calling an inmate in to inform him of the death of his father, and he wanted to know where I would be in would be in case the inmate wanted to see me. He did. I found a young man, not only grieving over the death of his father, but under deep conviction for sin. I don't know when I have witnessed in a long time such pungent conviction. He told me the following story.

His parents were very good, church-going people. When he was very young they were in an automobile accident and his mother was killed and his father crippled for life. He was the youngest of six children. His father remarried, but the older daughters never accepted their step mother and all of the children left home except him. He was brought up going to church and reading his Bible, but when he was sixteen, he rebelled against it all and went out to do his own thing. He did it, and is in prison.

For several weeks God has been dealing with him, and then he got word that his father had passed away. He called his mother and she told him that one of the last things his father had said was a prayer for his son who was in prison. His heart was broken with grief and sorrow.

As he told me all this, he said, "I know what the right way is; I know what this Bible says; I know I cannot ever be right with just a little profession of Christ; I really need to get right with God." He said he was doing all he knew to throw every sin out of his life and really come clean with God. Oh how my heart ached for him. How applicable the words of the old song, "I've wandered far away from God; now I'm coming home."

As we left that afternoon, I said to him what Jesus said to the rich young ruler, "Thou art not far from the kingdom of God." I've been trying to visit him very often, and he is earnestly seeking forgiveness from God. I told him I would ask the family of God to pray for him and he really wanted it. I gave him some of Brengle's books and he soon had them devoured and told me they were deeply convicting him of his need. Oh my, these dear souls pull my heart out until I feel there's nothing in all the world that attracts me outside of helping them to Jesus. Would you please bear him on your heart too?

The Puerto Rican man who is seeking to be sanctified is such a blessing as he walks closer and closer with God. The whole tier of cells where he lives was put on strict house discipline for the behavior of some of the men. I had several visits with men from that tier scheduled and when I called the unit I was asked if I really needed the men to come because they were trying to hold them in confinement for punishment and discipline. I asked them if it would be better for me to come to the tier instead of them coming to the chapel, and they said it really would. I went over and he walked up to me with a big smile and said, "Oh Chaplain, God is so precious. This isn't affecting me at all, I'm just happy in my heart with Jesus." He's still reading holiness books and he says he just wants it more than anything else. I believe he will find it soon, too.

Now, let me come back to earth—not all the inmates are shining stars by any means. There is one dear man, about six-foot five with well-padded bone frame, who is a burnout from Vietnam. I don't know what he was before Vietnam, but there is something distinctly less than perfection remaining now. He has been here a long time and wanted to see me the other day. He trembles and shakes, mentally and physically.

This Vietnam veteran proceeded to tell me that he had listened to me teach for several years and now he was having his own Bible study with some of the men on the tier. Just then I looked down at his paper, entitled, "Bible study on the tear." He said, "Chaplain, I need to ask you some questions so that I know I'm teaching this straight, because I want to teach it just like you do." He began to address his questions. I was quite at a loss; there was no coherence nor sense to it whatever. I said, "Lord, how hard must You try to keep me humble?"

Sometimes a chaplain has to be a comforter, sometimes a marriage counselor, sometimes a peace keeper, sometimes just a listening ear, and on and on. Sometimes he has to be a father. Two young men recently became cell mates. They are both seeking God and are showing steady interest and growth. Both were charged with murder while still in their mid-teens and are now in their late twenties. Both have many years yet to spend in prison.

It is almost inevitable that when a young man is incarcerated at such an early age, he becomes a product of prison mentality. His life was still in that pliable age at which the real visions and goals and directions of life should be formed, but now he is locked among wicked men and is subjected to do-ing whatever it takes to simply survive the system instead of being able to sort out and evaluate his priorities under normal circumstances and environments.

So now, here they are, with much more in common than they themselves realize, but without those skills of getting along with others that should have been developed in a home atmosphere. The one redeeming factor—they both really want to learn and do better. And so, "Daddy" has to bring them in together and have them sit down and just get it all out in the open. Then "Daddy" tries to point out to them what an excit-ing, beautiful, priceless opportunity they have before them in living with each other. They agree wholeheartedly and leave promising to make it work. Please pray for "my boys."

The men are so excited about the new classes in Christian Living. Between 75 and 100 have signed up so far. Please keep praying for these classes that God will use them to open many eyes and hearts to what it really means to "have grace, whereby we may serve God acceptably..."

I deeply thank each of you for your faithful prayers, I really mean it.

In Him,
William Cawman

August 1, 2002

"Chaplain, this is like being born all over again." Such is the observation of a newborn babe in Christ who cannot read well enough to have borrowed this sentiment from the Bible. Isn't it wonderful how God's work within, so exactly fits His Word? Then the inmate goes on; "When I read in the Bible" (this is the man who could not read but asked God to help him to read the Bible), "I see things that really make my heart rejoice. The Bible really speaks to me and it feels so good. But Chap-lain, I have a question—when I feel so happy, why do I cry? I can't help it, I just cry and tears come; why do I do this when I feel so good and I am so happy?"

I'm sure if you know Jesus you would enjoy explaining this to him just as much as I did. But you see, sin and the devil never made him happy enough to cry, and so he had never experienced such a thing as this before. Oh how precious to see a man trying to understand what has happened to him, as opposed to having all the knowledge with a barren heart.

Here are a few more comments from another dear soul. "I really missed you while you were gone." (We had been to several camp meetings.) "I prayed to God and asked Him if I loved you and depended on you too much, but really you have showed me the way to really be happy in God. And now, I desire only one thing. I am deeply in debt; you have showed me this wonderful way, and I know there are so many more out there where I came from who don't know yet. I just want God to get me ready to go and tell them. This is all that matters to me now."

I guess this is what Paul felt too when he declared, "I am debtor…" Jesus said, "To whom little is forgiven, the same loveth little." Perhaps God is going to use some of these forgiven ones to do what others are not doing because they feel so little indebtedness.

Let me update you a little as to the progress of our former Mormon. He told me yesterday that he is seeking just backwards from the way he always did before. He always went to the "prophet" for his answers, and if he did not find them then he would seek after God, which always got him in deep water with others around him. Now, he is finding the liberty to seek God first. At times this is severely attacked by a distorted conscience that warns him he is departing from what he was always taught to be the right way. He says it is always so meaningful to him when I assure him that it is safe to go directly to the hunger that God has placed within his heart for truth. Realizing that his trust has been terribly shattered, I constantly try to encourage him that any truth which draws his heart toward the light is safe to follow. And I can see that he is steadily learning to put his feet down on the Word of God. Do keep praying for him as God would lead you to.

Our dear "preacher" told me the other day that he was facing some issues he needed to talk to me about. We sat down yesterday and he began to tell me that his mind was being bombarded from all sides. He said that down deep he knows what the answer is, but his mind keeps going in a whirl like this; "If you really belong to God, and you are here in prison over something you did not even do, and there is so much need out there waiting for you, and your family needs you, and, and, and… Why does God just leave you here? Does He really care about the little details of your life? Is He really aware of your situation?"

The first parallel that came into my mind was John the Baptist in prison. "He sent two of his disciples, and said unto Him, Art Thou He that should come, or do we look for another?" This just doesn't seem right, Jesus. Don't You know that I am in prison? Don't You care? Aren't You going to do anything about it?

Even as we began to talk about what was bothering him and he exposed the devil's lies to the light, his face began to take on a big grin. He said, "I really know the answer. I know where this is coming from. And it's all right. I have peace with God and that's all that really matters."

I went on to talk to him about the Scriptural law that bread corn must be bruised; wine can only be produced from the grape that is crushed. We looked at the sweet balm that Job's afflictions have given to the entire world from his day to this. We ended up in the sweet presence of God and the devil disappeared "for a season." One of these days, dear friends, he will be cast down forever, "Bless the Lord, oh my soul." Until then, as we pray one for another, please do remember these dear men whose hearts God has forgiven and sanctified, and yet have to live on in conditions we cannot imagine—sin abounding and hell everywhere. Thank God for His all-sufficient grace.

The classes in Christian living are going well and God is helping us. The men are eager to learn and are so excited that it is a pleasure to teach them. I cannot emphasize too greatly the need of prayer for these classes. We are definitely plowing deeper furrows than just emotional experiences; we are aiming, by God's help, to look deeply into the "perfect law of liberty," and align our lives with what we find there. Please pray that as the unavoidable "offence of the Cross" divides and reveals, hearts will accept it and not be offended and go back into the shallow waters of sentimental human religion, which spares the thing that will keep them out of heaven.

Perhaps I will share in some detail another request with you. For several months a young black man who seems to be a very serious-minded, deep thinker has been coming to see me about his own spiritual need. He acknowledges that he is in need of a real life-changing work of God in his heart. He is very frank about his spiritual condition. As I pointed out to him the need of a clean break with every form of sin in his life, he said, "Chaplain, you are tough, but I know it's the truth. Down deep inside I know that you are telling me what I need to hear, not what I want to hear."

After we had been gone for some time in camp meetings, I called him in and asked him how he was getting along. He said, "Not good." He then told me he would tell me the truth just like I had always told him the truth, and then he proceeded with the following heart-breaking story.

He has a wife who is now twenty-five years old, and a little girl. After he was sent to prison, his wife began living with another man and after a time had a baby boy by him. He had already talked to me about the situation and asked me if he should get a divorce from her. I told him under no conditions would God be pleased with him entering into a divorce, but rather he should just trust God to work in her life as well as his and that he should pray for her. He said again that he knew that was right. Three weeks ago his wife came to the prison to visit him, bringing the little six-month old boy. He held him in his arms and he said he had no problem accepting and loving him, but his wife said she didn't have the love for the little boy that she had for their girl.

This past Sunday his mother came to the prison to visit and told him that his wife had just been arrested and sent to prison for murdering their baby boy. He was crushed over the news. He was allowed to give his wife one call between the two prisons, and he told her that it was all his fault, and that he still loved her. All she did was cry over the phone.

"Chaplain," he said, "I am torn apart. I know this isn't right, but I feel myself wanting to get angry at God. I just don't understand why a sovereign God would allow all this. And yet I know that is not the answer. I'm just on the bottom; where is this ever going to stop?" Such, want it or not, is the payback of sin.

I began with his distorted concept of a sovereign God. I went clear back to the pure, selfless, loving desire of God to create a being who could return His love by an act of its own will. I showed him that it was not the act of God, but the act of man that would choose to push aside the wonderful plan of God and choose the pleasures of sin, and that God stood by and wept over every act of sin and over every payback of sin. I told him that the worst thing he could do now was to scold or blame his wife, but that he needed to write to her and confess that they had both taken the wrong pathway and ask her to agree with him to seek the forgiveness and healing of God until He could bring them back into the life He planned for them. He said, "That's what I will do."

He looked at me with such pain in his face as he said, "I never dreamed what far-reaching effects sin could have. It seems like I have left a wake behind me that has hurt everyone I ever knew." Not ignoring this to be the truth, isn't it still true that "where sin abounded, grace [can] much more abound?"

Please pray that God can find access to both of their hearts until the course of sin can be reversed, and His grace can much more abound. Yes, these are tough cases, but for such Jesus shed His blood. "They that be whole need not a physician, but they that are sick." So often quoted, so desperately true— "Sin will take you farther than you intended to go, will cost you more than you wanted to pay, and will keep you longer than you wanted to stay." But—the Blood of Jesus!

I know that for a good reason I often try to tell mainly of the bright spots and the spiritual victories, but perhaps it is not always right to hide all the rest. Would you permit me to quote exactly a note handed to me today?

"My mother contracted ovarian cancer and in spite of the best medical treatment available her health deteriorated to the point of terminal illness. She did not complain of pain, not even to her doctors, but it was there! Ovarian cancer is not a fun disease! Finally she wanted me to put an end to her misery. Note that she had been doing this for a month. Twice I loaded the firearm and placed it on the nightstand next to her bed and told her to do it herself. Then I went out to lunch not looking forward to coming home to what I thought I would see. But in both instances she did not do anything. On the night of my mother's death I just could not bear to watch my mom suffer any longer. She was pleading with me to end it, so I shot her once in the head with a .357 magnum revolver. I am writing to you because I need any insight, guidance, wisdom and support that you can provide to me. Any help you can give in any way, shape or form is most gratefully appreciated! Thank you and God bless you."

I will add no comment except to say that you see why I covet and need your prayers for wisdom, guidance, firmness, compassion, love, hatred for sin, and ability to lean harder upon the One Whose idea this was in the first place.

Thank you so much once again for all those prayers which God is answering.

In Him,
William Cawman

September 1, 2002

How can I best share some good news with you? Do you remember Peter's words: "And God, which knoweth the hearts, bare them witness, giving them the Holy Ghost, even as he did unto us; And put no difference between us and them, purifying their hearts by faith"?

Well, back in May I briefly mentioned a man who has now been in my Bible studies since the beginning of this year. He was apprehensive about my coming to teach on his unit because he had been told that I was teaching a false theology. I can't blame him for not wanting a false theology. But as he began to listen, I saw his face just beaming with excitement, and finally he wanted to talk to me. He told me that he didn't yet understand all that I was teaching, but that his heart was just thrilled with what he was hearing.

As we continued visits from week to week, he told me this story, part of which I related in the May letter. He had gone into the army and then become a police officer. He had a very unhappy marriage and ended it by murdering his wife. After he was put into one of the other state prisons, he was in the mess hall one day when a huge man stood up, pointed at him and told who he was, what he had been, and what he had done. Immediately a core of riot-geared officers moved into the mess hall, took him away and placed him in protective custody. They knew he would never have survived after that was known.

For the next several years this man was in solitary confinement. He said that those years were the turning point of his life. He began to seek the forgiveness of God and found it and then began to study the Scriptures and walk in the light. God began to lead him into more and more of His grace.

As he began to listen in the Bible study and respond to the message of deliverance from all sin, his heart just latched onto it with delight. One day he said, "Chaplain, next time we visit I want to tell you something that happened to me some time ago." He began to tell me that after God had forgiven him, he would set aside a day every so often to fast, pray and go back over his life and repent of all that he had been. One day either in '97 or '98, he had set aside a day again to humble himself and fast before God. He said that as he went back over all that he was and was turning against all that had caused him to be what he was, suddenly God stood before him and said, "Son, you don't ever have to do this again. I have taken it all away."

He told me that he really had never known exactly what happened to him that day until he began to listen to the preaching of heart cleansing from all the nature of sin. He said that now as he reflects back upon that day and his life since then, he realizes that he has never struggled with inward sin from that point on like he did before. Such clearness was accompanying the new light that was dawning upon him. I gave him some books on the work of the Holy Spirit in cleansing the heart from sin, and he began to study them intently and really enjoy them.

Then, just a couple of weeks ago, he came in to see me again. His face was radiant. I asked him how he was getting along, and he said, "Wonderful, just wonderful." He then began to tell me that he had been reading one of the books over again which clearly described the wonderful work of the Holy Spirit and what it does within when the heart is cleansed from all sin. He said, "Chaplain, as I carefully read that book I find that everything within it agrees with what I find God has done in my heart." I looked at him and then began to praise the Lord. We just had a time of rejoicing together while the Holy Spirit bathed us with His precious witness.

Isn't God wonderful? All He needs is a hungry heart and He

knows how to get past every bit of mistaken theology and set the heart right. Now you can see why I quoted the Scripture above—it makes no difference to God that a man was once a murderer, that he has a long prison sentence yet ahead of him, or anything else. He loves to purify a heart by faith.

But then the dear brother went on; "There is only one thing that I am struggling with a little, and that is the concept that it is an instantaneous work of grace. It seems to me that it is an ongoing, never-ending work of the Spirit. I don't ever want to think that this will come to an end." I jumped right on that. I told him he did not need to change his viewpoint of it at all; that he was much safer to view it that way than to think the work was done and he could now rest on his attainments.

I could see that he was not clearly discerning yet that the work of the Holy Spirit is both instantaneous and progressive. I'd rather see him pressing on after more and more than to see him settle down where I have seen multitudes settle down and never really make any more progress spiritually. Oh how thrilling it is to see men plunge into the cleansing stream of Calvary's Blood and then learn what all happened afterwards. I do believe this is the way it came about in the lives of the early believers, and it still pleases the heart of God as much as it did then.

I did go on to explain to him just what the Holy Spirit did within his heart that wonderful day when he came to a full choice against all that he had ever been, for the Scripture does teach us that it is so important to fully claim all that God has promised to us. Oh my, but am I enjoying watching the light dawn upon his mind concerning what God has done in his heart.

Recently a man has been coming to see me who is a Romanian Gypsy. He is under deep conviction for his sin. He sat in my office the other day and said, "Oh Chaplain, I have to find God. I've been praying all morning that God would forgive me. I can't go on with this awful guilt on my heart. I feel so terribly guilty." Please remember him in prayer that he will not settle for less than a real relationship with God.

Some of you will remember a couple of months ago when I requested prayer for a man who was under deep conviction like this. Thank you for praying. I wish you could see the change in him. From the depths of sin and despair he is now rejoicing with a shining face. He is living a victorious life and is asking God to cleanse his heart from everything that is unlike Him. This man, now liberated from sin, says he is determined to never turn back and he is also determined to have all that God has for him. He is so changed that he doesn't even look like the same man. He is almost ready to be released from prison, and I know he would appreciate your prayers that he will go right on into the fullness of God for his heart, and the will of God for his life.

Once again I would beg you to remember the dear man I wrote about in last month's letter whose wife killed her baby and is also in prison. God is really working with both of them, and I really believe it is His will that this be the turning point in their lives. A sister from the church is visiting his wife in the prison where she is, and would really like you to remember her, too. It will take such wisdom from above to know how to show them the love of Jesus when they are so torn apart by the hatred of sin, but God is definitely working. He told me after church on Sunday night that his wife called him and that he would tell me more about it when we can visit.

There is just as much hope for this young couple as there is power in the Blood of Jesus. Anyone who can get a prayer through to God for them will certainly please the heart of Him who came, not to them who are whole, but to them who are sick. I don't know when I have felt more definitely that God wants to heal this broken-hearted couple, not just spiritually, but I believe He wants to put the whole family back together to the glory of His redemptive power.

And then, I am reminded again that you and I never know what lies behind the face we are looking into. A huge, middle-aged black man has come to my Bible studies for a long time; perhaps several years. He has come to see me a few times, but I never really felt that he was making any outstanding progress. He just seemed caught in a contentment to live today's shabby standard of a "Christian," pretty well convinced that sin was overlooked by God, and there was nothing more that could be done about it.

The other day he asked if he could see me again. I put him on the appointment sheet and he came in and sat down. He shakes constantly from a long history of drug use. But he was different than I had ever seen him. He began to tell me right out of his heart the story of his life.

He had grown up without his dad being there for him, and he said he was a "wild, uncontrollable kid." Then he enlisted and went to Vietnam. He was sent out in charge of a detachment of men who were supposed to stop the enemy convoys from coming into their territory. They would go out with two jeeps and heavy guns and were supposed to cripple the enemy until they had to turn back. He said he would just wipe them out instead of crippling them.

One day after he had turned his guns on the enemy, they went over to see what they had done and he said the men they had shot were just blood and guts all over the road. It unnerved him until his officer handed him a bottle of brandy and told him to drink it. It instantly made him feel better and he started drinking it regularly. Then someone introduced him to opium. It made him feel so good and so confident that he became a steady user of it. Now he began to take real pleasure in killing people just for the sake of killing them.

On one of the raids he was shot and had to lay off for a time to be healed. He went back at it again and was shot again. This time it pierced one of his lungs, and since they knew he would not heal right, he was given two discharges. One was a medical discharge because of his lung; the other was a mental discharge because they said he was enjoying killing people too much. He came home and continued to use drugs. He got

184 Voices from Prison Walls: William Cawman

married and tried to run his home like the military. That ended in divorce and he married again with the same results. Then he messed up and was sent to prison. He has to take medication all the time to keep himself under control, and even with that he wakes up in the night with terrible nightmares and cold sweats.

After unloading his sad wreck of a story, he looked at me and said, "Chaplain, what can I do? I can't go on like this." If you really believe in the miracle-working power of the Blood of Jesus, would you please pray for him?

Many of you know how often I feel burdened that I do not get as much time as I would like to spend in the prison hospital. It often bothers me that men might be slipping by us into eternity without knowing that there is One who can forgive them. Recently, my supervisor conceived the plan of training some of the best men among the inmates so that they could go over and sit by the bedside of dying men and minister to them in any way that they might need. I was fully supportive of the idea, and just recently it went into effect. Six of our best Christian men are now sitting by turns with these men who are terminal in order to help them die without being alone.

Friday morning, one of the men who was also in my class in Christian Living, came to me and told me that the man he was sitting with wanted to see me. I went over that evening just before time for my Bible studies, and I found a young black man dying from AIDS and cancer. He had lived in deep sin and homosexuality, but as soon as he saw me come in the door of his cell, he said, "Oh Chaplain, I'm so glad you came. I've been wanting to see you. I am so tired of living like this. I don't want to live in sin any longer, but I need to find God. I need peace in my heart."

I talked to him a little about some of his questions. He couldn't understand why God would allow suffering in the world when He is such a good God. I began to show him that suffering has nothing to do with God, that when we choose the pleasures of sin, we take the wages that come with it, and God weeps as He sees us suffer.

He seemed ready to hear anything that would bring relief from the guilt of sin in his life. I asked him to follow me as I prayed for him. As we prayed together and confessed his sins to God and asked Him to forgive him, he broke down and the tears flowed freely. Soon he was rejoicing while the tears continued to flow. I asked him if Jesus forgave his sins, and he said, "Yes, He does." He said he felt very happy inside. I told him that he had just made Jesus happy too and that all the angels of heaven were rejoicing that he had come home to God. Oh what mercy!

There is so much more that I could tell you, but let me say that God is answering your prayers in so many dear lives that I have to beg you to please pray on. Thank you each one.

In His love,
William Cawman

12
BLESSINGS AND THANKSGIVING

October 1, 2002

G OD IS NO MORE REAL in your life than you reflect Him." If you resent that statement, don't blame me. I am just quoting the words of a man in the prison who has no reason to blush about saying it. When this dear man gets up in church and begins to exhort, others around him do not look at him through their eyebrows with the reproach, "Physician, heal thyself." They listen with respect to one among them who is living up to what he talks.

Shall I give you a little more from him? He said, "We have heard it said many times, 'God said it—I believe it—that settles it.' Let me tell you that when God says it, that settles it, whether you want to believe it or not." Can you see why I never feel the need of asking him to sit down when he feels something on his heart? He doesn't claim to be a preacher, but he is a good one; and one of the things which makes him such a good one is that he knows just when to sit down and in turn pull the preach out of the preacher. His face shines with acceptance of the hottest truth and he backs it up with visible delight. Oh that every church had a few like him.

Last night in church I had just finished preaching on the subject "The Help of God." I had not been very soft-pedaled on cheap human religion that leaves one without any power from above to come clean from sin. But I had tried to really appeal to them to give up little false covers that were not working, and come to God for something that was real and really worked. I gave them a number of Scriptures to prove that God really wants to give them help from above to enable them to live above sin.

At the close of the message, a young black man raised his hand from the back row. I acknowledged him. He arose and said, "Chaplain, I really need what you are talking about. I came to prison a very young man and have been here for eight-and-a-half years, and I am going home tomorrow. I don't want to go out to live in sin. I need what you are talking about. Please pray for me."

I asked him to come up to the front and then asked several of the good Christian brothers to come up around him and pray. They came up and placed their hands on him and began to pray for him. I opened my eyes and the dear man was clutching his little New Testament with trembling hands while his tears were falling to the tile floor like rain. I couldn't help but wonder, "Jesus, how must Your heart have bled as You left those few disciples and thrust them out into a cruel world?" Oh for churches that would pick up these struggling souls and really lead them to Jesus instead of just patting them on the back and welcoming them into the choir. I'm afraid many of them go out as sheep having no shepherd. Please pray for them.

At the close of my last letter I told you of a dying young man in the hospital who found forgiveness through the mercy and Blood of Jesus as I was with him. I want to follow that story with an update. Let me first describe him to you a little so that you really get the whole picture of a divine miracle.

Let's remember first that Jesus Himself said, "They that be whole need not a physician, but they that are sick. But go ye and learn what that meaneth, I will have mercy, and not sacrifice: for I am not come to call the righteous, but sinners to repentance." Please pardon the following description, but it is just what you would have seen too, had you been there.

Here is a young black man, 27 years old. He has the face of a girl, long fingernails, fully formed breasts, and a woman's voice. He has been a homosexual for nearly all his life. But listen to his story. His mother died when he was very young and he became the constant companion of his father. His father was good to him and took him everywhere with him and did everything with him. When he was ten years old his father remarried and the new wife told him that he would have to put his boy out of the house because she would not allow him to be a companion to her boy. Without any further ado, the eleven-year-old boy was literally dumped out on the street and has not seen nor heard from his father for sixteen years. He said that his whole lifestyle from that point developed out of his need of mere survival. Now at the age of twenty-seven the fun is done and he lies dying of severe AIDS and cancer and who knows what else.

But thanks to our God and Father, Who through His abundant mercies sent His own dear Son to die in the place of such sickness as this. Ever since that night a few weeks ago that I told you about last month, when he repented of all his guilty past and asked the One Who came not for those who are whole but for the sick to come into his heart, he has had a sweet peace all around him. He studies the Bible with the inmates who sit with him, and he loves to learn. He asks many questions and it is so wonderful that these good men who also have been touched by the forgiveness of God, are able to lead him into an understanding of the God he now loves.

With tears welling up in his eyes he asked me what he should do about his father. He said that now that he knows he is dying he would like to be reconciled to his father but he is so afraid of being rejected that it tears him up inside. He said he doesn't know how to deal with it emotionally. I told him that he would never find the answer in his emotional responses. I asked him if he really wanted to keep the clear smile of God. He said with emphasis, "Oh yes, I don't ever want to lose Him or to do anything that would grieve Him, I love Him so much."

I said, "Then you have no choice but to obey Him, and He said that we must forgive others if we are to be forgiven." I told him that his torn-up emotions had nothing to do with his clear line of duty to obey God. But I also told him that he might be surprised at what a peace would come to him once he called his father and made things right. He resolved to do it as soon as he could make a phone call.

These inmates who are in what they term "hospice care," are discussed individually each week at a meeting of all who care for them. My supervisor usually attends, but the next meeting after these occurrences, he couldn't make it and asked me to go. We met around a table with perhaps fifteen people present: the doctor who sees him, the nurses, the social worker, the mental health doctor, the dietician, and several others from administration, and the chaplain. The doctor reports on him first and says that since last week a certain blood count which indicates the stage of his condition has dropped from nine to one. He says he has never before seen a one and that he doesn't understand why this inmate is still alive, let alone why he can sit up in his wheelchair to go outside in the courtyard. His verdict is that he may not live through the night. The social worker reports on his requests as to his family, etc, and also says that he has a date to be paroled in October, but no one there thinks he will live to see it.

Then they ask the chaplain if he has any report. He did. Some are strangely silent, while the administrator remarks that this is what the program is really about. The mental health doctor is then consulted. She observes that she doesn't really know what to think of him because he doesn't seem to need her. She says that he seems to be in a euphoria of some sort which isn't facing the reality of his condition and consequently seems very much at peace in his outlook. The chaplain sits across the table with pity and further observes once again that "They that be whole need not a physician, but they that are sick...for I am not come to call the righteous, but sinners to repentance."

I would not be very comfortable exchanging places with the dear man of whom I am writing, but I honestly believe I would sooner do it than exchange places with the mental health doctor. At least of this I am sure, unless things change, I would certainly sooner have his eternal reward.

We are stirring up some pretty interesting discussions as we move forward in the study of Biblical Christian living. I find it necessary to remind the men very often that when they come up gulping for air, staggered by some Biblical challenge to the way they have always lived and the things they have always considered acceptable, they must remember that is why they are taking the class.

We live in such an age of situational ethics, the end result of which has no more sense of direction than the modern goal of "If it feels good, do it," that they might as well be prepared to get knocked over a few times. Please do continue to pray that God will use these classes for more than just changing mental perspectives. I believe He wants to find a band of men who will dare to come out and be separate from the awful falling away of the churches of today, and live by Biblical principles, and do it because they love God with all their heart, soul, mind and strength.

One more thing—I cannot be specific, but as you can well imagine, a state institution is saturated and manipulated by political favors and political aggressions. God has opened a door here; please pray that He will keep it open by His precious Blood.

All for Jesus and these dear ones,
William Cawman

✝✝✝

November 1, 2002

Praise God from Whom all blessings flow! Let me start this letter with a testimony which was not asked for and was not given with any other motive than to give vent to that very Presence Jesus promised the woman at the well: "the water that I shall give him shall be in him a well of water springing up into everlasting life."

It was an ordinary Thursday morning in the worse than humdrum of prison existence. Our dear brother whom I call the preacher came into my office and sat down in a chair. His face was radiant—simply radiant. Without preamble or introduction he began to speak from the depths of a peace which flows like a river, and that in the middle of a prison hell-hole.

"Chaplain, I was just thinking; I know my sins are forgiven and that I am saved. I know my heart is cleansed and I am sanctified. I have the abiding Holy Spirit with me all the time; I have peace, joy, happiness; and heaven is yet to come." The heavenly Presence which accompanied the words left no room to even wonder if any word of it was less than genuine. Thank you, brothers and sisters, for praying. It is rewards like this that are too much for me to keep to myself and not share them with you.

Then to another facility with just a few minutes at the end of a busy day, to visit with another jewel of the grace of God. This is the man who has recently discovered in his mind what God had done for his heart some time back. As the truth of his spiritual position in Christ dawns upon him, his face just glows with reality. We sit down together, and he pulls out a few papers and says, "Chaplain, someone handed this to me and I read it. It is just wonderful!" I looked at the paper only to see that it was excerpts from John Wesley's *Plain Account of Christian Perfection*. I got the rest of it for him. Would you permit me to stop right here and thank my Heavenly Father for giving me, all unworthy of it, the glorious privilege of helping Him feed these sheep? Please pray that God will keep me emptied of self and filled with more and more of His blessed presence, until He will not find me hard to work with as His little shepherd boy.

And now, before I go further, I want to share in full a letter with you from the man whom many of you have prayed for again and again. To those who might not have followed or remembered his story, I will just briefly describe him so that you can appreciate and thank God for the letter as I did. You might even read it with moist eyes as I did.

Perhaps a couple of years ago now, this dear man whom I had not seen before stopped me late one afternoon outside of the cells and asked if he could talk to me. For the next two hours he poured out a story I have never completely related to anyone else. From earliest childhood he had been thrown into a tragic life of the deepest sin, finally leading him against his wishes into one of the bloodiest gangs in the country. He had experienced the hard drug traffic and all it entails and had seen murder in every form imaginable. His mind was torn to shreds; he would even look over his shoulder with shudders as he talked to me for fear someone was listening. He feared for his life in prison and out of prison. For months I visited with him regularly and he wanted me to, but it seemed like it was one step forward and two steps back.

About the time I thought he was beginning to come out of the past and look to God, he would slip right back into all the fears and trauma of his horrible past. There were times that I looked up to God and said, "God, this is the worst challenge of my life." I honestly never met anyone else so terribly torn up by sin. He was living in a literal hell on earth.

I cannot take the space here to retell the story of how he had four heart attacks about this time and ended up on the operating table, and how he nearly died. He went through some rough weeks after that, and God had to work on my own heart and mind in order for me to even understand how to relate to him.

No one had ever taught this man even the first principles of living a normal life, let alone a Christian life. My heart was so torn for him that I was out in the garage late one night pleading with God for him. God spoke so clearly to my heart the words of Paul to the Galatians: "My little children, of whom I travail in birth again until Christ be formed in you." "…until Christ be formed in you." Those words rang through and through my heart. God said to me, "He needs you to show him how to react like a Christian; he knows nothing about it."

It was about this time that in one of his upsetting experiences, he was put in detention. I went over to see him and he was beside himself with anger. He threatened a staff member in my hearing. I was obligated to report the threat to Special Investigations and he was sent out for a year of solitary confinement to a northern prison. As soon as he got there he wrote me a letter of apology, acknowledging that I did right and he was wrong. He freely forgave me and said he never wanted our friendship to cease. From then until now he has kept up a regular correspondence, and better than that, he has found peace and forgiveness with God. His letters grow richer and more Christ-like with each one. I do believe that through the marvelous grace of Calvary's redemption and your prayers, Christ is being formed in him. Here is the latest letter, unedited, from a man who was nearly illiterate two years ago.

"Dear Rev. Cawman

Hello, How are you & the family doing fine I hope, myself Im doing fine & hope you all are doing the same. I was just siting hear thinking of you so I thought Id write a few lines, Im still trying to get out on parole they want me to max out. They gave me a 8 year hit that was not so nice of them to do but its in God hands, I just think of how they nailed Jesus in the cross & how they had him in prison & I feel his love for me. I can feel Jesus right next to me so what ever they do to me it don't matter. Im not angry at them. I just pray for them all the more. Ive become hungry for the Word of God & the Holy Spirit is really moving in my heart. Im looking up above because I can feel Jesus is soon to come again. I keep telling people how I be come to know Jesus Christ & I tell them of the father & I can tell God has me in this max prison to tell of his love & power that can come to their hearts in hear & I pray that one day they will feel the desire for Gods love as I do. The lives that can be saved through Christ is many. Its important to me to tell people that their life can change as my life has.

   "Brother I could never thank you enough for helping me come to Christ. My heart is to always serve our lord Jesus Christ. Coming up to you that day in the prison was the first step to a new beganing in life to be with Christ for ever. Ive got a lot of feeling for other people in this world that need Jesus in their life. Ive promised the lord & my self that I will work with the church to help others to believe in the power of God & turn from their sins & put their trust in Jesus. I was a hot head in the past & a out law for many years so I don't fear people like that so I can walk up to them with the Word of God to help save them. Ill go any where the lord needs me to be & I will help people to change their life. Anyway its 12:00 pm right now so I better get to bed soon. I get up at 5:30 every day so Ill say good night. Love, Joy & Peace your Brother in Christ."

Last Friday night we had a very rewarding and profitable discussion in the Bible study in the minimum security unit and then I went back into the prison for the Bible study there, intending to cover the same area of study. God had something else in mind. The men gathered in and then began to sing the old song of Fanny Crosby's, "Blessed Assurance." Heaven came down in that room. My heart was melted as I looked at men's faces whom I had watched for some time. I had seen some of them come in all torn apart by sin and its merciless wages, and now some of those very same faces were lifted up in a song of praise that caused heaven to get all mixed up with earth inside of a state prison.

We finished singing the three verses and then sang them all over again. By that time, as good as the lesson was for the evening, we just followed the sacred Presence that was there and spoke to them right out of our heart on the reality of that "Blessed Assurance." And as so often happens, the Spirit just led right on into the central theme of the sacrifice of Calvary—complete deliverance from the nature of all that the devil ever put within us. It was a blessed time and we were reluctant to leave.

The dear man who lies dying in the hospital that I told you about in the last letter continues to walk in love for Jesus. He was somewhat tormented by a fear that if he gets out of prison he will be led back into sin by those in his life he was always with. Sunday afternoon I went in early and went to his cell to see him. He was in terrible pain but was so glad to see me. I began to expose to him the trick the devil was using on him of borrowing trials from tomorrow and making him fight them today. I asked him if he still loved Jesus.

"Oh yes, with all my heart."

"Are you holding on to Him?"

"With both hands."

"Then," I said, "you pray the prayer Jesus told you to pray, 'give us this day our daily bread.'" I told him that God would give him more grace when he got there. But I also told him to be on his guard, because God just might not let him enter heaven without facing the things which had always tempted him and then proving His grace sufficient to help him to say, "No."

Some of you might have been wondering about former inmate V——. I have hesitated to put much in the letters for fear he might find one of them somewhere, but let me tell you that he is an absolute blessing wherever he goes. God is really working with his family too. Keep him in prayer that he will never lose the simple but dynamic walk with God that he enjoys every moment of every day.

Dear friends, we may not have much longer to reap the

harvest; could we together raise our Ebenezer and reach for the prize set before us?

Your brother and fellow-laborer,
William Cawman

December 1, 2002

Rejoice with the angels in heaven; another sinner has come home. A new name is written down in glory, and here is the story.

At the end of the first page of September's letter I told of a Romanian Gypsy who was under deep conviction for his sins, and I asked you to pray for him. Friday afternoon, November 15, at 2:30, he came to my office with a face beaming like the sun. He immediately threw up both hands and said, "Chaplain, I got my answer; I'm saved, I'm saved! Do you have ten minutes?"

I have all day for things like this. He sat down and began: "It all started with this letter, and I don't even know who this is." (Several weeks ago a dear woman whom I have never met, wrote and told me that God had given her a desire to try to write to some inmates in need. She asked me to send her three names of men that I felt would profit from it. I asked that God would bring the right ones to my mind and sent her three names. The letter he laid on the desk was from her.)

He said that when he received that letter it just made him feel desperate to find an answer from God as to his forgiveness and he began to seek Him all the harder. He told several of the good men about it and they told him to just get on his knees and ask until God gave him the answer he was looking for. He asked them how he would know and they told him he would just know it. He went to his job the next morning but couldn't work for the conviction on his heart. He asked the officer to excuse him and went to his cell and got on his face before God. He told Him every sin in his life he could think of and asked God to let him know if he was forgiven or not. He prayed and prayed, but God did not seem to answer him. Finally he said he got angry because God would not answer him and he just lay on the bed and finally fell asleep.

The next day he was still under a heavy burden and began to ask God to forgive him for the way he felt the day before. He said, "God, I know that in Your own time you will answer me, and I'm sorry that I was angry with You." He suddenly felt a strong urge to get up and read his Bible. He had been reading his Bible for some time and had last stopped with II Corinthians 5, but for two days was under such distress that he hadn't read anything. He responded to the urging and opened his Bible and began to read with II Corinthians 6— "For he saith, I have heard thee in a time accepted, and in the day of salvation have I succoured thee: behold, now is the accepted time; behold, now is the day of salvation."

The words leaped from the Bible right into his heart and he jumped up saying, "God, I know I'm saved!" He read on and the last verse said, "I will receive you, and will be a Father unto you, and ye shall be my sons and daughters, saith the Lord Almighty." He said he had never dared to do it before, but he got on his knees and looked up and said, "Father," and it felt so good. He became so excited that he ran over to his totally ungodly cell mate and began to tell him how God had answered him and his cell mate got excited too.

He told me that he then ran out onto the compound to tell the good Christian brothers and to ask them when I would be back. They said they didn't know for sure, but just then the officer slipped a note under his door saying that I had scheduled an appointment with him. He said, "When I told the brothers in the yard they said, 'Brother, you are only this far (holding his fingers close together) from getting sanctified.' Chaplain, I don't know if I understand what that is, but I sure want it." Then he looked me straight in the eye and said, "Does this really mean that all my sins are forgiven?"

I said, "Yes, brother, that is exactly what it means; God has removed them as far as the east is from the west."

His eyes filled with tears and he said, "Oh I feel so clean; I feel so clean."

Now let me tell you another precious victory. We were in a revival in our church. Former inmate V—— came for the first weekend and brought his two children, a daughter, age 12, and a son, age 13, along with his nephew, age 16. Whether the nephew has ever been to church before in his life I do not know, but he was the typical product of today's street youth— the sides of his hair in little braids with a combination afro/ mohawk in the middle, earrings, band around his head, chain around his neck, etc. He listened intently in Sunday School class as we talked about the two choices in life and where they end up.

In the middle of that afternoon, V——'s daughter was walking around with a great big smile on her face and her father finally asked her why she was smiling so much. She said, "Because I have God in my heart."

He said, "Oh, did you ask Him to come into your heart and did you open it up and let Him in?" She said she had. In the middle of the service that night V—— asked if we could gather around the front and pray for his two boys. They came forward along with some other young people, and we gathered around to pray. The daughter became so happy that she testified about three times that night.

Finally the nephew got up from the altar and told us that God had saved him. Apparently by now, whatever statement was being made by the little braids was bothering him, and they had disappeared. After the service we were with him a while and suddenly he looked at us and began to open up. He said that before God saved him the devil (at least he knew who it was) was telling him that he did not want to be there and that it was going to be boring. But when he began to ask God to forgive him he felt his heart break down in tears and then he said, "It's like—well, it's sort of like I'm born all over again."

We told him that was why the Bible and those who have found it, call it "being born again." "Oh really," he said with surprise, "is that really what they call it?" I hear that since, he has been trying to tell his mother what happened to him that night. V——'s daughter has been happy in God ever since. Please keep these young people in your prayers, that God will guide their footsteps through all of the snares in the cruel world around them.

And now—I am aware that with this issue we complete three years of these letters. We want to stop and give thanks. First of all we thank God for His great and marvelous grace which reaches even to the worst of lost men. Great is His mercy and His patience and His loving kindness to us and to them. Oh won't it be wonderful to meet some of these dear souls among that "great multitude, which no man could number, of all nations, and kindreds, and people, and tongues, [who] stood before the throne, and before the Lamb, clothed with white robes, and palms in their hands; and cried with a loud voice, saying, Salvation to our God which sitteth upon the throne, and unto the Lamb."

Then we want to thank each one of you who have prayed for these dear souls. God does answer prayer! Thank you from our hearts, and also from the dear men who so often express it to us when it should go to you. Just recently as I told a man that someone was praying for him in a certain place he looked at me almost in awe, "Do you really mean that someone is praying for me halfway across the United States?" You, dear friends, by your prayers, have answered that pathetic wail which cries, "No man cared for my soul."

Then also, we want to thank all those who have felt the call of God on their hearts to volunteer their assistance and ministry in so many ways. Even though we would desire many times to do so, we cannot disclose the names of those who have become thus involved. For some of the same reasons that we cannot place names in this letter of men in the system, we also cannot identify by name those who are helping them. We have no way of knowing where all this letter goes, and we dare not run any chance of connections coming from it that would hurt the further cause of God.

Let me give you an example. The dear sister that I mentioned earlier in this issue who desired to write to three men has already proved a blessing to them, but those men have no idea that I was the one who gave her their names. What I did was perfectly legal; giving them a pen pal to correspond with; but if they knew that I knew who she was, they could be tempted to use me as a go-between for some ulterior motive. But, just because we cannot name who they are, we are thankful, so thankful just the same for those who have volunteered to fill in services and Bible studies for us when we are gone in evangelistic work.

One brother is visiting an inmate in the prison hospital who needs someone to talk to him in his own language. Others are coming in to help with music in the services. Some are preaching the Word, and oh yes! what a thrill it is to come back from being gone and hear an inmate say to us, "Oh my, that brother brought us a powerful message Sunday night; it really spoke to my heart." I know that the brother was right on track, and I thank God for brothers like this. At the same time I rejoice to see them too becoming "addicted" to this whitened harvest field.

Prison ministry is not something that fits everyone, and God knows that as well as we do. But it makes no difference to the cause of God as long as we are each one filling the place God has for us. Some of you have ministered in material ways that have meant more than you will ever know until that great day when all things are known.

We also want to thank the church we attend (except when we are in prison) for such support, such prayer, such encouragement. I thank God for a pastor who prays for me. Many is the time that I sit and listen to a message and a fire is kindled which in turn shows up in a message in the prison, but he does not know that, so indirectly he preaches there too. Oh how wonderful it is to be a part of the family of God.

I want also to thank my dear mother and father for their many prayers and strong support. They have given me a legacy that I want to pass on to other men who have not had the privileges that I have had.

Last but not least, I want to thank God for a good wife, and I want to thank her too. Jesus said, "Greater love hath no man than this, that a man lay down his life for his friends." In many ways known only to God and her husband, she has literally done this. Personal comforts and interests have been gladly laid aside and she has stood by her husband's side like a true, God-given help-meet. She will be thoroughly embarrassed by this insertion, but she will forgive me as she has so many of my other somewhat rash outbursts.

And so, on behalf of our Heavenly Father and on behalf of these to whom you have ministered, we say a deep, heart-felt thank you in complete trust that you will not grow weary in well doing.

In the love of Him Who first loved us,
William Cawman

13
WALKING THE WALK/TALKING THE TALK

January 1, 2003

GREETINGS TO EACH ONE as we enter another year of God's renewed mercies. One does not have to look around very far to realize that we have so much to thank Him for. Do we pause long enough in our busy lives to really thank Him as we should for the things we too often take for granted? Why do I ask this? Listen on.

On Christmas Eve we were gathering in the chapel of Facility Three when a man about my age came to me and wanted to tell me something. His children had just come to the prison to tell him that his wife of 36 years had just dropped dead of a massive heart attack. We stopped the service and had special prayer for him. At the close of the service several of the good men gathered around him and tried to extend their sympathies to him. I asked him if it would help him if I would come in to see him the next afternoon which was Christmas day. He said he would be so glad if I would.

So, after our Christmas dinner was over, I went to the prison and to his cell block and had him called out. We went into a small room together where he began to pour out his grief. He had had a happy home; had been married for 36 years, had five children and seven grandchildren. But he had made a wrong choice in something he did, which I will not disclose here, and had been sentenced to prison. He told me that after coming to prison he had really looked at his life and in his own words "I have turned every part of my life over to God." He had asked God to forgive him and he was so changed that his wife was thrilled to see it and was just waiting for him to come home. She was working 12 hours a day to keep their home together and suddenly dropped of the heart attack. He was grief-stricken through and through.

As he poured out his heart, he said over and over, "I will not blame God, but I just don't understand. All I wanted was to go home to her again. I know God is right, but I will never hold her in my arms again. I just wish God would talk to me and tell me something."

I told him to just keep listening and God would. I said, "You are too full of grief right now to hear anything. When a man is totally drunk he doesn't feel the cold; he doesn't feel the bruises; he is too filled to sense anything. That is how it is with you right now; you are so filled with grief that you cannot sense God near you, but He is, and you will hear His voice again. It is not wrong for you to be full of grief right now, just don't let your heart sin against God."

He said, "Oh I won't"—and then with tears again filling his eyes—"but I'll never hold her in my arms again." Need I tell you that I went home and held my wife? I spent some time with this inmate and for part of it we just cried together. He was to be released in just a couple of months.

A man, possibly in his mid-thirties, has been seeking to be sanctified for some time now. He has been just as open and receptive to teaching as an eager first-grader, and so often when I have presented some truth to him he has just acted dumb-founded with amazement and delight. On September 13, he felt that God sanctified his heart, and he has been bearing witness to it ever since. The other day he came to visit with me and as he was talking about his new victory he said, "Praise God, I have not sinned once since September 13." He is so hungry for more light and truth that he told me he looked around at all the other groups meeting in the prison, but said, "I really don't feel drawn to them. I can't say that I feel the need to examine other beliefs because I don't need any further proof. I have no question marks."

This man responds to any new truth that touches his heart with "Hallelujah! That's wonderful." At the close of our visit, I had prayed with him and then he wanted to "make a prayer." I wish you could have heard it. He had copied it from no one in the world. In the middle of it he became visibly excited and blurted out, "Man, I'm looking forward to life!" —then went right on with his prayer. And he is locked up in a state prison. Do you remember the song we love to sing, "Where Jesus is, 'tis heaven there."?

Just before Christmas I gave a five-page exam to all those who were enrolled in the Christian Living Class. I told them that if they liked exams, this would be their Christmas present; if they didn't, I guess I was a Scrooge. They seemed to enjoy it as well as I did, and it really helped to evaluate what they were learning from the class.

But this is why I told you about it. There were several who had enrolled in the class some time after it started, and they had missed a lot of the introductory material we had covered which mostly related to the internal equipment necessary to live the Christian life—the power of Christ dwelling within. To all those who had enrolled late, I assigned them to come and visit with me in small groups so that I could go over that subject material before they took the exam. So for several days, I took a few at a time and sat down with them for about an hour and a half. It was rich.

In one of those sessions a man sat at the end of the table with undivided attention like he had never heard truth like that before. Every little bit as it dawned on him that we really could be delivered from sin and live pleasing to God every moment without falling into sin, he would say with deep feeling, "Praise the Lord!" Isn't it so absolutely wonderful that God really does make sense? There is nothing in all the philosophies, creeds, codes of ethics, laws and psychiatric treatments that makes sense like the simple, powerful act of God in making us a "new creature" in Christ Jesus.

In another one of these sessions sat a young black man who had obviously lived "without God in the world" all of his life so far. As I was explaining the Christian life and the power of it to them, he broke in and said, "Chaplain, I have to say something. I've never read anything in my life like this Book." (It was not the *Reader's Digest* that he held up either.) "When I read this, I can't help it, it just brings tears out of my eyes. I never read it before, but this Book is really alive." Oh thank God for the Living Word of God!

Just before Christmas the inmates in Christian Living Class in Facility Two presented me with the most touching card I received for Christmas. They had put a lot of work into it and it was made to be a bookmark, not just a card. They had taken stiff paper and formed a sleeve, open at both ends, and then covered it with clear tape. On the back was listed all of their names. On the front was an expression of their appreciation, and then a square hole at the top. Inside of the sleeve was the bottom out of a muffin wrapper which was stiff cardboard covered with shiny aluminum foil. Into the foil they had indented in beautiful handwriting which I had to read with a magnifying glass, the Scripture from Matthew, "And thou shall call His name Jesus." In the bottom of the sleeve was a thumb nail hole and as you slide the inside piece down it has a touching presentation at the bottom while it reveals a picture of the manger scene in the hole at the top. It was really a work of art for the material and tools they had to work with.

Let me tell you of a very touching incident which illustrates the faithfulness of the Blessed Holy Spirit. We call Him the "Abiding Spirit." We sing, "He abides, He abides, Hallelujah He abides with me." Jesus said, "I will pray the Father, and He shall give you another Comforter, that He may abide with you for ever." And certainly He desires to abide forever; but it is all to the credit of His faithfulness, His patience, His love, and His chastening that He accomplishes this in us. We have so much to learn, so much to change, so much of our life styles to bring into conformity with His Son so that He can dwell in us and work through us. To see this "progressive holiness" working within your own life or the life of another is a heart-melting experience.

One of the men who has been living in the blessed experience of a pure heart, and who has been letting this great work of the Spirit be perfected in him, came in the other day to see me. He was somewhat troubled, or perplexed, and immediately began to open his heart without a trace of dishonesty or desire to hide anything.

For some time one of the officers had been miserable to him and would let it be known. The inmate would try to make the best of it and would greet the officer with all civility, but to no avail; the officer would tell him to get away from him, and all sorts of other insults. The inmate said he did not realize what was happening, but looking back now, he realizes that he had been allowing something to build up toward the officer.

He was in the chapel buffing the floor, which is his job, and the officer came into the control center. The inmate waved to him, and he motioned with his hand for him to get away and mouthed something to him. The inmate put down the buffer and went into the control center and asked if he wanted to say something to him. The officer exploded and told him to get out.

The inmate said, "I just thought you were trying to tell me something," and then, "Officer, I wish you would not treat me this way." He went out and picked up the buffer and burst into tears. He looked up to God and said, "Oh God, do I still have a nature of sin in my heart that would respond like that?"

About that time the officer went to leave and the inmate

called to him and apologized for speaking to him like that. But then he went back to the buffer and for two hours wept and searched his heart. As he told me about it, he obviously had no desire to shield anything that God wanted to show him. He said, "I don't understand just what happened, but when it was over I felt so cleansed. I hadn't realized that something was building up towards him, and now it is so cleansed away. But there is one thing I do know, I'll sure recognize anything that would build up like that next time."

I realized that only the Holy Spirit could witness to this man yea or nay, that was not my place to do. But I began to explain to him the possibility of even a pure heart momentarily reaching through an emotional door under pressure and touching forbidden fruit, and then instantly renouncing it when they became aware of what was happening. I told him that if there remained any element of the nature of sin in his heart, the Holy Spirit would not lift His finger from that hidden sin. But if sin had simply pressed hard at the door of his heart until he realized what it was and then renounced it, he would be left with no condemnation. As he simply and honestly laid his heart bare before God, that room filled with such glory that I cannot describe it. Oh thank God for the Blood which "CLEANSETH" (present tense) from all sin, whether that sin is within or without. "Hallelujah, He abides..." Please continue to pray for these as they learn to walk in the beauty of that treasure within the earthen vessel.

Your Brother in Jesus,
William Cawman

February 1, 2003

"Wonderful grace of Jesus, Reaching the most defiled,
   By its transforming power, Making him God's dear child...
   Oh, magnify the precious name of Jesus, Praise His name!"

Can the gentle, glowing man I am visiting really be the same man who murdered his wife? We sit together for three quarters of an hour with burning hearts, until I feel I have been in the very Holy of Holies. What a way to start a day! The glow of it lingers on and on.

What grace is this? It is none other than the grace of Jesus. And it is saving, keeping, sanctifying this very man, and that right in the middle of a prison atmosphere with all of its devilry, as well as all of its multi-religious factions. But the glorious fact is; it is Jesus. Let's come clear on this: Mohammed didn't die for this man, but Jesus did. Buddha didn't break his chains, but Jesus did. Confucius didn't dispel the darkness that he was groping in, but Jesus did. The virgin Mary didn't pray to the Father for him, but Jesus did. And what the law could not do, Jesus did! "In Whom we have redemption through His Blood, the forgiveness of sins…"

Now we are about to begin another Bible study, and I ask this same man to lead us in prayer. There is a deep and reverent pause, and he quietly but with great feeling begins: "I'm so glad I can call You Father. I'm so glad that Jesus is my Brother. I'm so glad I'm one day nearer home. I'm so glad for my Great High Priest."

Often I sit with men who spend the whole time complaining about the hard lot they are having trying to be a Christian in such a place as this. I've never heard a word about it from this saintly man. All he ever talks about is the marvelous grace of Jesus and the wonders of the holy life. This is not "jail-house religion," for he would have nothing to gain by it with nearly twenty years yet to go. There is never a trace of self-seeking, or wanting to be noticed, but instead a peace that flows from him with radiant contentment. This man is our "brother," friends; and he carries the title by just as much claim as you or I, not because of who he is or what he has done, but because of that redemption which is through the Blood of Jesus.

Those of you who have been receiving the letters will probably remember the sad case of the 27-year old, terribly abused, homosexual man who was dying in the hospital. We have to bury him some day soon; no one wants him. He will be one more little pile of ashes under that lonely tree along the road that leads into the prison. He will have nothing more for his epitaph than a number on a six-inch square stone; the number will be somewhere in the teens. But I believe he is in heaven. The last time I saw him alive, a day or so before he died, he said he loved Jesus with all his heart and that He forgave all of his sins. Oh the mercy of the Lord; David said that "His mercy endureth forever." He will have no jewels to present to Jesus. He will have no soul but his own to take with him. He will have nothing to commend himself before the Judge of all the earth, except the same thing that I have, the precious Blood of Jesus.

Recently one of the Christian inmates came to me very excitedly. He works in the hospital, cleaning floors, and as he was going down the hall one of the other Christian brothers who had been sitting by the bedside of a dying man came out to get him. He said, "Brother, come in here; I want you to meet a man who has just been born again." He had been sitting by his bedside feeding this inmate because he was too weak and too far gone to feed himself, and had been leading him to Jesus. As the second inmate entered the cell, the dying man was rejoicing and saying, "All the way!" The three of them had a time for themselves, and they truly believed the angels in heaven were rejoicing too. I'm sure they were.

And then there are the disappointments. As long as I have been writing these letters, I have mentioned the inmate labeled C——, and all that God was doing for him. He is bright and intelligent, and that in spite of a terribly trashed childhood. He never knew a father; his mother didn't love or want him and dumped him into a household of lesbians to raise him. She would come and get him at times and put him on the street to sell drugs for her. She would make him put the needles into her arm and then watch to see that she didn't die from the shock. She hit him and kicked him and shot a bullet through him, but never told him she loved him. For twenty years he has spent very little time out of prison.

I believe it was three years ago last August that God marvelously delivered him, and that completely, from a terrible addiction to heroin. He had gone right on walking in the light and letting God show him all the areas of his life that needed to be changed and cleansed. He swallowed down the truth of full deliverance from all sin and read every book he could get his hands on about it. He began taking correspondence courses and preparing himself for whatever God would call him to. He was a wonderful testimony to others around him, and he was influential in bringing others to the truth. He had a relish for the Word of God and for the truth of holiness, and again and again it seemed he came close to entering in.

Sometimes Inmate C—— would tell us of his excitement that it was soon to happen. But he didn't go far enough to get rid of the enemy within. He has at least temporarily been moved to a northern county prison for the last several months, and one of the inmates got a letter from him which he showed me. Inmate C—— is torn apart by the very thing he didn't get rid of. He is questioning his belief in God. He says he longs to just go back and get on heroin again, but he can't. Please pray for him; and please pray for me, that I will never, never cease to cry out against this deadly traitor within the heart of every man who has not been delivered from it by a death to all sin.

I must tell you about an interesting class session recently. I had gotten a cassette tape of the testimony of Charlie Wireman, and so I took it into the prison and played it for each of the three classes in Christian Living. I was following it up with what it really means to, in Charlie Wireman's words, "get religion," and what a change it brings into our lives.

A man on the front row put up his hand and said, "Some people take their car to the garage every day to get the battery charged, but they never get the short fixed." I confess, that set me off! I said, "Brother, I know all about that, because to my shame I tried it for twenty-five years." And then I spent the rest of the class period testifying to them of the wonderful change after I "got the short fixed." I believe I never felt more of the help of God in my life. I didn't hide a thing, nor put it under a bushel. I was glorying in the marvelous, transforming grace of being buried with Christ and alive in the Spirit.

I noticed after a while that the officer came out of his little windowed cell and seemed to need to spend some time slowly checking the locks on all the closet doors. Then I noticed that the Catholic chaplain had come out of the chaplain's office into the rear of the chapel and was wandering back and forth. I didn't care; I was feeling too much of what Peter felt on the day of Pentecost to fear any man. The men in the class listened with rapt attention, and no one offered to suggest that such a walk with God is not possible. The class is supposed to end at 10:30. We finally let them go at 10:45, just in time for them to be called in for count.

Later that day, the Catholic chaplain came into my office and said, "Chaplain, I just wanted to tell you that you were really filled with the power of God this morning in that class. My, we're so fortunate to have you here." Pray for him too. Some of the good men who were raised as Catholics feel that God wants them to go to his classes and use every opportunity they can get in to testify to the grace of Jesus. God bless them! Loose them and let them go! Someone asked me what I thought would happen if he got saved. I said I didn't know, but would certainly be willing to find out.

The last Sunday night of January, I had two services in Facility Three, and my supervisor, as part of the class work he is teaching, had two inmates prepare a short message, one for each service. The service began well. The dear brother I call "Preacher" led the singing, "Glory to His Name." Heaven bent low as they sang with deep worship, and then the "Preacher" got excited. He let loose with a vehement exhortation on being done with sin, and he wasn't preaching one thing and living another either. Then the first inmate got up to give his message. He told the men he had spent a lot of time that week searching his own heart to see if he measured up to the message God had given him. He then preached about Peter getting his eyes off of Jesus and going under his surroundings. It was an excellent message.

Before the second service an officer came in and said to me, "You know it's Super Bowl night, don't you? You probably won't get many of them out." I couldn't tell much difference in the crowd—that officer doesn't understand, does he? They began the second service by singing "Pass Me Not, Oh Gentle Savior," and the song leader paused and said, "Aren't you glad that God sees the Blood over the lintel?" Then another brother got up to give his message.

He announced that he wanted to preach about true repentance. He said, "First I'm going to tell you what repentance is not: it is not just a guilty feeling; it is not our own works, or penance; it is not an outward reformation; it is not just turning away from outward known sin, because your own will power will run out. That sin nature you were born with has to be dealt with. Repentance is a change of your mind, your heart, and your will. The prodigal came to himself; he had a change of mind. He confessed 'I have sinned;' he had a change of heart. And he said, 'I will arise and go;' he had a change of will. When that happens, you'll know it; it's real. When I have a bad headache, I don't have to go ask the Christian brothers if I have a headache; I know it. When you get the real thing you will know it." I was taking notes and saying "Amen" simultaneously.

When he was finished I jumped up and followed it up with the fruits of repentance—"Redemption through His Blood." The good brother who had just finished preaching sat grinning from ear to ear and taking it in just as happily as he had given it out. What a blessed service it was. It was hard to close when the door slid open.

Dear brothers and sisters, I can only make an effort at trying to share with you the fruits of your prayers. I trust the God you have prayed to so faithfully will somehow enable you to share the fruit of your faithfulness. I know you will in heaven, but I covet it for you now. These scenes are too much to absorb without sharing as best we can. And then, we meet in the parking lot with another brother and his wife and son who had a service in another facility and share the good reports. Thank you, thank you, for each of your parts too.

In His love,
William Cawman

March 1, 2003

Just after I sent out the last letter, the man I told about at the beginning of it came to me with this story. He had been assigned to the bedside of a dying inmate who had come from a northern prison and was only here for two weeks before he died. When the Christian inmate first entered the room to sit with him, he was utterly repulsed by the awful sight of the dying man. He was in the last stages of probably many diseases, and had ugly tumors all over his head. He had a tube from his stomach which was oozing blood. But worst of all, he was angry and would not let anyone talk to him. If someone would try, he would wave them off with his hand and refuse to speak.

For several days the Christian brother sat by his bed, tried to help him with his tube, and silently prayed for him. They did not say a word. When he would leave him it was with a heavy burden and a deep pain that the poor man was so far gone and so lost. He really did not know what to do to try to help him.

Then one afternoon as he entered the room he said he sensed a lift in the atmosphere. He went over and began to help the man with his trachea tube and as he was doing it, he felt an urge from within. He said, "Could I tell you something about myself?" Then he began to tell the dying man about his own life. He told him what an awful sinner he

214 Voices from Prison Walls: William Cawman

had been and told him about the crime he had committed. But then he told him that Jesus had forgiven all of his sins and that he was so happy now.

The man listened and did not wave him away. Then the Christian inmate followed with the parable of the lost sheep, and then about the dying thief on the cross. He said, "You can have forgiveness too. You can ask Jesus right now to forgive your sins and come into your heart." When he said that, the dying man brought up his bony arms and folded them together over his chest as one would in prayer.

That was the last response he ever made. The sick man died a few days later, but was unable to ever respond as far as anyone knew. Our dear brother was deeply affected as he told me, "Somehow I just have a warm assurance down in my heart that he asked God to forgive him."

Oh the mercy of our God! Certainly he too has nothing to offer, but that Jesus died for him. But that is enough, thank God.

A few weeks ago, a young man came into the chaplain's office for the first time and sat down in front of me. With a look in his eyes that emanated from way down deep within, he made a statement I think I'll never forget. He said, "Chaplain, I've gotta get it right this time." Perhaps had it not come from such a wellspring of desperation, I would not have felt it the way I did, but it fastened itself on my heart until I could not shake it off.

A few weeks later I found myself on Sunday night preaching from this subject, "I've gotta get it right this time." It was just a little over twenty-four hours after the space ship Columbia exploded only seventeen minutes from the landing strip—without a single further chance to "get it right." I poured out my heart to them as I plainly pled with them to quit playing around with God and religion and "get it right." I asked them if they could afford to go for another cycle of defeat and failure.

We looked hard at the Scripture in I Corinthians 9:24,26

"Know ye not that they which run in a race run all, but one receiveth the prize? So run, that ye may obtain. I therefore so run, not as uncertainly; so fight I, not as one that beateth the air…" I simply gave them back the cry of one of their own, "I've gotta get it right this time."

It was pretty quiet in the room, but the next day I heard about it everywhere I went. One man came to my office door and said, "Chaplain, I never heard you before, but that really got through to me; I've gotta get it right." He then signed up for Christian Living Class and I believe is really reaching for help. Another man called out as I was passing by the outside courtyard full of men, "Chaplain, that was pretty tough last night, but it was true; we've gotta get it right." Please pray for them. I believe I can honestly say that I preached it to them with love, even if it was tough. I don't want to see any of them lost without God.

Some days later another man came into my office with a look of deep pain in his eyes. I asked him how he was getting along and he shook his head. He began to tremble and I could see he was in trouble. He finally started in: "Chaplain, I'm forty-two years old. I was a pretty good kid, but I was a bad teen, and then I joined the army in 1979. In 1986 my officer called me in one day and said he had bad news for me. He told me that a blood test had revealed that I was HIV positive. They discharged me from the army and I went on with my life for all these years, but since I came to this prison my T-cells have dropped out the bottom and my viral load is way up. There's no way around it; I'm headed down the last hill. I listened to your message and I know I've gotta get it right."

Could I insert something at the end of this plea? Thank God for the mercy which never gives up on a man even down to the end of the road of sin. How rightfully we rejoice with the angels over every sinner that repents and comes home to Father's house from the far-off country. But oh how much greater is the grace which was given to enable us to "get it right" in the early bloom of life, before the scars and stains have been stamped upon the memory and the soul. Certainly this must bring more pleasure to the heart of Him who gave His life for the express purpose of putting away sin.

A few weeks ago a man that I don't remember seeing before, came to me in the chapel. He looked pretty old and worn out, but then I found out he was younger than myself. He asked to talk and then began to tell his story. His father was a rich and famous artist but not much of a father, and obviously not much of a husband either, as he went through nine wives. At the early age of fourteen this inmate began to take the rocky road of sinful pleasure and as a consequence had spent a good portion of his fifty-two years in and out of prison. He looked the part of the life he had lived. He knew well the feel of a bed in a cardboard box or a burned-out car, and he was well acquainted with the typical antidote to such discomfort—the chemical escape from reality. A few years ago he had a bad fall and suffered some brain damage for which he was placed in a nursing home, but as soon as he was recovered a little they came and took him out and returned him to prison to serve some more time.

I began to talk to him about the forgiving grace of Jesus Christ. He latched onto it like a drowning man, and as he did I felt such a compassion for the dear old broken wreck of humanity. He said he would really like to talk to me some more, but when I scheduled him again, he didn't come. I checked his whereabouts in the inmate locator and found that they had moved him out to the minimum security part of the prison. I placed him on the schedule for the next time I would be out there and what a change I found in him since I had seen him before. He honestly looked ten years younger and had a smile on his face. He began to tell me that he felt very sure that God had forgiven all his sins. He could hardly believe the fact, nor could he believe the wonderful peace and rest he was finding after all that stormy life. He said, "I just can't thank God enough for forgiving me. I read His Word and I just praise Him and thank Him." It wasn't hard to believe him, for it showed all over him. Didn't David say that "He will beautify the meek with salvation"?

I do want to thank each of you again for your prayers. One of the brightest spots in the week has become the three, two-hour classes in Christian Living on Monday, Tuesday, and Friday mornings. If you ever think of us during that time period and feel God pulling on your heart to pray, I beg you to please be faithful to Him. God is speaking to many of the men during these classes, and the more deeply we examine what it really means to live as a Christian, the more we realize how far today's religious programs have drifted from it. In every area from home life, to marital relationships, to child raising, to honesty, and on and on, eyes are being opened to what it means to walk pleasing to God. We are rigidly adhering to one and only one standard in everything—the Word of God. What a Book! It hasn't let us down once.

I have good news again from the inmate we have mentioned several times who is now in one of the northern prisons because of threatening a staff member. God has so changed him that you can see the spiritual growth in every letter. He even feels better physically, and is now working at a job in the prison. But the best of all is that God is healing all of the tragically damaged areas of his personality and attitudes. He feels so much love for everyone, even his former enemies. He has written to his ex-wife and made things right with her. And now, perhaps you should also pray for my faith, because I cannot say that I really believed some time back that one day he would write to me and tell me that he prays for me all the time. But even though I might have struggled to believe it, I am not struggling to accept it. I treasure his prayers more than I can say.

You and I cannot possibly comprehend what little if any love this man ever received from anyone, and how much hatred and violence he has wallowed in, and how terribly damaged his trust in everything and everyone was. And then to feel the love beaming from him now—this, friends, is not the work of psychiatry, or psychotherapy; this is the work of Him alone Who "according to His abundant mercy hath begotten us again unto a lively hope by the resurrection of Jesus Christ from the dead." And in case there should still be any doubt of whom we speak, it is that One whom "God also hath highly exalted…and given Him a name which is above every name…" And that name is Jesus.

I mentioned in the last letter that we would—and we did— we laid to rest in the little lonely cemetery, the young man who found peace in Jesus' forgiveness even while dying in his own sin. As we stood over the little hole in the ground I told the other two chaplains of that evening when he found forgiveness. I then said, "This is a sad moment; we hold in our hands all that is left of a young man that nobody wants, except Jesus." Oh the Friend of Sinners! I need Him just as much as that man did.

The atmosphere is solemn at times as the men watch the news of coming world events. No one needs to tell them that the time may be short, but we do anyway. Please pray that they will listen to the faithful warnings that they are feeling.

And again, I thank each one of you for your faithful prayers. And this thanks comes in great volume also from the ones for whom you are praying. They count you true brothers and sisters and love you even though they have not seen many of you. Only eternity will reveal where the crowns should be placed, but certainly those of you who are praying for us will not be counted among the least of them to whom it will please the harvest Master to bestow His smile.

Your brother and fellow-laborer in Christ,
William Cawman

14
STEPPING ON SOME TOES

April 1, 2003

T HE FOLLOWING ACCOUNT may not be altogether a typical afternoon, but it did happen. It was Tuesday, and I had five interviews scheduled, two in Facility One and three in Facility Two. I'll tell you about interviews two and three.

Interview two comes in and I ask him how he is getting along. He is only too ready to say, and he is getting along terribly. "This institution is really messed up. These officers are messed up. This place is a mess. I only have a few months to go until I max out, but I might have to get a fresh charge; I'm about to deck somebody; I can't take this any more."

I'm embarrassed to say that he had been attending the classes in Christian Living too. He is middle aged in years; not much over three in behavioral control. He sleeps on the top bunk. His cellmate always takes the only seat in the cell at the little table to eat his meals, so he has to climb up and eat on his bunk. He is really persecuted.

It eats away at him until one day he comes into his cell with his tray of food. His cellmate always goes to the head of the line and gets his so that he can get dibs on the little chair at the table. He's had it! He throws his meal, tray and all, at his ugly cellmate sitting at the little chair at the table. The tray hits him and he jumps up hollering and runs out and reports it to the officer. The officer comes in and handcuffs the disgruntled man, and he spends a couple of weeks in detention. This all happens in Facility Three. Now he has been moved to Facility One and has requested to see me.

I ask him if he wants to continue in the Christian Living classes; he guesses he does. But he continues to say that he is not having any better relationships with his new cellmate nor with the officers over here. He claims they are messing with his mail, and he might just have to do what he has to do and God will have to forgive him.

Sadly enough, friends, there is a "Christianity" being taught that allows for this lifestyle. I told him bluntly that what he needed was to get right with God. He said, "I am right with God."

I said, "No you are not; no child of God acts like that."

"Well," he said, "I'm not perfect yet." Sure enough! He then observed that maybe God was just trying him to see how much he could take. I told him that God was doing nothing of the kind, but that he had no God in his life to try him to begin with. I told him that God isn't in that kind of business. I told him he was just eating the fruit of his own sinful heart.

He rose to leave and said, "Well, Reverend, I know that I have God in my life. I know Jesus. I know what the Book says, 'Be angry and sin not.' I didn't act on it yet, but if I have to I have to and God will just have to forgive me."

I looked at him and said, "You don't know the Jesus I know." I dismissed him with a mixed feeling of pity and disgust—pity for him and disgust with such a concept of Christian living.

A few minutes later I've moved over to Facility Two and another inmate comes in. The moment he enters the door he nearly bursts into tears. "Oh Chaplain, God is so precious. I've just had a wonderful season of prayer with Him.

I'm telling you, He just came into my room and talked with me and put His arms all around me and I know He loves me. He's taken all my sin away and I just can't praise Him enough. Oh it's so precious; nothing else matters. Chaplain, I just want to thank you so much because I remember that several years ago when I was still playing around with my sin I didn't really want to come and see you. But you told me not to hide from you or you would come looking for me. That's just what God did too; He came looking for me, and He's found me. Oh I just love Him, He's so precious. Now I look back over my life and see how God's hand was following me all the time. I feel so bad I didn't listen to Him." The tears were choking his words.

By now I had my own tears too. I thought back over nearly five years that I have faithfully worked with this man. I've seen him pass through deep valleys of mental depression over what he had done to his dear wife and two little girls. I've seen him struggle with fierce attacks of Satan, trying to convince him that there was no way for him to quit sinning and come clean with God. He rose and fell so many times, but he never quit. Between these two inmates, only minutes apart, I felt like I'd been plunged from cold to hot almost more quickly than I could make the adjustment; but thank God there is a grace that works. There really is such a thing as genuine Christianity.

I confess I hate this raging plague of mealy-mouthed "Christianity" (minus Christ) which has perpetrated itself in today's religious sham as prolifically as houseflies around a garbage can. Sometimes it almost seems so deeply ingrained and imbedded in men's thoughts that one hardly knows where to attack it next. But by the grace and help of God I, for one, am determined to wage war against it until I die or Jesus comes back. It is damning souls by the millions while all the preparation it gives them for eternity is the preparation to hear those awful words, "I never knew you: depart from Me, ye that work iniquity."

Just as it is in the outside world, we have an abundance of those "Christians" (please note the quotes) who are totally captivated in a do-it-yourself religious endeavor and seem to know nothing whatsoever of that "power" promised to those who "receive Him." I hear the expression used so often of those who try and fail that they "came out of their character." They really profess to be good Christians, but sometimes they "come out of their character." One man in class even justified it by saying that Jesus "came out of His character" when He cleansed the temple. I rebuked it firmly and told him that rather than coming out of his character, his real character was only coming out. It was God's true character, hatred and anger for sin, which enabled Jesus to cleanse the temple. The inmate went on to justify himself by saying that we are all still in the flesh and that sometimes we will slip over into the flesh and do things we don't want to do and then we have to ask God to forgive us.

I told him he was pulling Christ right off of the Cross. If He didn't come to destroy the works of the devil then He is a liar, and that when that old nature of sin was cleansed away that Satan put within him, he would have no trouble with his flesh. It isn't our flesh that is the problem, it's sin. God gave us our flesh; the devil gave us sin; and Jesus Christ came for the express purpose of destroying sin.

I went on to tell him that I could introduce him to a few men who were living in the very same prison that he was living in and that all I ever heard from them was, "Oh this is joy unspeakable and full of glory!" I never hear a thing from them about their surroundings. They have no need to "come out of their character," for their character has been changed by the cleansing Blood of Jesus. They are new creatures just like the Bible says they are, and it works. Friends, please help me pray that more and more of these deceived and desperately needy souls will hear that voice in the wilderness crying, "Behold the Lamb of God, which taketh away the sin of the world."

The other night the men were coming into the Bible study.

The man I mentioned in a previous letter who feels that God has sanctified him and cleansed his heart from all sin, came in with a shine on his face and with obvious excitement. He gave me a hug and said, "Praise God, I'm six months old." I didn't catch it at first and so he said, "I've lived six months without sin."

Later he came in for a visit. He said, "God's just making Himself more awesome to me all the time. Uh, do you mind if I pray?" I didn't.

Friends there is not a show on earth that can compare with watching grace work in a soul. Hollywood grovels in the dust to produce anything more sensational, if that is what one is looking for, than a soul, cleansed of sin and walking in the light. But then, laying aside mere sensation, there is nothing which satisfies the deep, inborn longing of the soul of man except the marvelous grace of our Lord Jesus Christ.

I love to listen to this man. He is so absolutely unfettered by pre-conceived expectations and by religious tutoring. He sometimes even makes it difficult for me to keep back a grin as he tries to express in the only concepts he knows, what is going on in his thrilling new walk with God. And he is deeply concerned and careful that he does not sin. He doesn't want anything to do with it.

He felt an attack of the enemy against him the other day and told me that he immediately ran to God because he didn't know whether he had sinned or not. Then he said that God just cleared it all up and he went on rejoicing. He is to go home soon, so please pray that God will help him to get his feet firmly planted on the Rock until he will never fall again.

Please pray also for the inmates who are assigned to sit with the dying men in the hospital. This has proved over and over already to be a real means of salvation, not only to the men ministered to, but to the ones doing the ministering also. One of them told me that it is keeping his cup full and running over to minister to others who are so needy. Some of them are so far gone that it might take two hours just to get a meal into them through a tube, but what an opportunity to show the love of Jesus. Several of these dying men have been led to Jesus and forgiven of their sins right in their last hours by these inmates who really know the love of God.

Thank you each one once again for your faithful prayers, and may I beg that they continue? I believe in you; I know they will, and I thank you.

In the love of Jesus,
William Cawman

†††

May 1, 2003

WHERE SHALL I BEGIN? There is so much I want to share with you this month. Isn't it good to be employed in the service of One Who makes every day such a rewarding experience? And He does this in spite of the old devil, who hates it too. The "crown of life" which is promised to the faithful in Christ Jesus is not all reserved for that great day out ahead. Oh the "crown of life" He gives day by day as we simply walk with Him. That "crown" comes not to magnify or exalt us, but to anoint us with such convulsions of desire to be and do His will that it becomes our meat and drink.

I feel an urge to tell you something. I have no doubt that, without consulting any ideas or desires of mine, God led my life into this prison as one to tell others of this great salvation which saves from sin. But with humility and gratitude I look back and realize that He also brought me here to save my own soul. I confess that some of the men God has used me to minister to, have and are also being used of God to minister to my own heart.

Some of these men have become so fully God's; they have so completely yielded everything to Him, that they are living and walking under His smile and grace in "the fullness of Christ." These men fan the hunger and thirst for more of God in my own life. They drive me to live closer to God. They dig around my roots. I love them. Some of these men have not slipped into that "form of godliness" which "denies the power thereof;" please pray that they never will. After sitting with one of them recently I felt so overwhelmed with the presence of God that it left not one bone in me that didn't cry out, "Here, Lord, I give myself to Thee."

I told in a previous letter about an older man who had lived a horrible life. His father, an artist, had had nine wives and moved all over the country. This man had known well the life of sleeping in burned out cars and cardboard boxes, doing drugs, living in hell. He was imprisoned and after a while let out on parole, but instead of going to report to his parole officer, he had gone to New York and hit the streets again, had a terrible accident and ended in the hospital and then in a nursing home. When he was finally back on his feet the authorities came after him and imprisoned him again for parole violations.

I remember well the first day he asked to talk to me a few months ago. I thought he was older than myself, but found out he wasn't. He showed all the marks of a hard life of sin. But he was ready to listen and to change. He listened carefully as I told him that he could come to Jesus and be forgiven and have a change of heart that would make him a new creature. He began to pray and ask God for just that, and just like our great Jesus, He forgave him of all the past.

I wish you could have seen the change in this man. It was not just on the inside, but on the outside as well. I think in telling you of him before, I quoted the Scripture which says that "He will beautify the meek with salvation." What an example of it he is. What was once a face hardened by sin and sorrow has become the soft and gentle face of a "gentle-man," kind and loving. He began to love the Word of God and to read it with hunger. I gave him several books about the Christian life, some of which explained the way of de-liverance from the nature as well as the guilt of sin. He never stopped. He had set out to go all the way with God.

Well, last week he came to see me, and with that gentle face beaming with divine love, he said, "Chaplain, just between you and me and God, I believe He has sanctified me. All I want is Him, more of Him. I have no desire any more for any sin. God and this Book are all I want."

Isn't that what He came to do? These things may be hidden from the wise and prudent, but our Heavenly Father cannot withhold the fullness of His grace from those "babes" who cannot live without it. As he sat telling me of all that God was doing for him and showing him through His Word, I just listened and marveled at the words coming from his lips. As someone has expressed it, it is "from the guttermost to the uttermost." Thank God for the simplicity and the power of this great salvation.

The same afternoon in which we had this precious time, another inmate came in about an hour later. This man came to the prison a few months back, from another prison. He has told me his story of a pathetic background of sin and drugs and drinking. Some time ago, someone introduced him to the saving grace of Jesus. He yielded and God broke the power of those sins in his life. He started going to church and as he began to straighten up his life, he confessed to his wrong and is now serving time for it. He is a very energetic and enthusiastic man and is afflicted severely with a desire to be seen and heard. He is one of those whom Paul speaks of, who desire to teach while they still have need of being taught. His focus has been on getting into position and ministering to others, and I have had to put the brakes on him and hold him down for some time.

This formerly enthusiastic inmate came in to see me. I asked him how he was getting along. He sat down and looked at me for a minute and then shook his head. He said, "Chaplain, I'm sick; I'm just sick. I'm so sick in my heart that it is making me sick physically. I have been trying to preach to others and I'm seeing that I'm a mess myself. I have something in me that I am not getting the victory over, and there's no use going on fooling myself."

I looked straight at him and asked him if he ever read the Scripture in Romans 6 that says, "Know ye not, that so many of us as were baptized into Jesus Christ were baptized into His death?" I told him that the whole purpose of his becoming a child of God was to let that die in him that was unlike Jesus. I said, "Brother, that thing in you that wants to be seen and heard needs to die, and death isn't a picnic. You ought to thank God that He is showing you yourself and making you sick of how you are. Just let God continue to show you until you are sick enough to die. If you don't, you will never know the glory of the resurrection side."

He dropped his head and said, "Chaplain, I was so distressed and sick over this that I asked God before I came to see you to please let you tell me what I needed to hear, and I know you are." Here's another urgent need, friends; he will not remain long, sick at heart, without making a choice either against himself, or against the Cross of crucifixion. The difference between the choices, only God and eternity can measure.

I must tell you something about another man that I have worked with for quite a while. He does suffer quite severely from emotional and mental damages from drugs, but God did say, "I am the Lord that healeth thee," didn't He? Once again he sat with me and I saw him torn between the two forces determined to make the highest bid for his soul.

I tried to get him to see that his life will never be better until he forsakes all that he knows is displeasing to God and then gets down and prays through to a change of heart. He listened and I hoped that this time it will register. He did seem sincere; in fact he has longed for something different in his life for a long time. As I tried to impress upon him that he cannot just pray a little prayer and run away, but that he must pray until he really comes into the presence of God and becomes a new man, he suddenly lit up, "I'm going to do that! I'm going to go back to my cell and as soon as I get there I am going to pray for that." We had prayer together; first I prayed and then he started to pray. He closed his prayer quite abruptly with these words, "God, I'll be talking to You in a minute." Then he hurried out the door with a new hope in his eyes. I trust he does that, for I know God will.

I have been asked to tell you something. The man whom I have written about at times, calling him "The Preacher," because he was a pastor of a type before coming into the prison, has come into a whole new liberty in Christ. He wants you each one to know it because of the following facts. I have shared with you before in one of these letters that he was here on a false charge. Ever since he first led me to believe that, and that was months before God sanctified his heart, he has never again really said that he was innocent.

Whenever our conversation would refer back to that time, he would seem to be silent in a way that made me begin to wonder if he had told me the whole truth. This may sound strange, but at the same time I could not doubt that he was fully right with God and exhibiting the fruits of the Spirit.

By some circumstances which I could not relate here, I was told that he was deeply suffering over something. He was not innocent and he longed to tell me, but he had never in his life before known "Christians" who would not have cast him out over what he had done. He was torn between two feelings: "Oh that I could get this all out in the open! But if I do, I fear I will cut off the only source of real help I have ever found in my life."

When I heard of it, I went to prayer and laid it all out before God. God began to talk to me about my own life. He showed me that even after I was sanctified, there was a period of some time that I made a conscious effort to live up to what I thought would be expected of a sanctified life. He showed me how He had weaned me, by a growing trust in Him, from the false facades that I unknowingly had sheltered myself behind, and had brought me into a liberty of just genuine honesty in every area of life. He told me that what this dear man was doing was no different; he was not willfully hiding a falsehood, but was caught in a lifetime of fear that to be perfectly honest would deprive him of the help he was finding.

I went from prayer to talk with him. When I opened the door just a crack and he realized that I would not cut him off for being absolutely open about all his past, he just melted. He poured everything out in a heap and said, "Oh I can't tell you how I have longed for this; I've suffered and prayed before God and asked how I could get rid of covering the past without cutting off this lifeline to the help I've craved for years." He thanked me over and over for opening the door he was afraid to open.

He then said, "But now there's something that is bothering me; I know you have probably shared my story with others, and I feel so bad that I've put you in this position." I told him I could easily take care of that by just telling everyone the truth. He looked so relieved and said, "Would you please do that? I want perfect clearness." That's why I have told you. We went on to talk about it, and as we did, such glory and presence of God came into the room, that he threw his arms around me with tears and said, "Oh this is what I have longed for. It's all in the past now."

Oh the beauty of perfect transparency before God, and oh the freedom that comes even when a "sin of ignorance" is finally fully cleansed from the heart. Since God has sanctified him he says that God is working on him every day, but with a full-moon face he says, "But there is no struggle any longer."

The frequent letters from the man in the northern prison whom I have told you about several times, who had such a horrible background, get better and better. He says in a recent letter that God has broken all the power of sin in his life. All glory be to the One Who gave His all and then said, "It is finished." It is, too. To all who let Him do it; the power of all sin is broken!

Thank you each one again, until they can thank you for themselves.

In Him,
William Cawman

╫

June 1, 2003

I THANK GOD THAT you are praying, and I want to thank each of you, too. God is answering and the devil is fighting. I'll tell you about God's part first; if there's any room left on the page, I'll tell on the old rat.

God has been sending us a revival throughout the services, the classes, and the Bible studies. Didn't Jesus promise, "Blessed are they which do hunger and thirst after righteousness: for they shall be filled"? Through your prayers there has been an awakening of hunger and thirst, and God is answering just as He said He would. I want to tell you of some of these scenes so that you can rejoice with us and know how to pray for us.

I'll start with a Sunday night service a couple of weeks ago. We had sung a few songs and I asked if anyone would want to give a testimony. The chance never goes unused! One after another began to stand and in a few words just give God praise for what He meant to them. God's presence began to witness that He was pleased with the offering of praise.

A man then stood and said, "I'm glad I am here tonight. I haven't been coming, and I had a book I was reading and a movie I wanted to watch, but I heard a higher power telling me I ought to come down here, and I'm really glad I came."

The men began to clap, but I motioned to him not to sit down. When they finished I said, "I know that many of you in this facility are in a drug rehab program where you are not allowed to mention any thing other than "a higher power," but we are in church now, and I want to ask you, 'Who was that higher power?'" He immediately with a smile said, "It was the Lord God."

With that another man who was fairly new and had already said something, stood up. "Chaplain, I've got to say something; I've been hiding behind that too, and I want to say that Jesus Christ is my Lord."

By now there was an excitement all over the room and men were giving praise to Jesus Christ, and He was receiving it with a wide open heart. It felt so precious that I asked the men to get on their knees in His presence. No one had to lead them in prayer; they poured out their hearts to God—some thanking and praising and some praying and seeking. This went on for some time and I felt no inclination to change the order.

Even though God's presence was so near and He was helping so many of them, one dear young man who had undoubtedly been raised around some charismatic group began to act as he had seen others do. I do believe God was really dealing with him, but as he prayed to be free from the chains of sin that had bound him, he began saying "I am free, I am free," and then began to shake all over and fell from his knees to the floor. As most of the others had become quiet, I just got up and began to preach to them from Paul's words, "Whereupon, O king Agrippa, I was not disobedient unto the heavenly vision." Everyone ignored this inmate, and he soon got up and sat quietly for the rest of the service.

The next day he came to see me and sincerely asked, "Chaplain, can you tell me what happened to me last night? I really feel that God set me free from the chains that were around me." I began to point him to the completeness that is in the sin-handling power of God, and told him that he didn't need to seek after any strange sensations or experiences outside of being delivered from the power of sin. I told him that Jesus living and reigning and saving us from sin within and without was His own witness, and that he shouldn't seek after any signs or wonders or sensational experiences apart from that. I trust he did find help and that he will find Christ all he needs.

I also want to tell you about Mother's Day evening. I was scheduled to have a service in the prison hospital and then in the minimum camp. After a short service in the hospital I wanted to go upstairs and visit some of the men who are dying or else unable to get out to services. I took a few communion cups up with me and the first man I visited was the one I told you about a couple of years ago, whom I had found on his knees in his cell dying of AIDS.

If you remember the story of how the men prayed for him and God forgave him so wonderfully, you can appreciate the good news that he has been walking a new pathway ever since. He refuses to allow any of the old unforgiveness or bitterness that had torn him all apart, get back into his heart. Due to some very unusual circumstances which I cannot disclose here, he is actually being held in the prison unlawfully, and everyone seems to know it and just raise their eyebrows and shrug their shoulders when he is mentioned. He is never allowed out of his room to be with other prisoners or to go to any activities or to church, even though he longs to be there.

In spite of that, he refuses to blame God but just says over and over, "How can I ask for anything? God saved my life. I would have been dead and I know it."

I never expected him to last long when I first met him, but he has seemed better physically ever since God saved him. Well, we had a good visit and then he looked at me and said, "God has been really laying it on my heart to pray for a real revival to break out right here in this prison; I mean a revival from the administration right on down to us. I know too, that for God to answer that prayer, the revival must begin in me, and that's what I am praying for." I was so touched by it as I assured him that we would join with him in prayer for that very thing. I gave him communion which he hadn't had in years, possibly since childhood, and left him thanking God for His wonderful grace.

I then went to the next cell where lies a very sad case. He is a thin black man who has been in prison longer than anyone I can remember here (we can identify how long they have been in by their state number). A few weeks ago some of the inmates ganged up on him and beat him up so horribly that he is now a total paraplegic, and cannot move a single part of his body nor can he respond in any way. It looks pretty doubtful whether he will ever come out of it because he is wasting away to just a skeleton with no ability to eat. He has a trachea tube through which he frequently gurgles and coughs. His eyes are open, but it is hard to know whether he is seeing or not.

I spent some time with this pathethic man, standing over him and reading from the Bible and praying and singing choruses to him. I talked to him as though he could hear me; most of the doctors think he can. If you remember him, please say a prayer for him and maybe you will see the answer to your prayer some day on the other side. Across the hall I found another paraplegic who said he is a Christian and that Jesus has forgiven his sins. He wanted to take communion so I had to hold it to his lips as he cannot move any of his limbs.

After visiting a couple more, it was time for the service in the minimum camp. We opened the service with prayer and then I quickly sensed that these men had been thinking a lot about their mothers. I set aside what I had planned and just asked them if any of them would like to say something about their mother.

It would be hard to describe what followed. As one after another wanted to pay a tribute to a good mother, tears began to form; in fact I felt like crying myself. At that point I wanted to go give my own mother her third hug for the day. One dear man with no front teeth and with a far-away look in his eyes said, "I'd like to say that my mother was not just my mother; she was my best friend," and I could sense the longing—"Oh if I could just see her now." I couldn't help thinking of the song, "Could I Pray Like a Child Again." I really believe God was using the moments to break up some hearts that needed it, so I just let them go on with it for a while. It didn't seem that there was a man in the room who wasn't touched.

Finally one man said, "I'd like to say something to those of you who still have your mother; appreciate her." I was think-ing as I listened to them, of the tragedy that they had just now come to appreciate God's wonderful gift of "Mother." I set aside my message for them that night and talked to them for a while about the goodness of the Shepherd who sometimes has to break the leg of that wandering lamb in order for it to appreciate the Shepherd and the fold.

Then I must tell you (and I see my paper is running out) about the Christian Living classes the last two weeks. Oh how God is helping us! Please keep praying especially for these classes, from 8:30 to 10:30 on Monday, Tuesday and Friday mornings. Perhaps God is answering the prayer of that man in the hospital right in these classes. There has been such hun-ger and thirst for truth among the men.

Last Friday was a special visitation from heaven all through the class time. But then this Friday—how can I describe it? Early in the discussion a man asked, "Chaplain, you keep tell-ing us that the nature, the body of sin can be completely de-stroyed from our hearts. Why do so many teachers say, and why does the original Greek word indicate that in Romans 6:6 the body of sin is simply rendered powerless? That doesn't say that it is destroyed, does it? Where does the Bible say that sin is actually destroyed?"

I said, "Well, let's address your rendering of the subject first. Supposing the Greek word says that sin is rendered powerless. What on earth is sin anyway? Can you see it? Can you put a shape on it? Can you see the Holy Spirit or put a shape to Him? But is He not spoken of as a *Power?* What does sin consist of except a power within us to choose wrong? What is left if sin is rendered powerless? Isn't that the same as sinless? But here's the problem; many people want to think that grace just puts a harness on the power of sin, but didn't Jesus come for the express purpose of de-stroying it? Now what makes you think that an omnipo-tent God with all His desire for cleanliness, would kill the old giant of sin and then leave a stinking rotting carcass lying around in the temple that He indwells? Come on men, God makes sense, doesn't He?"

The discussion went on and on and God was just filling and thrilling me as I followed His lead and left no room for all the sin-sparing, mealy-mouthed, shabby and insufficient religions of today. Suddenly I realized an hour and a half had gone by. Just then a hand was meekly raised at one side. It was "The Preacher."

"Chaplain, it seems to me that where the whole problem lies is in this. Most of us here have been taught all our lives by teachers who were living in sin. When you are living in sin yourself, you cannot endorse the thought that you could be rid of it. But I'd like to say that when the old carnal mind dies, you'll see full deliverance from sin from cover to cover in this Book. It's not a matter of where is it; that's what this Book is all about, getting rid of sin."

Friends, I honestly believe that the same tongue of fire that sat on the disciples at Pentecost was moving his to speak those words. They went like lightning through the class, and the Holy Spirit was doing His office work in grand style. Oh bless God; please keep praying for these men as they begin to really awaken to the reality of Christ's work on the cross.

I need to tell you something very plainly, even if at the expense of appearing to abandon modesty. In times like these, again and again, I feel the Holy Spirit beginning to move in the tops of the trees and then like a rush of holy light, Scripture after Scripture, thought after thought falls from above and from nowhere else. Some Scriptures come that I had never connected before with the proof at hand, but God just pours them in.

Friends, in times like these, I know you are praying. I am humbled by it and overwhelmed by it, but please do not stop. I only wish I could in a more effective way share the glory of these moments with you. There is nothing on earth that equals the atmosphere created by the powerful agency of the answered prayer of Jesus, "And I will pray the Father, and He shall give you another Comforter, that He may abide with you forever...and when He is come, He will reprove the world of sin, and of righteousness, and of judgment...He will guide you into all truth..." Please pray earnestly that more of these men will also allow the fulfillment of His prayer, "Sanctify them through Thy truth."

There's so much more to tell, but let me wind up with an earnest request. Just as God is moving in a real way among the hearts here, the devil is mad about it. One of the officers here started a prayer and Bible study group for officers and staff every other week. We meet on our own time during lunch break and study the Bible and pray together. More and more have been joining the group. The idea came originally from a similar thing in the California state prisons. Now New York has started it, and it has been very good.

Just the other week a female officer was seriously wounded in an automobile accident. The officer in charge of the Bible studies went to the hospital to see her and she broke down. "I want to ask you something. I have joined many others in making fun of you up there in those Bible studies, but we all know where you are. I'm sorry and I want you to forgive me, and can you help me give my heart to Jesus?"

He could have shouted with joy, but instead he began to pray and talk with her until she felt God forgave her. She said, "I'll be joining you after this." Well, the powers to be in Trenton heard what was going on and demanded to know who started it and where they got the permission. Fortunately the proper permissions had been obtained and with blessing upon it. The chief, the administrator, the captain all informed Trenton that they had better not touch it, that it had done nothing but good. The California chapter was contacted and they sent all the proof that it was legal and even assigned an attorney to the officer who started it. It seemed it was over with, but you know Satan. The battle is raging over it and that is about all I could safely say in this letter, but please help us pray. I'll close with one blatantly politically incorrect observation—If it were not for the fact that it was in the name of Jesus, there would be no problem. But then, we know that Name, don't we?

With gratitude and love,
William Cawman

PS. One more note of victory: Since that Friday class I heard that "The Preacher" had to go to the hospital over the weekend. On Monday afternoon I went to visit him. He had suddenly started passing blood on Sunday and discovered that he had a bleeding ulcer. I found him sitting on the edge of the hospital bed. As I entered his room he laid back and the tears started coming to his eyes as he said, "I know that all things work together for good to them that love God. God is so good."

We visited for just a few minutes and had prayer together and only those of you who know the beauty of the bond of the family of God can imagine what a time it was. We shed tears together, put ourselves on the altar anew, and committed all things into the ever loving hands of that God Who is so good. As we visited, he referred back to the Friday class time. "Chaplain, as I listened to you and marveled at the work of God, it all came through so clearly. I had to say something, and the words that came out of my mouth were not my words. But I know one thing: I am more deeply convinced than ever, and it is sealed to my heart, that I can live without sin."

So what if the devil hates us as long as we can be possessed of this blessed assurance? Sorry about the extra page, but remember I told you that if you didn't stop praying I would not be able to get it all in one page. I'll try hard next time; please don't stop. Thank you again.

15
DEALING WITH DARKNESS

July 1, 2003

W
ELL, HERE WE ARE in Friday night Bible study again. You are there too, because you have prayed for us, so let me share it with you.

For months we have been working through a Bible study on the "Heart Life of Man." We started with the created heart, moved on to the fallen heart, and then have spent considerable time discussing the Biblical viewpoint of the awful disease of sin. Now we are ready to look at the way back to God from the end of the road of sin. We began to look at what it really means to be forgiven of God and to become a new creature in Christ.

We looked at the popular religious expression of today, "Accept the Lord Jesus Christ as your personal Savior." We saw that it is certainly Scriptural and necessary to do just that, but we asked if this is all that we are told to do in the Book of God. After all, we have seen Jesus words that "Man shall not live by bread alone, but by every word that proceedeth out of the mouth of God."

I used the illustration that several years before my wife-to-be received me, I had already received her; but my receiving did nothing to begin a relationship until she had received me. I asked them if this is a one-sided transaction that we can do all by ourselves. It would appear so from many religious exercises which claim to introduce one into the Christian life; but what about the other half of the relationship? What about God's word in II Corinthians 6:17, "Wherefore come out from among them, and be ye separate, saith the Lord, and touch not the unclean thing; and I will receive you"?

I asked them, "When you professed to receive the Lord Jesus Christ, did He receive you?" If He did, John says, "As many as received Him, to them gave He power to become the sons of God..." They are not only received of Him, but they receive from Him power to come away from sin and be separate from it and touch it not.

A man on the very front row had been listening intently along with the rest. Some who have found it to be true were glowing with the reality of it; others were pondering deeply. Our man lifted a finger. "Let me get this straight." He held out the case to his eyeglasses and pointed to it. "Here I am; I'm not saved." He moved his case to the other side. "Now here I am, I'm saved. Do you mean to tell me that now that I'm saved I will no longer be committing the sins that I committed when I was over here?" (pointing to the former position of his case.)

I answered, "Yes sir, that is exactly what I meant to say because that is exactly what God's Word says. John tells us that 'Whosoever is born of God doth not commit sin.'"

The Bible study erupted in clapping and praise to God. Those who are saved and know it were beaming with delight. Dear friends, these men have been lied to long enough. They want to know the truth. Way down deep in the hearts of men, they know better even when they are lied to by soft-pedaling, themselves-sinning, so-called preachers of the Word, who distort it to fit any state of rebellion against God they care to. Thank God there are yet hungry hearts who really want to hear the truth plain and clear and true to God's Word.

Well, we went on to discuss what grace really does when it transforms a man until he is acceptable to God. We made the statement that some of Paul's description of himself in Romans chapter seven is not the description of a born-again child of God. The time was up all too soon, but there was one more question from the front row of chairs. A big veteran of Vietnam said, "Well, Chaplain, I'm not sure if I understand. See this might work while we are in here, but I'll honestly confess that I have lived all my life in fornication and adultery, and I don't think I can help it. I don't know what to do because when I get out of here and the temptation faces me, I'm sure I'll commit adultery again."

I looked him straight in the face and simply asked, "Why?"

"Well, I just don't see how I can help it."

I looked at him again and stepping right in front of him said, "Sir, if you want to go to heaven, go back to your cell and get on your knees and place your finger on John 1:12 and don't get up until you have received that promised power to go and sin no more." Again the class broke into applause, but it was high time to leave.

Tuesday morning came and time for Christian Living class. We hadn't gone far before a man who has really been seeking to be made perfectly whole said, "Chaplain, I wish you could explain a little more about Romans seven. You said the other night in Bible study that Paul was not a born-again child of God at the time he was speaking about. I want to know because I really do love God and I believe I am His child, but I still find that law in me that is contrary to Him."

I started at the beginning of the chapter and showed them that in that one chapter is found every state of grace through which Paul passed from a dead Pharisee to a fully delivered man. I told them that the reason some get confused about Paul's state of grace is because Paul never stopped between the stages of his conformity to the entire call of God. First he is a dead legalist; next he says he sees what he ought to be and do but has no power to do it; next he finds a new life born within until he cries out, "I delight in the law of God after the inward man." That is certainly the mark of a regenerated heart, and yet he still finds "another law in my members..." and crying to be delivered from this "body of...death," he ends up, "I thank God through Jesus Christ our Lord." Paul never stopped in his quest to be obedient to the heavenly vision.

I then went on until before I knew it I was testifying to them to every detail of the work of God in my own heart and life, and I was so happy I was nearly shouting at them. The dear brother who had asked for more of Romans seven sat with his head in his hands and finally came up with both hands in the air. "Oh I thank the Holy Spirit; I thank the Holy Spirit; I never understood this before, but I want it!" Please pray that he will get it and get it soon, just like Paul did.

And then back for a minute to the Vietnam vet. By the way, this huge man was sent as an 18-year old to the conflict over there. The first time they attacked an enemy force he went to look at what they had done. As he put it, when he saw blood and guts all over the road it unnerved him, so someone gave him some brandy to drink. That calmed him down and then they introduced him to the world of drugs. He took drugs until it didn't bother him at all to kill, and he finally got to the place where he was enjoying killing so much that the army discharged him to get rid of him. From there on his life was one rocky road until he ended up in prison.

Well, a couple days after his question in Bible study, he came to see me and said, "Chaplain, I don't know what to do. I see now that I've been living in sin all my life. What do I do?" I asked him if he really honestly never knew he was living in sin. He said he never once thought about it, but just grew up living in sin without ever thinking about what he was doing. I told him to ask himself one honest question: "Do I really want to go to heaven?" Then if his answer was "Yes," he could go to God and He would tell him just what he needed to do to straighten up his life. Isn't it so restful to know that we can leave some tangles in the hands of Infinite Wisdom and not have to try to straighten them out ourselves?

In the Christian Living class in Facility Two that same week someone raised the question about really living entirely free from sin. As I began to point to the Scripture it came alive with great freshness to my own heart and again I began testifying to them. In those times I know that some of you are praying and oh how wonderfully God answers. Before long I felt so full of grace and glory I stopped and said, "Men I feel so full of God's presence right now that I believe I could break off a great big chunk for every one of the 3400 men in this prison and there would be some to spare, but I can't, I can only try to tell you about it."

Paul said, "I *know* Whom I have believed…" These are times I wish I could share with each of you who are praying in a more effective way than just trying to tell you about it. But how can I do this? My heart is melted with unworthiness and gratitude for each prayer that you have faithfully offered for us. I just received a little note in shaky handwriting. There is no name, but I recognize the address. "Dear Bro…I'm sending these tracts; hope you can use in jail services; confined to a wheelchair I can't. At 95 yrs old, wife 90, we enjoy His presence. We pray for you." Eternity alone will place the laurels where they truly belong.

A new inmate arrived a short while ago and placed a request to see a chaplain. I sat down with him and he began to tell his story. He had a good business, plenty of money, a nice home and fancy car—in short, he had the American dream. But he said, "I've got to find a new sense of direction. I need something different than women and drugs. I mean, this isn't what I had in mind for my life, to be sharing a toilet with another man."

I looked at him and said, "Is that all you want, just an escape from the wages of the sin you have been living in? Or do you really want to give your life to Jesus?" He wasn't sure yet; we have a ways to go. I asked if he would like to have continuing visits and he said he would. We will too, and I ask you to pray that light wiii dawn on his dark soul and that he will not become offended, but walk in it.

He went on to tell me that he had been reading the Bible, which he had never read before, but that he was really struggling with it. He said that he liked the words of Jesus, but that there were some stories in the Old Testament that he found it pretty difficult to swallow. But then, he said he couldn't really understand either why Jesus died on the cross. "Wasn't He already God? What did He gain by dying on the cross? It didn't help Him get to heaven, did it? I mean, He was already there before He died. What was it all about?"

And I thought to myself, "Is this 'Christian' America?" As I simply explained to him that Jesus died for him not for Himself, it seemed to be an entirely new thought to him. Such utter blindness one might expect from a derelict of the under life, but this man had at his fingertips all that America stands for. Isn't it sad beyond words? But there is hope if you will pray for him, for Paul told the Ephesians, "But now in Christ Jesus ye who sometimes were far off are made nigh by the blood of Christ."

I want to ask you to pray for the few men who are being assigned to sit with the dying inmates who are sent into the hospital here. Both men have told me the same thing, and that is this: they feel that God is testing them and trying their faith, and that sometimes the trial of sitting with men who are angry at everything and yet dying is almost too great to endure. But they both feel that God is stretching them through it to live closer to Him. I keep telling them to let it drive them deeper into the Blood of Jesus, and I believe it is.

Right now there are three dying men in the hospital. One of them is so angry and full of sin and the devil, that it is a real trial to even be around him, but they are doing their best to look for a door through which to get to him with the love of Jesus. One of the men just left my office and almost in tears told me that one of the other men is now in a coma and the nurse told him that the man cannot hear or understand anything he would tell him. Regardless of that the dear brother sits and reads chapter after chapter from the Word of God to him. Yesterday he said he went to him and took his hand in his. He spoke to the dying man and asked if he would like for him to pray for him, to squeeze his hand. The man squeezed his hand and he prayed with him. It brings tears to the brother's eyes as he tells me how God is increasing his own faith through this ministry. This brother is one who I have seen over the past five years come from the depths of spiritual devastation, through long and fierce struggles, into a relationship with God that will not waver. He has made his choice to go with God.

Another man who has been attending the Christian Living classes has recently asked to visit with me. He is a professional juggler and has worked in many of the famous circuses and known many of the top performers and entertainers in the world. He has traveled all over the world in his business. Now he is open and honest about how empty that whole life is. He has watched the backstage life of the world's best entertainment professionals and has seen first hand how empty and disappointing life is except for the few moments in the spotlight. I'm trying my best to show him how that whole thing is such a distortion of what man was created for, and how he must forsake it all if he is to find what his heart is missing. You might pray for him also.

But now let me close with an answer to your prayers. If you remember the last paragraph of last month's letter, I will go on from there. Yesterday we met together to celebrate the second anniversary of the correctional staff fellowship. We wanted to give thanks to the officer who has put it together and who was under attack for it and give him a gift certificate to a Bible book store. We also were privileged to have his wife with us who recently nearly died of a heart attack. She testified with tears and thanks for the prayers of the group. Then the officer spoke for a few minutes of the power of God's Word and how it really changes our lives into men and women who are fit to work with and be around.

At the very same time as we were honoring him here he has been selected at the national level as "Best in the Business" as a correctional officer. He openly attributes all he is and has done to his strong attachment to Jesus Christ.

Well, the commissioner's office in Trenton had sent a well-known man (I'll not put his name in here) to spy out what it was all about since there was such static coming out of head office to this Bible study in the prison. He came in and sat at the other end of the table from where I was so I could see him through the whole thing. As the officer spoke, he became absorbed in what he was saying. The assistant administrator was also listening and wiping tears from her eyes. As soon as it was over, the man walked directly toward me with a look in his eyes of "I can't believe it." He shook my hand and said, "I wouldn't have missed this for anything; I'm glad I was here." He then told all concerned that he was going back to Trenton to tell them this should spread through the whole state. Isn't God wonderfully able to handle His own business? Thank you for praying. Will you do it again?

With deep gratitude to Him and you,
William Cawman

August 1, 2003

THREE THOUSAND, FOUR HUNDRED men, each with a soul that is just as precious to Jesus as yours and mine, are one month closer to eternity. I do believe that a few of them are closer to heaven—but what of the ninety and nine? How many of these are still held in chains of addiction and sin? How many of them are shut up in the narrow confines of unforgiveness and bitterness? How many just plain don't care? How many are full of hatred and revenge; and how many have been released this month who will go out to repeat the pattern of sin all over again?

How many of these men are caught in the deadly snare of sinning religion, whether that be Muslim, Jewish, or a form of godliness which denies any power? I'm sorry to start out like this, but I'm also sorry that there are still way too many on their way to an eternal hell.

Sometimes it overwhelms one to think that perhaps there's something more that could be done which would make the difference in where some precious soul spends that eternal forever. Somehow, too many are still slipping through our fingers. Too few are really waking up to the reality of what life is all about. God forgive me if I have been guilty of painting the picture with too few colors. Thank God for every victory, but oh the burden for the many who are as dark within as sin itself. Some of these even sit in church with us; they listen to Gospel truth; they sing the hymns together; but they are lost— just plain lost. I do thank you each one, friends, for your prayers, but we are far from finished yet. The harvest is ripe, and the false prophets abound. Oh may God help us yet to reach as many as possible before it is too late, forever too late.

It is painful to see a man begin to respond to the pull from heaven, make some steps in the right direction, look the Gospel right in the face and acknowledge it is the answer, and then turn back to his nothingness again. It makes you want to scream in his ear sometimes, *"What on earth is there to go back to? Haven't you had enough yet? Will it go any better this time?" Is the devil going to be your friend now?"* Oh the insanity of the carnal mind.

I want to share a request with you because the inmate has asked me to. Perhaps for as long as I have been writing these letters I have mentioned a man by the name of C——. God worked miracles in his life a few years ago, delivering him instantaneously from years of heavy addiction to heroin and other drugs. He sought God fervently for some time, and faced the clear light of holiness within. At times he felt he was just around the corner from that full cleansing that he needed. He is gifted in working with people. Wherever he is, he doubles the attendance at church. He has the respect of the prison officers, and they trust him with many privileges.

But for all that, the devil tripped him up. He got his eyes off of the prize and onto doing some legal work that he felt would help others out of their trouble. Then he felt he could better himself by a change of custody and went back for a retrial. During all this time, he was deaf to the call he had been listening to. The devil had his ear almost entirely. But oh the faithful "Hound of Heaven."

Everything fell through; he came back to this prison broken and needy and ready to listen again. God is really dealing with his heart again, and one day as we sat together I got a little rough with him. I asked him if he was happy with the turnout of the past few months. He said, "Absolutely not."

I said, "Do you know why? You have too many friends who love you and want to see you make it for God, praying for you. God would not let you find satisfaction in those pursuits you were after over top of their prayers. Now tell me something. Do you want them to stop praying for you so that you can get what you were wanting?"

He looked at me with terror in his eyes and said, "Oh no, please. Please tell them to keep praying for me."

Just last Friday he asked me, "Did you tell my friends my message? Will they pray for me?"

Will you? I know you will. God is not finished with this man yet, and if we were able to relate to his background we would not lose patience with him, either. Remember, he never knew the existence of a father, nor the love of a mother. His earthly mother did not want him and what little she had to do with him was to push him into the drug traffic to satisfy her cravings. At the age of seventeen, having just gotten out of prison for stealing a car to take his mother on a drug deal, he brought her some money from another deal and she bought a dose of drugs with it and overdosed and died. Can you place yourself, even remotely, in his shell and try to look out of his windows? But God has already worked miracles of change in him; let's pray him clear through it all.

Oh my, let me tell you something. I had a few minutes this morning between class in Facility Two and visits in Facility Three, and that is when I wrote the paragraphs above. I closed down the computer and stepped out into the compound to come over to Facility Three, and one of the good brothers was just walking out also to go to the hospital to sit with patients. His face was beaming.

He started right in. "Chaplain, how are you? I'm so blessed. This is such a wonderful pathway, walking with Jesus. He's just giving me the victory over sin and the devil and it's so wonderful. Oh yeah, the old dirty devil comes to my mind and tells me to take a look at what's on the television, or to think a certain thought, but I just tell him, 'Not today, devil; I'm walking with Jesus.' I just feel so blest; I just love the Lord."

Now if that isn't a case of the Monday blues—that is, I mean clear blue skies over your head on Monday. These dear trophies of the redeeming grace of Jesus make the burdens lighter and make one feel like traveling onward and upward. If others don't want Him, these do, and they are proving so beautifully the words of Peter, "Unto you therefore which believe He is precious." This is what I was trying so clumsily to say in the first couple of paragraphs, friends. Please pray a few more through to this kind of victorious grace, will you? I thank you in advance. Praise His name!

Now for another precious scene. My wife and I had been away for a couple of days at a camp meeting in central Pennsylvania, and we hated to leave. But I had promised myself that I would not miss the Christian Living class and the Bible studies on Friday, as we have been gone quite a bit lately. We stayed as long as we dared, leaving the camp around ten o'clock Thursday evening and driving home. We crawled into bed around three or three-thirty and got up and into the prison in time for class at 8:30. It was a good class, followed by visiting inmates and then the Bible study in the minimum camp.

I was now in the chapel in Facility One, ready for Bible study at 7:30 that evening. I'll admit, I was feeling a little run down. The men started coming in, and soon two of them who minister to the dying inmates in the hospital came in and began to tell me of a man who had died that morning. They had been working with him for some time, and he felt he had given his heart to God. They were called in early that morning as he was slipping away, and as they sat by his bedside they began to read to him from the Bible. They read on and on, and finally asked him if he wanted them to stop. He said, "No, don't stop," so they kept on reading, and about 5:20 in the morning he slipped on to heaven. As they told me about it, it seemed that a heavenly presence settled down in the room.

We began to speak about him to the men. We began together to imagine what he must be enjoying just then, only fourteen hours in heaven. We talked about how he must be looking on the face of Jesus and seeing "Him as He is." We talked about how he left his sick body, his aches and pains, his temptations as well as the tempter all behind, and was now made perfectly whole. We imagined that he had already met Abraham and Noah and Moses and Joseph, and that when he met them they did not look down their noses at him and say, "You old jail bird, you; just sit over there." Oh no, in the presence of Him who died for us, we are all just sinners saved by grace; Christ is all in all. Before long it seemed the very heaven was open over us; he had joined that heavenly "cloud of witnesses," and was looking down upon us.

I said to them, "Men, he is calling us to come. He is saying to us, 'Leave everything else behind; it doesn't matter; nothing else matters, just come.'" For quite a while we couldn't move away from that peculiar presence. One of our own had gone to be with Jesus forever and forever. I believe the veil was rent for a few short moments, letting us hear first-hand the call of those beyond.

Then we started into the topic of our Bible study for the evening. We have been trying to come clear on the need for a real work of grace which leaves us a changed, new creation in Christ, so we told them this: "It is not correct theology to say that God does it all." They began to look a little strangely. I said, "It's not; that's not Biblically correct to say that, because God has told us to do some things. He told us to seek Him. He told us to cleanse our hands. He told us to confess and forsake our sins. All of these God is expecting us to do."

They just began to see the truth of it when I said, "All right, now listen: It is correct theology to say that God does it all." Again they looked a little puzzled until I told them, "There is nothing you can do to save yourself; there is nothing you can do to merit your salvation, or to earn it. God does it all; but He will not do it until you do what He has told you to do."

Grins appeared everywhere as they began to see the truth. It is so necessary at times to preach *"line upon line,"* until they see through the false teaching they have been immersed in that God requires nothing at all of us. He paid it all, and we can go scot free, and go right on sinning as before and He will love us anyway. No one was asleep; no one was bored; no one was wanting to quit, and I forgot all about the tired feelings I had a little while before.

The next Friday night in the minimum unit once again God visited us with wonderful power. We were studying the marks of a new creature in Christ. The men were listening with such rapt attention that it was a thrill to give them the truth of God's Word and His work in the soul. I would sincerely ask that you pray God to follow up this seed with His convicting Spirit. I do believe that many of these men are realizing, perhaps for the first time, that there is reality in salvation, and that what they have heard all of their lives is totally a human religion which has failed to do anything for them. Pray that they will believe it to the saving of their souls.

One more thing—a few months ago I told you about how "The Preacher" finally emptied out the last false cover he was living under and came clear with it all. Since then he has been living with such a hunger to grow and let God make him all that he needs to be.

He came to me again wanting to talk about something. He was feeling a burden upon him to write to some people that he had damaged and let them know he was forever finished with that lifestyle and tell them what God had done for him. But he said along with it, he felt the need of God's help to do it in such a way that it would close that door in his life forever. As he spoke about it I felt God powerfully witnessing to my own heart that he was doing exactly the right thing. Once again, the faithful Holy Spirit is doing His work, and doing it so wondrously. Isn't God good? Thank you each one; I really mean it.

In His love,
William Cawman

+++

September 1, 2003

Don't deny it; we all like to be loved. Listen to this prayer from a dear brother in prison who has listened and loved and learned for several years now. "Oh God, we want to thank you for our dear chaplain who we love with all our heart. Now help him to decrease so that You can increase."

Oh how that thrills my heart. Will you help him pray that prayer? Will you pray that these men can see, even as the three disciples saw as the cloud of transfiguring glory lifted from them, "No man, save Jesus only"?

Thank you so much for your prayers through another month. Let me tell you a few scenes from how God is answering them.

I must start one more time with a man I have told you about often. You will remember the one who presented to me the greatest challenge I have ever met in my life. I hope to never again meet a man so wrecked by sin. But many of you prayed for him at his lowest state, and God heard—did He ever! This man is a glorious miracle of redeeming grace as well as of heal-ing power, physically and spiritually. He is, as you will remem-ber, in one of the northern state prisons now, but writes very often, and his letters simply glow with love and grace.

But I have a confession to make to all those who have prayed for him. I have searched my own heart over something that occurs when I get a letter from him. To be honest, I open the letter with trembling fingers and a pounding heart. I do be-lieve I trust the power of God's redeeming grace, but I have also seen many turn back and become offended at the claims of the Cross. And so, I open the envelope and unfold the letter with some degree of anxiety. I'm sorry if that is lack of faith or lack of something that I should have, but I admit the way it is. Then I begin to read, but soon it is difficult to see through the moisture in my eyes. Yes, praying friends, God answers prayer! He is answering your prayers! And if you continue to so pray that God has to stretch my faith, go ahead. I'll do my best to keep up. But then, if we are to spend all eternity entranced by an ever-expanding vision of Who God really is, perhaps it's not a bad exercise to let Him stretch our capacity and vision here. I'm willing—go ahead!

One of the inmates who ministers to the dying patients in the hospital asked me if I could go see one of them. As soon as I saw him I remembered him from being in the Bible studies and in church. He is fast dying of cancer that has spread all through him. As we had prayer together, I felt such a bond with his spirit. No sooner did I finish praying than he looked up, apologized for not being able to turn over because of the pain, and said, "Oh that prayer felt so good." It did to me too. He is my brother; he is as black as I am white—the Blood of Jesus Christ God's Son has made us one in Him.

This is one of the most precious ministries in the prison; inmates sitting by the bedsides of dying men and watching for the door to crack open. In fact, (I'm smiling right now) they sometimes push on it pretty hard. They are not allowed to proselytize or to offensively cross faith boundaries, but the fact is that when you really love Jesus it's awfully hard to hold it back. And so, like determined and zealous salesmen, they often get their toes in a very small crack.

One of them recently told me the following: he was assigned to sit by a certain man, and the social workers and officers told him that there was no use even trying to communicate with him, he was so far gone. They said, "He's just a dead man."

The inmate told me he couldn't do that. He said, "I felt in my heart that I wanted to treat him just like he was my father." He began to talk with the dying man, and then he began to read the Bible to him. He read on and on and soon he found his eyes filling with tears as God was talking to him out of His Word while he was trying to read it to the other man. He said, "I just felt so melted as I realized that God was talking to me. Oh, God is so good to me."

These inmates say that it is not easy to sit beside one dying man after another, especially if they have no assurance that they opened their hearts to God before they died. But every one of the men doing this ministry say that it drives them closer to God. They feel so deeply the need of His help to reach the other man.

For some time now I have noticed a very quiet, small-framed man who faithfully attends the classes in Christian Living and is very regular at church and Bible study. I was drawn to his open countenance and to his ready response to close truth, so I decided to schedule a visit with him and get better acquainted.

We hadn't visited long before I found a man who had been just drinking it all in and living it out in his own quiet corner of his world. He was not struggling with truth nor with the sinning business, but was just as happy as could be in the new life that God has given him. It was an especially heart-warming visit, and it reminded me again of a verse in II Timothy which says, "Nevertheless the foundation of God standeth sure, having this seal, The Lord knoweth them that are His..."

How many souls, God only knows, are His and His alone,

and are walking with Him right in the midst of a crooked and perverse world around them. I would never have known how precious this dear soul was, had I not for some reason decided to have a visit with him. But then on the other hand, something did attract me to him; that shine of contentment and peace on his face did rather resemble quite strongly one of our family's traits, didn't it?

We have plenty enough of the type of "Christians" who are obsessed with an appetite to be seen and heard, and who are more interested in doing than in being. It is so rewarding to find a man who is not seeking to be noticed, who is not trying to rule over others, but is just walking in contentment with his hand in God's. Believe me, we will become better acquainted.

And then I must tell you of another man who has me excited. He recently came here from another prison, and my supervisor told me that he has been a troublemaker everywhere he has gone. The first time he came to see me this inmate brought a typed-out program that he was very interested in getting off the ground and into the church. He presented a whole plan of developing a "worship team" in the church, and he had already talked several of the men into signing up for it. They would practice together and then would present the worship part of the services.

I very kindly began to ask him where he could see any foundation for such a thing in the Word of God, either by example or precept. I told him it was a modern concept that was totally adverse to what God is looking for in His desire for us to worship Him. I told him that worship must spring from the love and devotion of the heart, not be produced by the talents of humanity manipulating the emotions. I suggested that it would be well for him to just sit back a while and dig in and see what God might want to do for him before he tried to do something for others.

Amazingly enough, he let go of it and began to do just that. A few weeks later here are some of his comments: "I never knew I was such a mess. Oh, God is just cleansing me and cleansing me. I never knew all this was wrong with me. Chaplain, you told me that God wanted me to die to self. I never knew it would be like this. It hurts but it feels good. He is showing me things that I never knew were part of me. I want to die to this, whatever it takes."

A church from the outside contacted him and offered him a position when he gets out. He told them he is not interested. He said, "I'm not ready for that; I need my own heart cleansed."

My supervisor teaches classes he calls Deacon Classes, in which he trains the men to take a responsible position in the church. It is good training for them. But when he approached this man who he had said has always been a troublemaker and asked him if he wanted to join the deacon classes, he backed away. He was told that was the only way to become active in the church, but this inmate replied that he was not ready to become active in the church because there was too much work that needed to be done in his own heart. He said he needed to be cleansed of what he is seeing wrong in his own heart. My supervisor said to him, "You've been in chaplain Cawman's classes," and dropped the subject. I've given him some books on holiness and he is devouring them. Please pray for him that he will "die."

Another older man arrived recently from one of the other prisons. He looks to be in his sixties, a black man with gray hair and a very grandfatherly look. I do wish you would remember him too in your prayers. He is not the typical repeat offender "doing another bid." He signed up for the classes in Christian Living, and twice last week he tried to express himself and his need of help and just broke down in tears. When that happens, believe it or not, the other men become broken themselves. One will get up and go get him some tissue, and then they will rally around with such amazing support.

Friday night this inmate asked the men to pray for him and then just sat down with his head in his hands and began to weep. He is so crushed over the life he has lived and how he has disappointed God and his family. I asked the men to gather around him and have prayer, and nearly every man in the room formed a circle around him and began to pray.

He touches my heart so deeply. It is bad enough to see the young and careless serving time for their folly while they can still flip their heads and think life is still going to be all right. But it is really sad to see an older man who has allowed some awful sin to tear him away from his family, away from his life, away from his manhood and self-respect. Oh the cruelty of the mastery of sin. One moment of sin, a lifetime of regret; it is the story told over and over again.

With a new influx of men into the facility where we have the Friday night Bible study, we have backtracked a little and gone back over the groundwork of what it really means to be a child of God. Last Friday night we were dwelling on that wonderful Scripture, I John 3:9. We were pointing out how good it was to seek to measure up to the Scripture rather than explain the passage to our carnal minds.

We told them that when we are "born of God," and "His seed remains" in us, it is just as fully against our nature to sin as it would be against the capacity of a snake to fly like an eagle. I said, "Men I feel so in love with Jesus right now that I have no capacity to rob a bank on my way home. I don't want to do it, and I won't. It's no struggle at all. I'm born of God and I am not sinning. But if I should begin to cool off in my love for Jesus, and then should begin to yield to the attraction of something else, I could let His seed slip away from me and take on some other seed. I could begin to develop a love for money and finally yield to avarice and little by little develop a capacity to rob a bank. I can't imagine doing it now however, because the seed of Jesus is filling and thrilling me with desire to do His will."

As we went on examining the inner heart of a real child of God and trying to steer them to something higher than the concept of today's sick religious mental acceptance of a "Jesus" who can do no more than cover up who they are and mop up after them, the atmosphere became electric. They were all eyes and ears. Just as we finished trying to Scripturally paint the portrait of a child of God, I said, "But now I must tell you this, that even within this heart so in love with Jesus, there is still a nature of sin that you were born with."

They answered that they fully understood that. I said, "It won't be long before you will be aware that it is still there and not dead yet. You have been a child of God for a few days now. It is getting better and better and you love Jesus more and more. You get up one morning and have a wonderful time of prayer and communion with God. You ask Him to help you to walk with Him all day long and to please Him in everything you do.

You then go out and get the lawnmower out of the shed and begin to mow the grass. You mow for about an hour, and the sun gets hot and you begin to sweat and get very thirsty. Just then the lawnmower gives an explosion and quits dead. You push down on the handles and look under it, and you see that you have run over a baseball and bent the blade out of shape. You go to the garage and get a wrench and take the blade off, take it to the garage and straighten it out and go put it back on. You put up the wrench and go back to the lawnmower and check the gas and pull the cord again. The cord jerks out of the lawnmower in your hand. Just about then you become fully aware that there is a nature of sin still in your heart. You feel something that wants to go get a twenty-pound sledge hammer and break the lawnmower into a thousand pieces. You had better not do it or you will sin, but that nature is there." I said, "Do you know what I'm talking about?"

They all burst out laughing and said, "Sure we know."

I said, "Can we get rid of that ugly thing down inside of us?" They sat there tense, waiting for an answer and it was time to leave the Bible study. I said, "We'll be back next week," and dismissed them. Will you please pray that the soaking pot will do its work?

On the way out, the dear brother who is living so wonderfully in the blessing came to shake my hand with a smile all over his face. I said, "Brother, do you know the answer to the question?"

"Oh yes, do I ever!" Oh that some more will find the answer to the question, not in their heads alone, but way down deep—as deep as the stain has gone.

Here is something else very exciting that I wish you would pray about. The former administrator of this prison retired about two years ago, but finding retirement very boring, he took on another job. He is now the administrator of a nearby county prison. He was always quite friendly and warm and is very open to volunteers. Several weeks ago he said he needed all kinds of volunteers at his prison. Through that medium it has come about that a couple from the church are starting Bible study groups once a week at both the men's and women's county prisons. The response was good at the first gathering. Please pray that yet another door of opportunity will reach a few more gems for the crown of Jesus.

I know you are praying; I thank you; but I beg you to keep it up, for Jesus' sake.

Your brother in Christ,
William Cawman

16
SHEEP WHO NEED THE SHEPHERD

October 1, 2003

HOW OFTEN HAVE WE SUNG in our foreign missionary songs, the statement, "Behold how many thousand still are lying, bound in the darksome prison house of sin; with none to tell them of a Savior's dying, nor of the life He died for them to win?" But how many thousands still are lying across the street from us, or around the corner, or next door?

A young Spanish man came to see me for the first time. He hasn't been in this prison very long, and he's only 21 or 22 years of age. He is just as darkened as if he had grown up on a never-visited island of the south seas, as far as knowing anything about God or salvation. But now in prison, someone told him about the church services and about the Bible. He has begun to read it, and he came across the word *humility.*

"What does that word mean? Does it mean to be real relaxed? And what does it mean to deny one's self?" As he goes on to unburden his disappointment with his short life, he describes his feelings the best he can. He takes his shirt front in his fingers and begins jerking it outward and says, "I feel my heart is jumping out like this to Jesus. It seems I can see Him standing right in front of me and my heart wants to get to Him, and it feels like this," still pulling outward on his shirt. "I want Him to take my heart; my heart wants to love Jesus." Aren't you glad with me that Jesus, through the Blessed Holy Spirit, speaks in such a way that anyone can understand Him? This man is one of the many who still are lying in darkness, and need your prayers.

Let me relate a couple of very sad deaths since I last wrote to you. A couple of Sunday nights ago, the superintendent came in during the service and told me that one of the inmates in the hospital was not expected to live through the night, and wondered if we would want to pray for him. Of course we did, and then they asked some of the men who sit with dying inmates to sit with him through the night.

After the service another brother and I went over to the hospital to see him. He was half sitting up in the bed and after we introduced ourselves, I asked him if Jesus had forgiven all of his sins. He said, "I hope so." I told him he could know that they were all forgiven and that he could ask Jesus right there to forgive him. The other brother prayed and then I asked him to repeat a prayer after me. I prayed in short sentences, but he could only get the first few words and then would become confused. We left him with rather heavy hearts. He was supposed to be released from the prison on the following Friday.

During that week the Christian men did all they could for him. When he was in pain, he would listen to them and respond to a certain point, but when the medication brought him some relief, all he wanted to talk about was going home. He felt if he could just get out on his own he would be all right.

On Thursday night he took a turn for the worse again. One of the Christian inmates was with him and suddenly this patient went into a panic. He climbed out of bed and went to the toilet. Suddenly he started trying to pull his shirt off and then collapsed into the other inmate's arms. The Christian inmate lowered him to the floor and ran for help, but it was too late. It looked as though the dying man had put off his spiritual need in hopes of getting home. He missed out on both. He died the night before his release and never left a clear testimony behind.

These times are especially hard for the men who sit with them with burdened hearts, wanting to see them come to Jesus. The inmate who held him in his arms had just been telling me the struggles he was having over the last one that had died with him. It is not easy for them to know that the soul they tried to help, slipped through their fingers. They need your prayers.

The next Sunday night I was just finishing my message in the second service for the evening, when the officer came in and said the men would have to leave. He held one unit back until all the others were out and then let them go last; then he told me that there had been a death on their tier.

The next day several of the good Christian inmates came to me and they were very heavy hearted. They said the man who died was just about 31 years old, a very tall husky white man who was very racist. He had just been making a lot of fun of the Christians and their beliefs and was openly ridiculing them. He claimed to be an Aryan and was very intolerant and hateful of blacks and foreigners. This man had collapsed during the church service time and they had called an ambulance, but before the ambulance got there they called it off. They moved his cellmate out of the room and said the body might have to lie there all night waiting for a coroner. It was pretty obvious that the inmate had died of drug overdose; whether self-inflicted or whether he was the victim of gang activity we may never know.

I had a very precious visit recently with the man I have told you about who allowed God to sanctify him before he ever knew what it was. Toward the end of our visit time, he said, "I'd like to share something with you." He then went on to tell of a certain area of his personal life that he had battled with and struggled over for years. He said part of the battle was that he could never really decide whether it was something God was pleased or not pleased with. He had reasoned a lot about it and did not feel that he was committing sin in it, but it still remained a cloudy area in his life.

One day about six months before our visit, he was reading in the Book of Joshua where in the possessing of the land of promise one tribe after another had failed to cast out the inhabitants of the land. God began to speak to him very clearly. He said, "God showed me that what I was struggling over and partly justifying was an inhabitant that He did not want remaining in my life. To have gone beyond that point without getting rid of that would have been a sin, because now I knew how God felt about it."

He immediately renounced it and put it out of his life. The devil badgered him over it, but he held fast. Just the night before we were visiting he had been awakened for a spell in the night with the devil pounding at his heart's door fiercely, but he sat in front of me with a glow on his face and said, "I have the victory. I have not given place to that in my life once since God spoke to me about it."

How could I help but rejoice with him as he stood triumphantly with his heel on that giant's neck? Later as he was praying before he left, he prayed, "Lord, just purge out everything that is not fully like You!" I believe there is a crown of righteousness awaiting him, don't you?

There is another young man I would like to ask you to pray for. He is 22 years old, but has had a very sad background. He never knew his father, and his mother was so addicted to drugs and neglect of her children that the law took them away and put them into the foster care system. He was only six and his brother was two.

The little six-year-old felt very protective of his little brother as he was all he had left of his family. They were in an orphanage and his brother got sick in the night. No one took care of him so he stayed up all night cleaning up after his beloved brother . In the morning he told someone that his little brother was sick, so they took him away saying that they were taking him to the doctor. He wanted to go with them as he did not want to lose sight of him, but he was so tired from staying up all night that he fell asleep. He never saw his little brother again.

From there on he was sent from one home to another. Finally a family adopted him, but they were very mean to him and finally he went back to the orphanage. A second family adopted him but that didn't work much better. Every time he changed environments he was introduced to a new religious belief until he is so confused that he doesn't know what is right. But for all that he is very hungry to know the truth and to find the right life. The Christian men are trying to help him, and I will too, but he needs prayer. It is so hard to see a life so young in years and so old in sin.

Here's another sad story—I'm sorry, but they are all around us. A man who was obviously burned badly by drug use stopped me after a Sunday night service and said, "Chaplain, I need to talk to you." The following week he came in, and judging from his looks I expected an incoherent story. I got just the opposite. Yes, he was badly damaged by heavy drug use, but his memory was as clear as a bell and he did not fumble at all with his words.

When he was only five years old, a man across the street from his apartment took him and abused him. After he had done it three times, his father found out about it and went over and began to beat the man up. The police found them and sentenced the man to 15 years in prison.

That incident so damaged the poor boy that he still wakes up with cold sweat nightmares, thinking the man is grabbing him again. He carries a false sense of guilt over it yet, asking me, "Chaplain, did I do something wrong? Did I look at him wrong? Did I say something to him wrong? Why did he do that to me?"

He began to wish he could just die and get away from it all. His little heart was so crushed and confused that he was angry at God for letting it happen to him, yet he prayed all the time for God to just take him to heaven. His grandmother had just gotten a prescription filled for Valium and he saw the bottle and took the whole thing. He was only eleven years old. When he passed out they took him to the hospital and pumped his stomach, but even so it was a miracle that he recovered.

As if that wasn't enough trauma for a boy, his own father would beat him mercilessly with a cat-o-nine-tails until his back was bleeding. When his grandfather died, he was so sad he began to cry. His father began to beat him for crying, but the more he beat him the more he cried out with pain. No telling what would have happened had not his uncle happened to come into the house just then, and when he saw what his father was doing to him, he tore into the father. The two men were brothers and were both weight lifters; one of them weighed four hundred and some pounds and the other one over five hundred. They got into it so hard that suddenly the door opened and the police broke in on them. With that the son ran out of the house into the fire chief's arms and then left home.

To get away from it all he went to the Marine recruiter's office and enlisted. They asked him how long he wanted to enlist for, and he told them he wanted to enlist for life. They had never heard of that before, and took him on. They placed him after a while in charge of hand grenade training. He heard so many grenades go off that he had a nervous break. Then they sent him to Desert Storm.

That became the second nightmare of his life. He said, "We had no time to put on the gear they gave us; we just had to shoot back—I can't get it out of my mind." After three or four nervous breaks over it all, they discharged him from the Marines; breaking his heart. Now it seemed no one wanted him. He could find no way of coping with all of his trauma except through heavy drug use. This deluded soul got a large room and began throwing big drug parties. And then—a big party, a stupid head, a night in bed with a strange, intoxicated woman, an accusation, and prison.

Now he sits in front of me and says, "Chaplain, if you professional religious people can't do anything for me I'm just going to end it all; I really am. I've tried all the doctors and they just load me up with more drugs. They tell me I either take them myself or they will put me in the rubber room and shoot them into me. I can't live like this."

Do you wonder, friends, that sometimes I feel I could nearly scream out without mercy against that terrible plague of the heart called SIN? In its "nicer" forms we kiss it and cuddle it and excuse it; but it is hideous when the cover comes off.

A few months back I was nearly becoming discouraged with the services and Bible studies out in the minimum camp. Only five or six would show up, and it seemed these were so dull, but over the past few months God has given a real revival out there. We are having between twenty to thirty attend the Bible studies and services. I asked my supervisor if he thought I should extend my Christian Living classes out there, and he thought it would be good. I asked how many would want to sign up for a Tuesday afternoon class in Christian Living and there are presently twenty-seven names on the list. It is exciting too. God has really been helping us.

One young man grew up in the Methodist Church, but he never paid much attention to anything, and does not seem to know the first thing about salvation. He is all ears, and listens with such riveted attention. At the end of class he comes and says, "I never knew that; this really has me doing some thinking." Once again we are reminded that we are living in an extremely post-Christian America. If Jesus tarries much longer, one would wonder if we will not need missionaries from other countries to come and teach us the true Gospel message.

Here is a real prayer request. Of all the men we have told you about over the past several years, every one of them has come to us, or come to the Christian services or classes on his own. Many of them have deep inner struggles that we know nothing about. They have been ripped apart by the cruel monster of sin in all its forms.

Some of them come seriously, some—well, they are like the one who came recently and unloaded thus. "Chaplain, I need something different. I've been a success all my life until now. I have fabulous houses, nice cars, tennis courts, women; I've had it all, and now I'm shut up here in this prison. This is not what I had in mind for my life. It's not my idea of living to be sharing a toilet with another man. I'd like to see if God can help me." Probably not yet; God is not a 911 repair service for the messes one cannot put up with any longer. I can only trust the inmate will become more serious than this.

But, of all those who have come and are coming, there are many who have never come. Their needs are just as great, but for some reason, God only knows why, they will not come to Him for help. Would you please pray for these also? Please pray that the Holy Spirit will so infill some who are seeking Him that it will open the eyes of others who will be lost forever, unless they come. Oh the sad words of Jesus, "And ye will not come to Me, that ye might have life." Perhaps I have shared more requests than victories this month. Thank you for your faithful prayers.

Your Brother,
William Cawman

┼┼┼

November 1, 2003

LAST NIGHT IN THE CHURCH service, one of the older men asked if all the brothers there would be willing to join him in a commitment with each other. It was that they would get alone with God at five o'clock for the next seven days and ask God to send a revival to the prison. Might God lay it on your heart to join them?

Last month I told you of another challenging man who was

coming to see me. I told you of his story as he told it to me, how from early childhood he was plunged into the depths of sin until he has nearly lost his reason over it. Let me follow it up to date.

I was gone for a few days to a convention, and during that time this man had a terribly dark night in which he felt he couldn't handle his life any longer. He told his mother that the only way he could think to get the nightmares over his past to end, was for him to end.

At seven-thirty one evening, he called the officer on his tier to come. When the officer came into his cell, he said, "Officer, can you call Chaplain Cawman for me? I need to talk to him." The officer told him I was gone. He said, "Well then, officer, would you do something for me? Would you take all the razor blades out of my room?"

The next thing he knew he was handcuffed, taken to the hospital, and injected with drugs to alter his mind. When they felt he was stable again they sent him back to his cell. A couple days later when I had returned, he came to see me. "Chaplain, can you help me? I don't want to live. I can't stand these flashbacks anymore. I don't want to live on drugs."

Let me say without hesitation, I need your prayers at times like these. I tried to point him to the pathway of repentance and asking Jesus to come into his heart. I told him I knew that Jesus could heal and make him whole again if he was really sorry for his sin and wanted to be God's man. I made him promise me that he would not hurt himself, and that he would really pray and ask Jesus to come into his heart. We had prayer together and then he left.

This man told me later when I met him on his tier that he had asked Jesus to come in and forgive all his sins and take his past away. He smiled and said, "I haven't had any flashbacks since." I told him to keep right on seeking until God witnessed that he belonged to Him completely. A few days later he came and told me he was getting closer to God and that he wasn't taking the drugs, and God was keeping the bad dreams away.

He said, "I believe Jesus forgave my sins, but I still want to get closer to Him." I urged him to do it.

Then he told me that he was sitting in his cell listening to some gospel music. He said it made him so happy that he was smiling when the officer walked by. The officer looked in his cell and said, "What are you taking now?"

He said, "Officer, it isn't what you think it is; I'm taking Jesus."

The officer laughed and said, "Oh I know just what you'll do; as soon as you get out of here, you'll go get a jug of your favorite whiskey and drink it up."

"No I won't either, officer. Jesus took all that away from me, and I don't want that anymore. I'll tell you what I will do though; as soon as I get out I'm going to get me a big cigar and celebrate with Jesus for breaking my chains."

Aren't you glad, friends, that God made abundant provision for those many places where "if any of you lack wisdom"?

Let me include a little letter here that was sent to you from a young man who (you would never guess it by looking at him now) brutally murdered his grandfather and the woman his grandfather was living with. Let him express himself to you in his own words:

Dear Brothers and Sisters,

I hope and pray that this letter reaches you in the blessedness of God's grace. I count it a joy to know that your faithfulness stands as an example in this dark world.

I have been seeking God day and night for the second blessing. Temptations and trials have arose [sic], but praise be to God that His grace is sufficient. I have been asking God the what, where, when, why, and hows, but in His mercy He spares me the impatient requests and like a tender mother suckles me on the milk that will foster growth. I weep, I grumble, I have even, dare I say, pouted; but thank God that unlike the parents of today, He spares not the rod. Always in retrospect I see the wisdom of His ways, but oh the cries of protest that arise within when He sets the inviolable terms. I know the land of milk and honey is before me. I can smell its

sweetness on the breeze. I will enter in. I may be halt like
Jacob with a new name, but I will not rest until it is the rest
where I have ceased from my own works. God bless my sisters and brothers. Your brother——.

Are you selective in who you pray for? Would you find it in
your heart to pray sincerely for a professional juggler? I mean,
one who became second from the top in circus jugglers? He
traveled the world performing his little stunt, but friends, God
is knocking at his door. At first he didn't know how to inter-
pret that Knock. Shame on today's religious teachings; he was
sure that God was telling him that now it was time to perform
for Him.

I faced him squarely with the demands of Jesus; that one
must forsake the old to have the new. I told him not to try to
drag the old life over into the new, but that God was calling
him to "be with Him," not to do something for Him. He seemed
to hug right up to that and said, "I want it." Since it is beyond
the ability of either you or I to start with him anywhere else
than where he is, let's do it. I'd love to see how Jesus could
change the entire life of a professional entertainer; after all, He
already undertook a tax collector, a fisherman, a Pharisee, and
you and me.

And then there is a tour bus driver. He sits in class and
enters in with great interest, but just like many others, behind
the front is a broken and shattered and disappointed life.
"Could I talk to you, Chaplain?" And one more life story begins. Soon the religious front disappears. The tears fall like
rain. "I've lost it all; I've lost it all. Jesus is all I have, and if I
miss the mark in serving Him, I've got nothing." He freely
confesses that he is not happy with his relationship to God.
He is sick of sin, but he is also sick of a religious front that
does nothing for the deep, hollow ache on the inside. God
have mercy on religious teachers who can lead a soul on like
this for years and leave him just as empty of the grace of God
as the devil himself would.

I've been watching another man in the weekly classes. He is absolutely vibrant with hunger and agreement with truth. His face beams with joy as the class goes on. Recently he came to see me. He said he has been listening to the teaching, and that he goes and searches the Bible and finds it all so true that he just loves it. He says, "I just love truth."

He told me that one day he got tired of his own life and the way he did everything He said he just gave everything to Jesus, and it has been wonderful ever since. He knows he is God's child, and lives with the conscious knowledge of the love of Jesus every day. Oh the faithful Holy Spirit; we have perhaps no idea how many hearts and lives around us have heard Him knocking and have opened the door. And guess what else— when they do, He comes in just like He said He would, and sups with them and they with Him.

It is quite obvious at times that those demons which inhabited "Legion" are not finished with their hateful plague of entering in and making men feel like they want to torment themselves. We were just getting ready for a Sunday night service when a Hispanic man came up to me and said, "Chaplain, could I talk to you a minute? Do you think you could say a prayer for me? I think I have a demon in me. I get so angry that I bite myself." He held out his arm, and he had actually bitten a chunk right out of his arm, bigger than a fifty-cent piece. How correctly the old Methodists appraised the disease of sin, "'Tis palsy, plague, and fever, and madness all combined; and none but a believer, the least relief can find." I did have several of the men gather around him and pray for him.

I also told you last month of a man who has been seeking to die to sin and self. He told me the other day, "God is putting me through a mirror experience. He's showing me traits of my character I never knew I had before. I've been reading those books you gave me, and that one called *Death Route Holiness* I've read again and again. I read in there about the danger of just getting the knowledge of the way in our heads and missing it in our hearts. I'm scared of that. I want to die. I want to be cleansed. I'm sick of hearing my name. I sit in my cell with tears of hunger just to die to myself. I love my brothers, but some of them seem offended at the route I'm taking, but it's all right. I just want to die."

The inmate continued, "The head chaplain wanted me to organize some music practice for the men." (He is gifted at this.) "I just don't want to do it right now. If the music is not holy, I don't want it. It took me a long time to discover that I don't have anything to offer."

Please pray that this soul will not be sidetracked or miss the mark. This is the man I told you about last month that my supervisor had said to, "It sounds like you've been in Chaplain Cawman's classes." That's not it at all, for if it was, there should be over a hundred dying just like him. He has been in the class of the Holy Spirit, and I trust Him to do His great work if the man will stay there.

There are also a couple of inmates in the minimum unit who are really seeking to be fully sanctified. One of these has struggled for several years now, and for some reason it seems the full light of what holiness really is, just did not get through to him. Notwithstanding, he has consistently endeavored to live free from sin, and has had many severe tussles with failure because of that nature remaining in him. I would think at times he was understanding that he could get rid of it, but oh how hard it is at times to break the deadly spell of religious teachings which leave man incapable of rising any higher than the devil wants him to.

Suddenly, it seems the light has dawned upon him. He is so hungry that he is seeking it definitely now. The other inmate who is pressing his claims told me that they go to the chapel each day and study the Word and pray together, and he said this dear man seeks and prays with many tears, desiring to be made fully whole. I visited with him yesterday and he told me that he feels so terrible that he has been so dull all of this time. He said, "I look back now and realize this is what people have been trying to tell me for several years. You have told me I needed this over and over, but I just couldn't seem to see it. But I do now, as clear as can be, and I want it with all my heart." Will you help them pray?

There is another young man, twenty-seven years old, out at the minimum unit who began to come to me and seemed to want to get through to God and have his life changed. I haven't seen him for several weeks, but his name is still on the roster, so I called for him. He came into the room, and immediately I knew something was wrong. His face was the picture of discouragement and trouble. I asked him about it.

He said that he had tried to live life to the fullest in the world. He tried everything, and tried it hard. At twenty-six he sat on a park bench and realized he had nothing more to live for. When he came to prison he started seeking God, and then everything went wrong. He found he had hepatitis C; his family cut him off; he felt like everything was gone.

"Why can't I find God? I ask Him, but He doesn't answer me. What can I do that I'm not doing? I'm afraid I'm going to get out of prison and go down the same path again." Would you remember him, too, in prayer?

Yours in His love,
William Cawman

┼┼┼

December 1, 2003

THANK GOD, "THE BLOOD still reaches deeper than the stain has gone." I'm speaking just now of a thirty-four-year-old man whom I have known for several years. How long he has been in prison, how long he has to go, and what the nature of his crime is, I don't know. All I know is that his life has been steadily going downhill for some time.

He became very ill about a year ago, started running high fevers and having pain throughout his body, but didn't know what was the matter with him. He finally convinced the nurses to take him to the dispensary where they found he had a temperature of over 106 degrees. The nurse started to put a stethoscope to his chest and he said, "Nurse you don't need that; listen." He turned from side to side and the fluid sloshed audibly in his chest. They sent him right away to Trenton hospital, and there he was diagnosed with lupus. He spent some time in the hospital here when he came back, and from then on has walked with a cane because of swelling joints, etc.

Worse than the physical condition, he just about quit coming to Christian classes and to church and Bible study, and became confused and discouraged. A few days ago he turned in a written request to see me. I scheduled him for three o'clock on a Monday afternoon.

Another inmate came down at three and said that he wasn't coming to see me. I said it was all right, but God had other plans. The officer in charge, seeing his name on the list, called his unit and had him sent down. He came in and sat down, cane between his legs, the picture of dejection and woe.

He started in, "Chaplain, I wasn't going to come down, even though I requested it. I don't know what to think. I can't find anything. I am really wondering if I am even in the right faith group. I have been going to the Catholic services and I'm just questioning everything. I don't know what I believe anymore. I saw another inmate who was a real mess, get his life turned around a few months ago, and his face just glows with it. I know it's real, but I can't find anything."

I looked at his broken body and his sad face and said, "Well, sir, the first thing you should do is to look up and thank God that you are not happy, because if you were, you would continue right on into hell." With that he bowed his head over his cane and burst into tears.

I let him weep for a minute (the tears just ran like a faucet), and then I said, "My brother, since you don't know what faith group you should belong to, could I ask you something? Is that Mohammed, knocking at your door right now?" He shook his head emphatically, "No." "Is it Buddha? Is it Confucius? Is it the Virgin Mary?" "No." "My brother, Jesus is knocking right now at your heart's door. Why don't you open the door and let Him in?"

We began to pray. I prayed first and then asked him to pray. He poured out his heart to God and it was no modern, typical prayer that he prayed. The tears fell freely until his sleeve was wet. Just then the officer signaled that it was lock down time. I urged him to keep asking Jesus to come in and forgive all his sins and make him a new man. I promised him that if he would keep reaching for God, his tears would turn to joy. I quoted the Scripture that says, "For He hath torn, and He will heal us; He hath smitten, and He will bind us up."

I was scheduled to go in at six the next morning anyway to have prayer with several of the officers, so I asked this inmate if he would come back down to see me at seven-forty-five. He was only too ready. I told him he could come back down a new man.

He was there right on time. He sat down again, cane between his knees, and said, "I've been asking God all night to forgive me and come into my heart; I do feel some light coming."

I said, "Don't stop, brother. Many people stop when they feel a little better, but God wants to change you completely. Do you really want to be His child?"

"Oh yes, I do."

I said, "Then why don't you just do it? Tell the devil you don't belong to him anymore, and tell God you are going to be His child from here on out."

We had prayer again. After I had prayed, he started praying again, tears flowing freely. Suddenly his tears of conviction changed to tears of joy — "Oh I can't believe what I feel. I never knew I could have such peace. Oh Chaplain, I thank God and I thank you for opening my eyes; this is wonderful!"

For the next few minutes we just sat and rejoiced in the glow of forgiving grace while the angels of heaven rejoiced over a sinner who had repented. He rose to leave, but it was difficult. "I can't believe it. I never had such peace in my life."

He came down the next day again, and then again on Friday, and each time his face was glowing with the wonder of it. "Chaplain, I can't express it. I don't ever want to lose this. I'll never let go of God's hand." He would talk about it a bit, then just shake his head and look out into space, and then the tears would start all over again. Then he would just bow his head on his cane and begin to love and thank God for it all over again.

Could I tell you something? This, friends, is what they used to call SALVATION! God did a lot for this dear man, but He didn't miss me either. I need to see this once in a while at least to keep my own vision clear in a day of anemic conversions that are powerless to produce a new creature in Christ. I'd love to see it more often that once in a while too, believe me. Oh I could live in the atmosphere of a seeking soul and a seeking Savior making that first contact. Thank God for SALVATION!

And then, still another victory. The man I wrote about recently who has been longing to die out to self and sin, and has said he was sick of hearing his own name and just wanted to be cleansed of all sin—well, are you ready? He crossed over Jordan, just like the Holy Spirit always does His work. He was sitting in the courtyard alone, looking up to God and begging once more to be cleansed from all that God had been showing him. He had told me that God was showing him things about his nature he never knew existed, and he hated it.

Well, praise God, when a person gets sick enough, death looks inviting. So as he was sitting there in the courtyard, he said the Holy Spirit spoke to him and said, "It's now!" From that moment he has been consciously clean and free from sin. I met him in passing yesterday, and I bumped his shoulder and said, "Brother, is it better on this side of the Jordan River?"

His face beamed, "Oh yes, it sure is." Oh friends, God is making up His Son's bride, and if those on the padded pews are not coming, those in the highways and hedges might take their place around that great table.

In light of these victories, I want to make a special request. There are several other men who are on a hot trail for the same work of the Holy Spirit. One told me he is seeking it night and day, and feels he must have it, regardless of all else. Could you help pray for them? If you have ever prayed through to this blessed cleansing of the heart from sin, you know full well how the devil hates it, and how desperately he will try to sidetrack or detour the soul from getting it. With the same vengeance that he tried to get Jesus to come down from the cross, so he will use every means available to him to get these men to stop short of that one thing needful, and that is for the corn of wheat to fall into the ground and die. Let me say this very plainly: the crying need in the prison is no different from the world outside, and that is for more souls who will obey the command of Jesus and "tarry until" every last trace of self and sin is dead, and Christ is all in all.

And, while we rejoice in every new victory, many are still lost in the night. A man who has been in my classes for quite a while but who has never really been awakened spiritually that I can tell, was recently going through some type of mental gyrations. He came to class one morning, barely able to walk in and sit down because of whatever medication they had him on. His eyes looked like he had not slept for days and he couldn't keep them open. He sat for a few minutes right in front of me and then got up and left. I asked the men who knew him if he would be all right, because I didn't know whether he could make it back to his cell. I guess when he got back he went ballistic and ended up in confinement in the hospital. I went over to visit him, only to view once more, one of those graphic, deplorable pictures of the wages of sin.

As I looked into the little hole in his door, I took a quick inventory. A small stainless steel bed, bolted to the wall, with a thin mattress on it and one blanket. A toilet in the other corner of the room, and that was it. Nothing to do, nothing to read, nothing to see but cement blocks, nowhere to go except eight feet across the room and back; and worst of all, a heart far away from God. When he saw me he came over to the hole and tried to communicate. I watched him for a few minutes as he leaned over with his hands on his knees and swayed back and forth, barely able to keep his balance, his eyes still glazed over with stupefaction from the medications. A lost soul! Lost, and for all that I could tell, barely enough desire for God to bother His ear. I got him a Bible; I hope he read it. Oh the drab and dismal colors which appear on the canvas of life, when the Scripture is painted, "Having no hope, and without God in the world."

A few months back, the spiritual tide in the minimum security unit of the prison was really discouraging. Only five or six would come most of the time, and they seemed to have no real settled purpose for being there. But God has really given a reviving out there. The Sunday services, the Bible study on Friday night, and the class in Christian Living has been packed out, with new ones coming all the time. And it is not just numbers, but the interest is inspiring.

The other night in Bible study I felt as though I was trying to feed a nest of baby birds, with their mouths wide open waiting their turn to be fed. The time goes by so quickly and they are disappointed to leave.

A chaplain's job is two-fold; he is employed by the state to help rehabilitate men so that they will cease being a liability to the state and to society, but he is also employed by God to lead them to the path to heaven. Please help us pray that these men will find something so solid and lasting that they will do more than just stay out of prison. Oh that God would make some of them such a terror to the devil that he will wish he had never tampered with them. There is so much that still needs to be done before Jesus comes, and some of these men could reach hearts that some of the rest of us might not know how to. Pray that God will raise up an army of them to go out and pay back the world they have harmed by rescuing some more victims out of its clutches.

And then, please do remember their hurting hearts as Christmas time approaches. A few have been in the system so long that they do not really feel it much anymore, but most of them will, and will feel it keenly too. It is overwhelming to walk through a prison tier on Christmas Day. Grown men are crying with loneliness and broken hearts. Perhaps God could speak to some that would not otherwise hear Him, and if they do hear—oh blessed thought—Christ could be born in a prison just as truly as in a manger.

To all who have faithfully prayed this past year, could I on their behalf thank you and wish you a Blessed Christmas. They would want me to do it, and please keep praying.

Yours in His love,
William Cawman

17
GRACE AMID TRIALS

January 1, 2004

ANOTHER YEAR HAS SLIPPED so quickly into those unchangeable things which have been. Not one single accomplishment of the year 2003 is worth talking about except the ones which prepared immortal souls for the world that is so soon to come. If ever we needed to hear the cry of the coming Bridegroom it is now—"Go out into the highways and hedges, and compel them to come in." The night is coming fast. Please pray that God will keep every door open that He is not finished with, for a little longer.

Opposition is mounting from all directions against the central theme of a Jesus who came to save His people from (not in) their sins. Any other gospel can be excused and tolerated, but sin-sparing, antichrist teachers are becoming alarmingly aggressive in opposing the very thought that Christ can save us from sinning.

We are feeling it strongly here in the prison; not from the inmates, but from the churches about, who just want to come in and "celebrate" their emotional infatuation with a cross-less Christ. We sense more all the time that many of these so-called teachers of the Word, encountering the fact that a Gospel is being preached that declares freedom from sin, are becoming vicious in open opposition. It is that very antichrist "Who opposeth and exalteth himself above all that is called God…" Antichrist? Yes indeed; anti everything Christ died to accomplish, for if He cannot save from all sin, just really what did He do anyway? Could I beg that you help us pray that God will hold this "man of sin…the son of perdition" in check just a little longer?

And there is glorious good news too. The inmate that I told you about last month who got saved, is just blossoming day by day into the Scriptural description of a babe in Christ. He comes to see me and is no sooner in the door than his face begins to beam, "Pastor, it's working; it's really working."

After a few minutes with him I feel like I've been through a precious altar service. He tells me just where the devil is trying him and lying to him. As I explain to him the tactics of the enemy and point him to the ever-present Blood, he catches it immediately and then just leans over his cane and begins to pray his heart out in praise to God. "This is overwhelming, but glorious; I never knew it would be like this." (*Insert:* He just left my office two minutes ago after praying with tears, "Oh God, I just thank You for saving a wretch like me. Now, save some more wretches." It brought tears and glory to my heart, too.)

Last week he had been sitting in the day room when another Christian man came in. The second man has evidenced a real work of forgiving grace in his life for some time, but has never gotten rid of the old man of sin within. He got into an argument with a Muslim man bigger than he, and lost his temper. The man who had previously been saved, went to his cell and dropped a tin can of soup or something into a sock and went back to the dayroom to attack the man. The big man saw him coming at him and grabbed him and slammed him to the floor on his head. Blood spurted out and he lay unconscious in the doorway. The inmates all went out, step-

ping over his body, and the ambulance was called and took
him to the outside hospital.

When someone told me about it, I left and went to the hospital and found the inmate semi-conscious and in bad shape.
I talked to him, had prayer with him and then they took him
to the hospital in Trenton where he is now.

Anyway, our dear brother was under a real attack of Satan,
because the devil was accusing him that he should have
stepped up to help this man. I told him that it was not God
who was condemning him, and that regardless of the fact that
the man had been a Christian, he was not acting like one at
that moment, and furthermore had lost his Christianity by
his choices. He was so relieved to know that it was not God
condemning him; he doesn't want God's frown again, ever.

Just today I saw in the roster of inmates that the man who
had been so beaten up had returned to the prison hospital. I
took a few minutes and went over to see him. They told me
he had been sent to the detention unit just an hour before, so
I went over there. Because he had been in a fight, he will be
held there for a few days at least to see how he reacts.

I started visiting with him through the door. He hung his
head and told me he felt so sorry and had been asking God to
forgive him. I told him if he was really sorry and was finished
with that kind of action, God would most certainly forgive
him again, but I told him he really needed to ask God to take
that thing out of his heart that made him do what he did. He
hung his head and said meekly, "I know that, Chaplain
Cawman."

As I turned to leave his cell after having prayer with him,
the man in the next cell called to me and asked to see me. He
was the one who had thrown him to the floor. I don't think
you would need me to explain why they have them in solitary
confinement cells right next to each other. The man, even
though a Muslim, started to tell me how sorry he was for what
had happened. He said that for the past several days he had
been in that cell all alone and all he had heard was that the

other inmate was in critical condition. The last he had seen of him was a smashed head in a pool of blood on the floor. He had been really suffering for those several days, and when the other inmate was led into the cell beside him just an hour before, he was so relieved.

He said to me, "I don't know what made him go off like that. I have known him for a long time and he was really a very God-fearing man. I don't understand what happened to him."

I didn't hesitate to witness to him also about the awful disease of sin and how we need to get rid of it. He listened carefully and then said, "I know; I pray for God to take that away from me five times a day." Oh that he would pray to the right God; He still answers by fire.

Every once in a while I call in some man that I see has really been responding in class, but who is backward and not needing to be seen and heard by everyone. Sometimes this is so rewarding. The other day I called in a black man with one blind eye, and within minutes we were united in the bond of the Spirit. He had been just sitting there walking in the light, going back to his cell and reading and studying the Word, and growing in grace. He told me he had let the Holy Spirit come into his life in His fullness, and he said, "I can't live without Him. If I don't feel His presence in my heart, I go to prayer and stay there until He comes back again. I can't live a single day without Him."

Yes, the devil may be a roaring lion, walking about seeking whom he may devour; but praise God, the Holy Spirit is also brooding over the hearts of men, and He is finding those who will open the door and let Him in.

A brilliant young man, raised totally in Catholicism, has recently also found new life in Christ. He told me that people think he is really strange, because he is so enraptured with what he is finding in God. He said, "I just feel euphoric at times, and then I feel a lot of pressure from those around me to tone it down a little."

I said, "When you were euphoric for the devil did they want you to tone it down?"

"Oh my, no."

"Well then, just let God have all there is of you."

Remember the old song, "What you are speaks so loud, the world can't hear what you say?" Well, there are two Christian inmates living together in the same cell. They are having a wonderful time of it, too. They have a little study chamber all to themselves with their little bookshelf full of Christian books and their Bibles and studies spread out on their beds. They pray and worship together, and oh, how my heart was touched when they said that they get down together every night and pray for me and my wife.

It is standard procedure when an officer comes on a tier for his shift, that he picks two cells at random and inspects them; this keeps everyone on guard. Well, the other morning the officer picked the cell of these two Christian inmates. Neither of them were in there at the moment, but another Christian inmate saw the officer go in, and come right back out, and then heard him say to another officer, "Man! I couldn't stay in there very long, or I'd have gotten saved." Wouldn't that be tragic?

The other night we were again in Bible study and we were discussing the Scriptural marks of a sanctified life. An inmate raised his hand and said, "Chaplain, I was talking to a staff member this week, and they said that it is impossible in this life to live free from sin, because we are in the flesh and we will always fall into sin, either in thought, word or deed."

I said, "Well, let's look at that. Let me ask you a question: When you were living totally for sin and the flesh, you did it pretty good, didn't you?"

"Oh yes," they said.

"All right, when you were running after the devil's offers, and you really wanted to follow the lusts of your flesh, did any of you ever find that, in spite of all your efforts and desires to live in the flesh, you suddenly fell into righteousness?

You really didn't want to, but suddenly, in spite of yourself, you found yourself in the Spirit and loving God?"

They burst out laughing, "Absolutely not; no chance of it!"

"Well," I said, "so you are telling me that Satan had the power to make you a consistently perfect sinner, is that right?"

"Oh yes, he sure did, not a question about it."

I told them to take a deep breath. "Now, are you saying that Jesus Christ and the Blood He shed on the Cross of Calvary does not have sufficient power to make me consistently, perfectly righteous? Are you saying that Satan possesses greater power than Jesus Christ?"

Amens erupted all over the room, and those who have found already that the Blood of Jesus cleanses from all sin and stops the sinning business, just beamed with delight. Aren't you glad that this great salvation makes sense? It is because of this that a fool need not err therein. It might take a Ph.D. to explain just how satisfactory it is to a holy God that man can do nothing but go right on sinning, but any feeble mind can grasp that if He came to destroy the works of the devil, He either succeeded or He didn't.

This very morning in Christian Living class, a man who has been rising to the top more and more with an insatiable need to be the teacher, got clear out of line and self-destructed. I was wondering just how to handle him, but God allowed him to do it himself. He became so argumentative for his point of view that finally the whole class recognized that he didn't want to see the light; he just wanted to be right. Finally one man said, "Chaplain, could we pray?"

We did. We prayed clear through. As we finished a man from the back shouted, "I feel better." I did too. I hope someone else did also.

I must tell you also that the man who recently prayed through to holiness of heart is thoroughly enjoying being dead to himself and alive to God. He says he never wants anything of himself again. The Holy Spirit is teaching and guiding and showing him just how to live. Wasn't that included in the promise of His coming? This man will be released about the time you read this, so please follow him with your prayers as he goes out to walk in newness of life.

I am reminded once again at the beginning of a new year that this great battle for souls is God's idea, not ours. We are just laborers with Him; the power is His; the glory is His; and the great harvest moment when the shining sickle is thrust among the souls of men is also His and His alone.

Thank you each and every one, and renewing our vow, let's be true till He comes.

William Cawman

╫

February 1, 2004

THERE IS A STORY I have been wanting to tell you for a while, but it seems there is so much else to tell that I haven't gotten it in. The only reason I want to share the story with you is to show that many hearts and lives that we might look upon with disdain and disgust are really worthy of our reaching hand. They have honestly, hardly ever had a chance to be anything different.

The subject of the narrative is a large-boned black man in his very late fifties. At the early age of four or five, he was sexually molested over and over by a cruel perpetrator. He grew to youth hating the man who did it, and as soon as he was of age, acquired a double-barreled automatic shotgun and went driving around looking for him. The man heard he was after him and fled the state.

Our subject then joined the forces going to Vietnam, with every intention of taking out his rage on human life somewhere. He was sent on a raid to wipe out enemy resistance, and the tactic was to use flame throwers and burn the jungle while they covered it with gunfire. He heard the screams of innocent women and children, and saw them burning to death and dismembered in every way. It began to unnerve him, until someone slipped up and handed him a bottle of strong liquor.

"Drink this," they said, "We've got a lot more of this to do." It became almost a delight, a vent to his long pent-up hatred for what had been done to him, to kill. He also learned to torture the prisoners they took by war.

This man told me recently that he had seen on TV where nine Iraqi children had been killed. He said, "We killed thousands of them with our big guns. I found many of their little feet and legs on the ground as we pressed onward."

He was given orders that he and his men were to stop any convoys of the enemy from coming down a certain road. He stopped them by shooting the tires out from under their lead vehicles and blocking the road like they were supposed to, but he couldn't be satisfied with that. He turned the big guns on them and blew the whole convoy apart. He said it unnerved him again when he went over to the scene and viewed what he had done. There were body parts, blood, and guts all over the road. He told me with pathos in his voice that when he saw what he had done and knew he didn't have to do it, he flipped out and has never been right since. He found a fix this time by using strong drugs, and was soon hooked on them completely.

Five times over, as he walked through the jungles, he was hit by sniper bullets. Two of them are still in him as they lodged in his lungs and cannot be safely removed. He was burnt by Agent Orange as they sprayed it to clear the jungles of their foliage, and he still suffers from awful-looking rashes in the summer heat.

For all of this, the man received a congressional honor for performing beyond the call of duty. But—now he wakes up in the night with horrible nightmares. He still hears the screams coming from the jungle trees. He wakes up with cold sweats and it all replays over and over. Still struggling with grudges, with revenge, with hatred, he now adds to all of that the awful disease of Hepatitis C.

But now for the most tragic part of all: As he listens diligently to us teach and preach a salvation which can save a man from sin, he says, "I have gone to church all of my life, but I never heard that before. I got out of the army and married a wife. She couldn't live with me because I ordered her around like the army, so we got divorced. I have lived with another woman for 30 years without being married to her. Nobody ever told me it was wrong. I don't know what to do; I'm convicted; I've lived in sin for years and nobody ever told me. We were just taught that if we went to church, all would be all right. I don't know how to get rid of all this. As long as I keep busy studying the Bible and reading books I'm OK, but if I stop it all comes back over me again."

All the light he has ever had is enough knowledge about God that it works at times for a cork to plug the volcano that's raging within. And friends, this man was raised in "Christian America!" God have mercy in that Great Day for false shepherds who willfully allow such cesspools of sin, trouble, and anguish to fester for almost sixty years and never tell them of a Jesus Who can heal their sin-sick, bleeding soul.

I apologize for relating such a graphic tragedy of a life, but I feel sometimes like pleading—how many more of them are out there with no one to tell them that there is a real, forgiving, life-changing Jesus? How many of them have we dumped into prison with our backs turned, passed by on the other side of the road, and they still have not a ray of light in their dark world? Forgive me, but I cannot take cases like these without pain in my heart, when I face the truth that had I been raised in their hell hole of a world, I might have been just as hopeless and unwanted as they.

Oh God, why have You been so good to me? Why me, Lord? All I can do is reach for them like I would wish someone would for me, if I were them. Isn't there a song that says, "The world's great heart is aching; aching fiercely in the night?" Please don't forget it, my friend.

But now let me turn to the brighter side of what God is doing for others. I told you in a recent letter about the inmate who recently got sanctified, and is being released from prison to go home to his family. He was called in to the parole board to review his status just a few days before his release date. Several others were before him, and most of them gave the board a hard time, arguing about the verdict, etc.

When it came this inmate's turn, the parole officer told him that since he was being released to another state, the paper work had not come in from that state yet, and that he might not get to go home on his date. He calmly looked at the board and said, "Well, that's all right. It will work out somehow."

The officer looked at him very searchingly and said, "Are you all right? I said you might not get to go home on your date."

"Yes, I heard you, but that's just fine; I'll go whenever you release me."

The officer said, "I don't understand you; something has to be wrong with you."

"Oh no", he said, "what was wrong with me died. I'm just fine now. I belong to God and whatever He wants for me is just right."

They looked at him some more and shook their heads and dismissed him. On the way out the door the sergeant stopped him and said, "Man is there something wrong with you?"

"Oh no, Sergeant, the old man inside of me that something was wrong with, died, and now I just belong to God. I'm just fine, Sergeant."

When he told me about it we both had a good laugh and I let him know that he will meet many more who don't understand him. He is so happy that it doesn't even affect him.

And yes, the dear man who got saved a few weeks ago continues to find God's grace a match for the devil's tricks. That is not to say he does not face them. The other day he came to see me, and I could tell immediately that something was bothering him more than usual. He sat down and said, "Pastor, something is really troubling me, and I don't know exactly how to explain it; but I'm bothered about it." I asked him to try to tell me about it.

He then said that he had attended a Bible study the night before, and one of the inmates who had recently professed to be a Christian stood up and asked the Bible teacher this question: "Now that I'm a Christian, how do I get others to see it?"

Apparently the Bible teacher had detected that the man was motivated by a desire to be promoted and seen, so he answered him thus: "You need to ask yourself this question, 'Am I into this for what I can get out of it?'"

He said, "I have been thinking about that question all night; in fact I hardly slept because it is really bothering me. To be real honest, Chaplain, I would have to say that yes, I really do want to get something out of this."

I could just see how the devil had beat him up over that all night long. I told him that first of all, the answer the Bible teacher gave the man was entirely correct, that the motive for living the Christian life is not what we can get out of it. But then I told him that he had tried to swallow a chunk of beef, and his heart was still crying for more milk.

I pointed out to him how it is perfectly normal and necessary for a new baby to be totally consumed with its needs, without regard for anyone else. It wakes up at two in the morning without a thought of how Mother feels, and wants to be fed; and it really needs to be fed too. I told him that the time would come when he would be so filled with the presence of God, and that he would develop such a trust in Jesus, that he would look up and say, "Jesus, You don't have to bless me today, but what can I do to please Your great heart?" But for now, the reason he feels he needs to get something out of it is simply because God is putting that ravenous appetite in him so that he will reach out for more and grow up spiritually.

I told him that the devil was taking advantage of him by trying to accuse him of not being in a realm of maturity that he had not grown into yet. I just encouraged him to give place to the hunger he felt and reach out with both hands for more of God.

Once again the devil was shown up, and as this man's face relaxed, big tears welled up and ran down his face, and over on his cane he went again. "Oh God, I thank You; I just thank You. I just want more of You. I thank You that You have shown me again what the devil is doing; Oh God, I just thank You." He reluctantly left the room breathing out deeply, "Oh thank God, and thank you, Chaplain."

Oh how many little ones in Christ are suffering and stumbling at the hand of this awful accuser. My heart cries out with a passion, that for any I can reach, Jesus will not have to see them also "as sheep not having a shepherd."

Let me tell you one more story before this page runs out. On December 26, the night after Christmas, my wife and daughters went with me into the prison for two Bible studies. We had some special music and tried to share the message of Christmas with them.

Right after New Year's I made a trip to Guatemala, and when I returned a man wanted to talk to me. I went to his cell block and he told me that he was the youngest of seventeen children, ten boys and seven girls. The whole family was strongly and actively Muslim. He had been struggling with his confidence in that religion, and so had come down that night to the Bible study. I had noticed that after the service while I was shaking hands with the men on their way out, a small group gathered around a man and prayed with him. It was this man, and that night he received Jesus into his heart.

He said when he woke up the next morning, he couldn't understand why he felt so different. And he said, "I still feel so different; I'm not the same. Now I see a fight and I just walk away and have nothing to do with it." He said he really wants to understand more about what has happened to him.

Oh the blessed Jesus; He doesn't wait until we have learned all about Him. We rightfully say that there is nothing God cannot do, but there are certainly some things He will not do, and one of them is to fail to enter the broken and contrite heart. That is our Jesus; praise His name!

Please remember this man and remember me as I try to guide his footsteps in this new walk. I had just returned from a land where I saw some little brown eyed, black-haired babies that I could hardly keep from touching. I came back to some babies I can hardly wait to see drink their milk and grow.

Your Brother in the love of Jesus,
William Cawman

March 1, 2004

WE ARE ONE MONTH CLOSER to Home, if we are walking with Jesus. Can you imagine this following comparison? A man has lived for ten, fifteen, or twenty years in a little stark, gray prison cell. He has one little window to what is on the outside of his cell, and maybe that window simply looks out on a blacktop courtyard surrounded by a tall, chain link fence. Inside his cell, he has a stainless steel platform about 30 inches wide and six feet long, with a three-inch-thick rubber mattress on it for his bed. He has a little locker in the corner of the room in which to keep his private belongings, and that locker is subject to search at any time. He has a little stainless steel table, about 2 feet wide, fastened to the wall, with one stationary, round stainless chair with no cushion. Above the table are two open shelves. This little area he must learn to share with his cellmate. There is a toilet in the room with a small sink on top of the toilet tank. That is all.

And then the great trumpet of the Lord sounds. He suddenly rises up through the concrete ceiling of his little "home" and "in the twinkling of an eye," he is ushered into all the glorious splendor of God's eternal heaven. Friends, this will necessitate that glorious "we shall all be changed," if he is to physically, emotionally, and every other way be able for that glorious transition. "What a day that will be!"

But— if you keep praying for these dear men, that is exactly what is going to happen one of these days. I have not been able to ever describe to you the feelings (can I really describe them as feelings?) while sitting together with a few of these precious souls. I will try once again.

Yesterday, I had a list of names that I needed to visit. Near the middle of the afternoon, I called out the man I have told you about a number of times. Although in prison for two murders and with many years yet to serve, he lives and walks and talks with God and carries a glow of divine glory wherever he goes. I lose immediately the concept of chaplain and inmate—we are brothers.

As we sit and share the battles we have encountered, and the all-sufficient and ever-present grace of God so abundant for them, our hearts burn together. We laugh together; we cry together; we literally "sit together in heavenly places in Christ Jesus." We could spend much longer than we have together, as we share the riches of God's Word and grace. Then I ask him if he would pray. There is silence for a moment, and then with such deep respect and awe he begins, "Glorious and gracious God, our Father…" I cannot hold back the tears as God's presence fills the room.

There are two windows from the room into the dayroom where many inmates are sitting, playing cards, telling dirty jokes, and all that sinners do. They can look in the windows and may wonder what is wrong with us. We wonder what is wrong with them.

His prayer continues: "Father we know that as we hold You up before men we will be the savor of life to some and the savor of death to others." He is not magnifying himself; he is not bragging on his brother next to him; he is exalting Jesus. We see God "high and lifted up; and His train [fills] the temple," and as I leave him I feel I have been ministered to clear down to the roots of my soul by one of God's own.

There is no question that we are living in perilous times. Seduction and deception are hard at work everywhere to tear apart the pure truth of God. But in these times of visitation, my own vision is cleared and my heart renewed and challenged. I can only try to tell you about it, but honestly I envy for you that you could share it too. These simple followers of the Lamb are not holding any positions that they have to protect. They are not trying to prove anything about themselves. They are simply bathed in the presence of the God Who loves them and fills them "with all joy and peace in believing."

They are not complaining about their circumstances; they are not having trouble with the authorities; they are not overcome by the hell hole they are living in; they are walking in the fire with the Fourth Man by their side. I love them, believe me, I do. You would too if you knew them; and I believe you do anyway. I will freely confess something to you: I never dreamed that God had this in store for me when He called me into this corner of His harvest field. I thought He was calling me to minister to others; it has ministered to and saved my own soul.

We have six housing units in the main part of the prison. Each housing unit holds about 500 men. It is laid out with two wings in the shape of a V, and each wing has two floors, and on each floor there are two layers of cells with a balcony to reach the top ones. The man I was just telling you about was on the left wing of the top floor. When I left him, I went directly across in the same housing unit to the other wing on the top floor. Filled to overflowing by the visit I had just experienced, I learned God had more yet in store.

This man is a very quiet, unassuming person who never seeks to be seen or heard, but in spite of that you cannot help but see him because of the glow on his face. He sits quietly in classes and Bible studies with beaming face and a nodding head. He came toward me and from halfway across the tier floor his face broke into a big grin.

"Chaplain, you have just made my day by coming to see me." His heart is so full that he starts right in spilling another dose of heavenly glory all over me. He also has a long

time yet to be in prison, but he would be an effective antidote for anyone's depression. He has no time to elaborate
on the trials and battles he is passing through. He simply
says that he takes everything to the throne of grace, and
God gives more and more.

He says many don't understand him, and they cannot fig-
ure out what makes him so happy all the time, but others are
perturbed by it and come against him in various ways. He
says he just simply goes directly to his cell and lays it before
the throne of grace, and God brings him through everything
with complete victory. He even seems to have obtained this
great peace in his own typical way.

He has told me before that, as he sat in the classes and
Bible studies and listened to the truth of full salvation, he
just simply walked in the light and walked right into the
blessing he lives in so beautifully. Isn't that the promised
way after all? "If we walk in the light, as He is in the light,
we have fellowship one with another, and the blood of Jesus
Christ His Son cleanseth us from all sin" (I John 1:7). What
fellowship indeed! What a bond exists between those who
have walked and are walking in the light.

Thank you friends, for praying for these men. Please pray
that the Lord will add many more to their number.

I wish that I could only tell you stories like that, but that
would not be a fair picture. There are also so many misled and
desperately needy hearts still bound in darkness. The other
day I went to visit again a man I have worked with for several
years. I would guess he is not really retarded, but definitely a
little slow, as well as badly damaged by years of drug use. He
has had one desperately tragic childhood as well as adult life,
but for several years has really had a desire to find reality in
God. My heart aches for him. He seems to bang his head into
one wall after another without ever finding real peace with
God. Whether he has ever really known what it is to be saved
I wouldn't know, but oh, how viciously the devil tries to get
people to cling to their rags to keep them from the true riches.

He has been roughed up a lot by the officers, possibly because of his own actions, and recently he has been really angry and upset. His counselor told me he was deeply filled with anger at the officers and the whole system, and yet he wanted to see me.

He began by telling me that God had told him that he was to fight this system, not only for his own sake but for the sake of others also who were being mistreated. I immediately told him that God did not tell him any such thing.

He said, "Oh yes, He did. And my pastor on the outside told me that I am doing just the right thing. He told me that God would use me to expose and bring justice to the system."

I told him that he was totally mistaken; that God would never tell him to do something that was contrary to His written word. I began to read some Scripture to him where it is said "Blessed are ye, when men shall revile you, and persecute you, and shall say all manner of evil against you falsely, for My sake. Rejoice, and be exceeding glad…"

Of course I pointed out the difference between being persecuted for righteousness sake and being persecuted for our own actions. Then we went to where Peter said, "For even hereunto were ye called: because Christ also suffered for us, leaving us an example, that ye should follow His steps: Who did no sin, neither was guile found in His mouth: Who, when He was reviled, reviled not again; when He suffered, He threatened not; but committed Himself to Him that judgeth righteously."

It was hard for him to listen to me because he was so angry and upset, but as I showed him that Christ's example was so contrary to the path he was taking, he finally calmed down and said, "Chaplain, I have always loved and trusted you and wanted what you have; I will go and pray about it." Please help him pray.

There is something that places a heavy burden upon my heart. A state chaplain is actually hired to perform a task for the state. He is to try to bring about a rehabilitation that will keep men from having to come back and be a liability to the system again. Over and over I receive letters from men who have left, and who are very thankful for all that was done for them. They want me to know that things are going well for them. But I look at the religious mess that has swallowed them up and I cry out to God; "Where will they spend eternity?" Will they simply go to the same fire of damnation by a different route? Did we only succeed in changing their route number to the same destination? I honestly cannot sense any degree of satisfaction for any success of this nature, even though that is what I am paid for by the state. Please help me pray for the many who have left without the solid foundation they so badly need, the Rock Christ Jesus. Please also help pray that the number will increase who are finding the real "pearl of great price."

One more request. There has been an overpopulation crisis lately which has caused a lot of shaking around of inmates between prisons. Many who have more than ten years yet to serve are being transferred from this prison to another, and among them one very precious man who has seemed so close to receiving the blessing of holiness. He is taking a very Christ-like attitude about it, but he is so disappointed. There is nothing of the help he was receiving at the prison where he is now, and he writes and begs for prayer. I have told him that God makes no mistakes, and that he can make it his Arabian desert where God can help him to die to all but Him. He wants that and asks that you pray for him, that he will be able to very soon enter into the promised blessing.

May the Lord pour out His Spirit of grace and supplication upon each of us as we labor together till He comes. Thank you again, and may God reward you.

In His love,
William Cawman

18
ALONE AND UNWANTED

The Last Chapter Until Then—

JUST ONE MORE INMATE of the New Jersey State Prison system; just one more burden on the grumbling taxpayers; just one more six-digit identification number. But he lies dying on the second floor of the prison hospital, another victim of that grim reaper—sin.

His wasted body is already beginning to resemble more and more of a skeletal form; his eyes are sinking deeper into their sockets. We ask him if he ever prays. He frowns deeply and shakes his head, "No." We ask him if he would like us to pray; he shakes it, "Yes." His name reveals his having come from Puerto Rico, otherwise we know nothing about his history. We could go search it out in the prison records, but perhaps it would only hinder the hope that we can help him.

For a few weeks he vacillates from better to worse, hovering for a little longer before the light goes out. We visit him often. After a few visits we ask him if Jesus forgives his sins. He shakes his head, "Yes," but there is little other assurance we can grasp. The next time he is asked the same question, there is a look of uncertainty in his face. He gradually sinks lower and lower until they find him one September morning, dead in his cell.

His mother is notified of his death but she seems to care about his death no more than about his life. Time is given her to claim the body, but there is no response. She is notified again, but still it appears that he is in death as he was in life—unwanted.

It is now November 16, Thursday afternoon. My supervisory chaplain and I climb into his vehicle and start out across the few miles to the lonely little graveyard of those whom nobody wants. On my lap I hold a plastic bag from Staples Office Store. Inside the bag is a small but heavy green plastic box. Inside the box are the pitiful ashes of all that the sins of the flesh have left behind. I look over the death certificate and the cremation papers. I then understand why the dear man never answered me except by the shaking of his head. He never learned to speak English.

We arrive at the other prison; the place where the unwanted ones are laid to rest. We go in and deliver the papers and then an officer escorts us to the simple graveyard. It is an isolated spot of ground, perhaps fifteen feet by forty feet, surrounded by a low white picket fence. It lies under a spreading tree, a few feet off the lane leading into the prison. We park near the fence, walk to the spot and step over the gateless fence. I carry the green box by the handholds in the Staples bag. The officer moves away and leaves it to us.

I remove the Staples bag and hold in my hands the little green box. The other chaplain prays a short prayer and reads a few portions of Scripture. I then make a few comments and offer another prayer. We each take a side of the little green box. Within it is all that remains of the hopes and aspirations, the promises of the father of lies, the ambitions of life, the short-lived thrills and pleasures of sin, in short, all that composed the earthly part of a human life.

He was a man; I am too. He had desires; he had dreams; he had had a childhood, a youth, a manhood; but now we hold him in a little green box. The cold November wind cuts through our overcoats.

Together we lower him into a hole that has been dug for his arrival. It is perhaps sixteen inches in diameter and two feet deep. There are a few late autumn leaves in the bottom of the hole from the tree overhead, but not a single flower, not a single wreath, not a single tear. If he had been dear to anyone, they are not here now; only two chaplains who had cared enough to try, in the fading embers of his life, to rescue his soul from the same fate as his body. Whether it was accomplished, God only knows; my heart aches that I could have known.

As we step over the little white picket fence again, the officer motions to two inmates waiting at a distance. With humped shoulders and somber faces they drag their shovels to the spot and begin to fill the little hole with the dirt that had been taken out of it. Their work is nearly done by the time we reach the pavement. And there, at the foot of a little six-inch - square headstone which bears testimony to nothing other than that he is number six, we leave what is left of a human being like ourselves, to await that resurrection in which the Judge of all the earth will do what is right.

Just one more inmate of the New Jersey State Prison system; just one more burden removed from the taxpayer; just one more story of one more life.

We are reminded that there is definitely more than melancholy in the words of Bryant:

...and what if thou withdraw
  In silence from the living; and no friend
  Take note of thy departure? All that breathe
  Will share thy destiny. The gay will laugh
  When thou art gone, the solemn brood of care
  Plod on, and each one as before shall chase
  His favorite phantom; yet all these shall leave
  Their mirth and their employments, and shall come

And make their bed with thee. As the long train
Of ages glides away, the sons of men —
The youth in life's green spring, and he who goes
In the full strength of years, matron and maid,
And the sweet babe, and the gray-headed man —
Shall one by one be gathered to thy side,
By those, who in their turn shall follow them."

Thanatopsis

But there are still those among the living, and we must return to them before they too pass this way.

Appendix
ANCESTRAL ACKNOWLEDGMENTS

ON A DAY UNKNOWN, in the year of our Lord 1500, a baby boy was born into a home in Birmingham, England and was given the name of John Rogers. He was graduated B.A. at Cambridge, 1525, and received an invitation to Christ Church, Oxford. About 1534 he became chaplain to the Merchant Adventurers at Antwerp. There he made the acquaintance of William Tyndale and Miles Coverdale, and became a Protestant.

On October 31, 1517, a young German monk by the name of Martin Luther, having been visited with the soul-thrilling and life-enduing Scripture, "The just shall live by faith," boldly walked up to the church door of Wittenberg and nailed to it a large manuscript containing ninety-five protestations to the corruptions of the Church of Rome. With that act of heroism, the Protestant Reformation was launched. However, as a result there followed almost immediately, one and one-half centuries of persecution and bloodshed that blighted the whole of Europe and England. Both Catholics and Protestants grasped the sword of carnal weapons and deluged the land with human blood.

On October 6, 1536, William Tyndale was tried as a heretic, imprisoned and then strangled and burnt. His last words were:

"Lord, open the king of England's eyes." As he was being led away to prison he handed a packet of manuscripts to John Rogers containing his years of secret labor in translating the Bible from its original languages into English. John Rogers subsequently set about to complete it. Filling in unfinished portions of Tyndale's work from a just-finished translation by William Coverdale, he completed the English Bible and named it with the pen name of Thomas Matthew. The work was delivered to King Henry VIII who had it examined, and approved it for the press in 1537, not knowing that much of it was the work of William Tyndale.

The Matthews Bible, as it came to be known, was the first English Bible to be printed in quantities and used in the protestant churches. This Bible was practically the basis of the text of the Authorized Version. When Bloody Mary (daughter of Henry VIII) ascended the throne in 1553, she had John Rogers arrested and tried for his vigorous denunciation of Romanism. After months of imprisonment he was led to the stake and his wife and ten children, the youngest still on its mother's breast, were brought before him in an effort to get him to recant. Instead he washed his hands in the flames and was burned alive at the stake on Feb. 4, 1555 at Smithfield—the first Marian martyr. Eyewitnesses said that his children began to sing, making the occasion more like a wedding than a funeral. His dying words were, "Lord Jesus, receive my spirit." On Oct. 20, 1883, his bust was unveiled at Birmingham, England by the mayor.

Thus the following list of his descendants:

1. John Rogers (the martyr in 1555) .... married Adriana Pratt
2. Bernard Rogers .... married ?
3. Thomas Rogers (on *Mayflower* in 1620) .... married ?
4. John Rogers .... married Ann Churchman
5. Abigail Rogers .... married John Richmond
6. Edward Richmond .... married Mercy Thurston
7. Nathaniel Richmond .... married Alice Haskett
8. Nathaniel Richmond, Jr. .... married Saron Damon

9. Sally Richmond .... married Lester Stuart

10. Aravilla Stuart .... married Benjamin Bump

11. Elmer Bump .... married Alice Pettingill[1]

12. Lester Bump .... married Mary Perry[2]

13. Luella Bump .... married William Cawman[3]

14. William Cawman (author of this book) ...... married Peggy Carroll[4]

Notes

1. Alice Pettingill was the daughter of Captain George Pettingill and his wife, Clara. George was a sea captain and his wife was left for long periods of time with her children in their home in Maine. Clara was a Bible-loving and praying Christian. At one time when her husband was gone to sea, she heard that smallpox was coming across the land. Long before any thought of vaccinations was known, she walked to a village a distance from her home and requested some infected pus from the pox of some children. This she took home and made a scratch in each of her children and rubbed it in. None of them contracted the dreaded disease. George and Clara and Alice are buried on the southwest corner of Rosehill Cemetery in Newfield, New Jersey.

2. Lester and Mary Perry Bump were the maternal grandparents of this author. When the author's mother was very young, a pastor by the name of Benjamin Rickenbach came to the little Methodist church in Minotola, New Jersey, and began preaching to them the foundational doctrine of Methodism: a work of sanctification subsequent to regeneration. Their hearts responded to the message and so were led, as were their subsequent family into the way of holiness.

3. William and Luella Bump Cawman, the parents of author, were the providers of one of the best Christian homes in America. William Cawman was a model father, a patriarch indeed, and through the last day of his ninety years on earth his son never saw his father engage in any form of sin.

Luella Bump Cawman, the author's mother, was sanctified wholly at the living room couch in their home when the author was but five years of age. The author of these letters never knew an unsanctified mother; all glory be to God! One of the strongest reasons why this author is a firm believer in the way of holiness is that he saw it lived and loved at home. When God led into the prison ministry, this dear mother (the best the world ever knew) said, "If God wants to fill our little church with ex-prisoners, let Him do it!" Oh how much the author misses those precious moments when walking into the unlocked door of his boyhood home, he would hear the sound of prayer and find two godly octogenarians facing each other in their recliners, praying for their boy.

4. Thank you Dear Lord for my precious wife of forty-one and one-half years. What a blessing indeed, not only to the calling God had laid upon her husband's heart, but to the men in prison. They all felt she was their mother, and when God in His infinite wisdom translated her to His home in glory, they were among the most affectionate of all comforters, outside of the Holy Spirit Himself.

God never loses track of a prayer of one of His children. He only knows the extent of impact the prayers of John Rogers, Clara Pettingill, Lester and Mary Bump, William and Luella Cawman and Peggy Joyce Cawman may have had in the answers to prayer recorded in these letters.

Here is the patience of the saints: here are they that keep the commandments of God, and the faith of Jesus. And I heard a voice from heaven saying unto me, Write, Blessed are the dead which die in the Lord from henceforth: Yea, saith the Spirit, that they may rest from their labours; and their works do follow them. (Revelation 14:12,13)